Understanding and Engaging
Under-Resourced College Students

A Fresh Look at Economic Class and Its Influence on Teaching and Learning in Higher Education

Understanding and Engaging Under-Resourced College Students

A Fresh Look at Economic Class and Its Influence on Teaching and Learning in Higher Education

College of the Ouachitas

Karen A. Becker, Ph.D. ◆ Karla M. Krodel, M.B.A. ◆ Bethanie H. Tucker, Ed.D.

Understanding and Engaging Under-Resourced College Students: A Fresh Look at
  Economic Class and Its Influence on Teaching and Learning in Higher Education.
  Revised 2010.
Karen A. Becker, Ph.D., Karla M. Krodel, M.B.A., Bethanie H. Tucker, Ed.D.
314 pp.
References pp. 273–290

Publisher's Cataloging in Publication

Becker, Karen A., 1963-
    Understanding and engaging under-resourced college students : a
    fresh look at economic class and its influence on teaching and
    learning in higher education / Karen A. Becker, Karla M. Krodel,
    Bethanie H. Tucker. -- 1st ed. -- Highlands, TX : aha! Process, Inc.,
    c2009.

        p. ; cm.
        ISBN: 978-1-934583-33-3 ; 1-934583-33-2
        Includes bibliography and index.

        1. Low-income college students--Services for--United States.
    2. Education, Higher--Economic aspects--United States. 3. College
    students--United States--Economic conditions. 4. College student
    development programs--United States. 5. Academic achievement--
    Social aspects--United States. 6. College dropouts--United States--
    Prevention. 7. Social classes--United States. I. Krodel, Karla M.
    II. Tucker, Bethanie H. III. Title.

LC4069.6 .B43 2009   2009904470
371.826/9420973--dc22   0905

Copy editing by Dan Shenk and Jesse Conrad
Book design by Paula Nicolella
Cover design by Naylor Design

Printed in the United States of America

Special thanks for the contributions of Henry Ingle, Ph.D., San Diego Community College
District; Susan S. Jakes, Ph.D., North Carolina State University; Jan Lewis, M.S.N., R.N.,
Pueblo Community College; Donna Magee, Ed.D., aha! Process, Inc.; and Victoria K.
VanSteenhouse, M.A.T., Delta College.

Grateful acknowledgment is made for permission to use portions of the following copyrighted material:

Bridges Out of Poverty: Strategies for Professionals and Communities (3rd ed.), by Ruby K. Payne, Philip E. DeVol, and Terie Dreussi Smith. Copyright 2006 by aha! Process, Inc.

Bridges Out of Poverty: Strategies for Professionals and Communities Workbook, by Philip E. DeVol, Ruby K. Payne, and Terie Dreussi Smith. Copyright 2006 by aha! Process, Inc.

"Building Bridges Communities," by Philip E. DeVol. Copyright 2008 by aha! Process, Inc.

CAS Professional Standards for Higher Education (6th ed). Copyright 2006 by Council for the Advancement of Standards.

Changing Children's Minds: Feuerstein's Revolution in the Teaching of Intelligence, by Howard Sharron and Martha Coulter. Copyright 2004 by aha! Process, Inc.

Collaboration: What Makes It Work, by Paul Mattessich and Barbara R. Monsey. Copyright 2004 by Fieldstone Alliance.

Collaboration: What Makes It Work (2nd ed.), by Paul Mattessich, Marta Murray-Close, Barbara R. Monsey, and Wilder Research Center. Copyright 2004 by Fieldstone Alliance.

Crossing the Tracks for Love: What to Do When You and Your Partner Grew Up in Different Worlds, by Ruby K. Payne. Copyright 2005 by aha! Process, Inc.

The Development of Learning for Nontraditional Adult Students: An Investigation of Personal Meaning-Making in a Community College Reading and Study Skills Course, by Karen A. Becker. Copyright 1993 by Karen A. Becker.

"Double Whammy of Disadvantage," by Doug Lederman. Copyright 2009 by Inside Higher Ed.

Facilitator Notes for Getting Ahead in a Just-Gettin'-By World: Building Your Resources for a Better Life (2nd ed.), by Philip E. DeVol. Copyright 2006 by aha! Process, Inc.

Flowchart: Nomination & Confirmation. Copyright 2009 by SmartDraw.com.

A Framework for Understanding Poverty (4th ed.), by Ruby K. Payne. Copyright 1996 by aha! Process, Inc.

Getting Ahead in a Just-Gettin'-By World: Building Your Resources for a Better Life (2nd ed.), by Philip E. DeVol. Copyright 2004 by aha! Process, Inc.

"Getting Them Unstuck: Some Strategies for the Teaching of Reading in Science," by Jim Walker. Copyright 1989 by School Science and Mathematics Association.

Helping Under-Resourced Learners Succeed at the College and University Level: What Works, What Doesn't, and Why, by Karla Krodel, Karen Becker, Henry Ingle, and Susan Jakes. Copyright 2008 by aha! Process, Inc.

Learning Strategies Database. Copyright 2009 by Muskingum College.

Learning Structures (3rd ed.), by Ruby K. Payne. Copyright 1998 by aha! Process, Inc.

Meaningful Differences in the Everyday Experience of Young American Children, by Betty Hart and Todd R. Risley. Copyright 1995 by P. H. Brookes.

Mental Models for English/Language Arts: Grades 6–12. Copyright 2007 by aha! Process, Inc.

Mental Models for Social Studies/History: Grades 6–12. Copyright 2008 by aha! Process, Inc.

"Motivational Design of Instruction," by John M. Keller. Copyright 1983 by Erlbaum.

Moving Beyond Access: College Success for Low-Income, First-Generation Students, by Jennifer Engle and Vincent Tinto. Copyright 2008 by The Pell Institute for the Study of Opportunity in Higher Education.

New Models of Economic Development: White Paper Version 0.5, by Ed Morrison. Copyright 2006 by Ed Morrison.

On Course Workshop II: Innovative Strategies for Promoting Student Success Across the Curriculum, by Skip Downing. Copyright 2002 by Skip Downing. www.OnCourseWorkshop.com

PowerPoint Presentation on Preventing Dropouts, by Ruby K. Payne. Copyright 2008 by aha! Process, Inc.

Rubric for the Assessment of Computer Programming, by Shane Bauman. Copyright 2009 by Shane Bauman.

"Situated Cognition and the Culture of Learning," by John S. Brown, Allan Collins, and Paul Duguid. Copyright 1989 by American Educational Research Association.

Student Responses: English 101A. Copyright 2007 by Chabot College.

Student Responses: English 102. Copyright 2007 by Chabot College.

Trainer Certification Manual: A Framework for Understanding Poverty, by Ruby K. Payne. Copyright 2001 by aha! Process, Inc.

The Triarchic Mind: A New Theory of Human Intelligence, by Robert J. Sternberg. Copyright 1989 by Penguin.

Under-Resourced Learners: 8 Strategies to Boost Student Achievement, by Ruby K. Payne. Copyright 2008 by aha! Process, Inc.

Understanding by Design, by Grant P. Wiggins and Jay McTighe. Copyright 2005 by Association for Supervision and Curriculum Development.

Understanding Learning: the How, the Why, the What, by Ruby K. Payne. Copyright 2002 by aha! Process, Inc.

Word Atlas: Mapping Your Way to SAT Success. Copyright 1981 by Townsend Learning Center.

Table of Contents

Section IV. *How* to Shift Institutions and Communities

Foreword

In 1964 Bob Dylan told us, "The times, they are a-changin'." Forty-five years later higher education is still facing change. Students are different, teaching is different, learning is different, technology is different, curriculum is different … the world is different. The mission and functions of higher education have been altered, largely from outside the academy, and this has led to the greatest change of all—an expectation, often a demand, that higher education move away from its traditional role of identifying those whose innate academic skills allow them to succeed in a competitive college environment and move toward a commitment to ensure academic success for the vast majority of those who enter college, including an increasing number of under-resourced learners.

This paradigm change carries with it a clear need to reconsider the strategies and methods we use to help our students learn and adjust to the demands of achieving a degree. Chief among these is the recognition that the students who step into (or login to) our classrooms have widely different sets of experiences and backgrounds that significantly affect their opportunity and ability to succeed. A narrow, traditional view of college teaching and learning—and the resources allocated for student services—simply cannot accommodate this new diversity. In this book Becker, Krodel, and Tucker consider previous work on issues outside the classroom that affect student learning, then extend that work into the classroom by examining what college instructors and student services personnel need to know and do in order to respond to the experiences, beliefs, attitudes, and expectations of a changing student population.

One can argue that new expectations and demands for accountability are contrary to valued traditions—or that the purpose of "higher" education is to sort those who can learn effectively and step into leadership positions from those who cannot learn effectively and who step into the workforce at different levels. We cannot survive in these changing times if we adhere to this view, but at the same time we do not have to sacrifice quality, dedication, or acceptance of the simple fact that a teaching-learning partnership must be based on mutual respect and mutual acceptance of responsibility. This book is about building that partnership—whether in the classroom, seminar room, office, small group setting, or online.

Indeed, for both instructors and student services staff, the most powerful personal motivation to serve in the college setting and the strongest affirmation of the teaching-learning process come from observing student progress: gains in knowledge, skills, and thinking. Such gains reflect not only the acquisition of information but engagement with that information, along with the development of complex and sophisticated habits of thought that are the hallmarks of "an educated person" who will go on to make significant differences in the world beyond college. This book has that motivational intent as its subtext and undercurrent. It provides instructors with a new framework from which to design effective instruction, and that framework is built around understanding students as individuals whose sum of life experiences may help or hinder academic progress. One might ask why this focus instead of an emphasis on the ideas, concepts, and principles of disciplinary content. That question would miss the point because this book does not propose to supplant content with process. Rather, *Understanding and Engaging Under-Resourced College Students* deals with an approach that can be used to help more students acquire content knowledge more effectively. If, as instructors and student services personnel, our strongest motivation is to have our students "learn the material," then we must consider all the factors that relate to learning. Content is only print on a page, pixels on a screen, or talk in a classroom, absent the engagement of a student's mind and heart. Becker et al. tell us about enhancing and deepening that engagement because it is what makes content and learning real.

When we are asked "What do you teach?" we often think first as disciplinary specialists and respond with the names of our disciplines. This is understandable because, as teaching and student services professionals, many of us have devoted a large part of our lives to our disciplines, but *what* we teach must be considered in light of the fact that both teaching and learning are essentially human interactions. *Who* we teach is equally important, and it follows, then, that consideration of the persons involved (students and those who help them learn) is as important as consideration of the content. Learning happens when those persons and that content interact or, as Palmer says, "[w]hen my students and I discover uncharted territory to explore, when the pathway out of a thicket opens up before us, when our experience is illuminated by the lightning-life of the mind. ..." But Palmer makes another important point. He says, "In our rush to reform education, we have forgotten a simple truth: reform will never be achieved ... if we continue to demean and dishearten the human resource called teacher on whom so much depends" (1998, pp. 1–4).

The purpose of this book is to promote the "lightning-life of the mind" by opening new pathways out of the thicket: the tangle of human experience and emotion that can make learning either a daunting threat or a thrilling journey for any student. We have gone on that journey ourselves on our way to becoming higher education instructors and staff. What a gift to find even more effective ways of being guides as our students embark on their journeys, perhaps bringing with them experiences we could never envision, but which this book reminds us we might use as advantages. This book is not about "reform," and it does not demean higher education or the people in it. Instead, it reminds us of the intimate nature of both teaching and learning, and it gives us a powerful new mindset as we travel the path toward shared understanding.

—Michael Theall, Ph.D.
Associate Professor of Education,
Youngstown State University
President, Professional and Organizational
Development Network in Higher Education

CHAPTER 1

Colleges, Resources, and Economic Class

In today's economy, institutions of higher education are invaluable forces for community change through both the students they educate and the engagement and advancement of the larger community. Economic forces are bringing an increasingly diverse student population to the doorsteps of these institutions compared with the past. Many more of today's students are under-resourced—that is, students without the advantage of fully available financial, personal, and support system resources necessary to well-being. Many cannot read, write, and compute at the college level and have years of baggage from their school experience. For college personnel to achieve maximal effectiveness in reaching these students, paradigm shifts are needed in the ways teaching and learning are understood and actualized on campuses.

This is a sensitive subject, and so it is important from the outset to note the distinction between social class and economic class. Social class tends to be about comparisons, envy, and judgment while economic class, at a personal level, is about resources and gathering strength to build a future based upon one's own choices. Describing patterns is a useful means of beginning to understand groups of people. Applying the patterns associated with economic class to assess under-resourced learners—and analyzing and adjusting the strategies available to support and educate them—offers a different perspective for faculty and staff to consider. The patterns that emerge within economic classes are an adaptation to living within the wealth structures in the environment. Patterns always have exceptions. Thus if a pattern is applied to all people in a particular group or used to prejudge an individual, stereotyping has occurred. This book focuses on the patterns of under-resourced students from generational poverty—those whose families have been in poverty for two or more generations.

While poverty is typically thought of in terms of a lack of financial resources, "poverty" is defined for our purposes as "the extent to which an individual does without resources" (Payne, 2005b, p. 7). The term "under-resourced" is grounded in UNICEF's (2007) term "resources" to identify well-being. It is important to note that the financial resource, often considered a prime reason that poverty exists, is only one of many resources. This is not to gloss over the brutal reality created by having little money over a long period of time. Rather, it is to emphasize that there are other sources of strength, achievement, and pride—and that the more resources a person has the easier it is to make changes and live well. This book focuses on under-resourced college students, explaining ***what*** causes them to be under-resourced, ***why*** that may affect their ability to persevere in the postsecondary setting, and ***how*** to address this in the classroom and student services arenas.

These resources constitute the knowledge and means necessary to move between classes—in particular for the poor to climb out of poverty and for the middle class to be able to competently and comfortably interact with those in poverty. Eleven resources, possessed to one degree or another by all people in myriad manifestations, are:

- Knowledge of hidden rules
- Mental/cognitive
- Emotional
- Motivation/persistence
- Integrity/trust
- Physical
- Spiritual
- Language
- Relationships/role models
- Support systems
- Financial

Understanding and Engaging Under-Resourced College Students explores the application of a set of theories, strategies, and processes intentionally designed to address the effects of poverty and improve teaching and learning that were first pioneered by Ruby Payne with K–12 students. The effects of poverty explored in her first book, *A Framework for Understanding Poverty* (1996, 2005b), were later applied to social services organizations to help agency personnel better understand their services from their clients' perspectives. Philip DeVol (2004), in collaboration with groups of adults from poverty, then created a workbook and process called *Getting Ahead in a Just-Gettin'-By World* to be used by people from generational poverty in acquiring the tools essential for making the transition out of poverty. Unlike so many soft-skill training programs, this workbook and process open doors to rich areas of academic study related to economic class theory, theories of change, language development, and research into the causes of poverty. For this reason, several community colleges and universities have adapted the semester-long *Getting Ahead* process. These colleges are finding that *Getting Ahead* creates a different type of invitation for students and accelerates their ability to engage and reach college-level performance.

School success can depend on students' ability to access and develop resources. The good news is that most resources can be developed at any stage in life (Payne, 2008b, p. 2)—and institutions of higher education are particularly well positioned to cultivate this development for students and their families. College faculty and support staff can more effectively facilitate resource development by first considering the challenges faced by postsecondary students who come from generational poverty. Here are four such challenges.

First, under-resourced students usually lack the intergenerational transfer of knowledge about higher education because few or no family members have college experiences to share with them. To first-generation college students, the concepts of provosts, major advisers, independent studies, financial aid rules, and scholarships often are unfamiliar, making the landscape of the college and its departments quite literally "foreign" territory.

Second, there is in every institution and among economic classes a set of "hidden rules"—cueing mechanisms that are not deliberately taught by parents nor are they deliberately taught at a college; they are modeled and implied. Those who know the hidden rules of a particular group or institution assume that everyone should know them. Unfortunately, at college, not knowing or using the hidden rules of middle class is often equated with not being intelligent. Thus staff members with knowledge of the hidden rules of generational poverty are more likely to be successful with their teaching and advising. "Academe," however, is notoriously slow to change and adapt. Therefore, as yet there is a limited knowledge base about students from generational poverty. Likewise, given multiple systemic barriers for low-income students to accessing college, resources tend to be inadequate or unavailable to support their efforts. Some educators mistakenly think students are unsuccessful largely because of the effect of socioeconomic status—including the

K–12 schools they attended, the values placed on education in their families, and their ability to fund and access higher education programs, not fully aware of the complex interrelationship of factors and forces that affect students' lives and perspectives.

Third, under-resourced students might not have developed "future stories," as described in *Getting Ahead in a Just-Gettin'-By World*: building "individual plans for gaining economic stability ... for moving from poverty to prosperity" (DeVol, 2006, p. 5). As students learn to plan through guidance and course expectations, they free themselves from the "tyranny of the moment" (Freire, 1970) and make decisions based on their larger goals and dreams. It is very difficult to build and execute individual plans for gaining economic stability—indeed, their future stories—without such guidance.

And fourth, individuals from poverty also may be lacking the social capital or bridging relationships (Putnam, 2000) that give them the linkages to overcome the challenges of college and subsequent career exploration. Bridging relationships are one of the keys to college and university students' success. The professors, advisers, mentors, on-campus employers, and fellow students who form relationships with under-resourced students become a primary source of information and support to effect changes in their lives, thereby completing their transition from poverty to middle class.

College students, to be sure, are a select audience—that is, they have taken many steps to be admitted, to be enrolled, and to attend classes at an institution that is probably unfamiliar to them. In a sense, they have taken steps that many under-resourced people or individuals in poverty may not have even considered taking. Personnel in postsecondary institutions can help students build their resources in order to stay in college and persist in their efforts toward a certificate, a two- or four-year degree (or beyond), and eventual economic stability. What individuals do with that economic stability, where they decide to live and work, how they engage or do not engage in society, and what they do with their leisure time all constitute choices—choices made possible by the acquisition of a level of education and income that releases them from most of the day-to-day pressures that generational poverty imposes.

What is exciting about bringing this work to higher education is how ready most students in postsecondary institutions—technical schools, colleges, universities, etc.—are to discover it, to receive it, and, by finding meaning, to own it. Whether the ideas outlined in this book are implemented by one instructor in one classroom or by entire institutions and communities, the potential for transformation is significant.

CHAPTER 2

What Are the Causes of Poverty?

The Research Continuum

In the United States many of us tend to be confused about the causes of poverty and, therefore, not sure what to do about it (Shipler, 2004). A review of research on poverty indicates that the dialogue has been polarized between those who believe poverty is caused by individual behaviors and those who believe poverty is caused by political/economic structures. Proponents of both of these views often make "either/or" assertions: If poverty is caused by individual behaviors, then political or economic structures are not at fault and vice versa. Taking a "both/and" approach, however, is more productive. "Poverty is caused by both the behavior of the individual and political/economic structures—and everything in between" (Payne, DeVol, & Smith, 2006, p. 266). This book's authors categorize the research into four clusters along a continuum of causes of poverty:

- Behaviors of the individual
- Absence of human and social capital
- Exploitation
- Political/economic structures

Alice O'Connor, in her book *Poverty Knowledge,* states that society typically focuses on race and gender when considering poverty. She suggests that efforts to ameliorate poverty would be better served by examining it through the prism of economic class instead (O'Connor, 2001). In the postsecondary arena, this approach emphasizes faculty interaction with students, support services, and student programming to give more attention to building students' resources and creating sustainable communities.

There is valid research that points to strategies and/or solutions to the causes of poverty. As long as there is a range of strategies following the continuum of causes, it is possible to consider how to end poverty. The lists and examples that follow are not exhaustive but rather examples of what might fall into each area of research.

Behaviors of the Individual	Absence of Human and Social Capital	Exploitation	Political/ Economic Structures
Definition: Research on the choices, behaviors, characteristics, and habits of people in poverty	*Definition:* Research on the resources available to individuals, communities, and businesses	*Definition:* Research on how people in poverty are exploited because they are in poverty	*Definition:* Research on the economic, political, and social policies at the international, national, state, and local levels
Sample topics: Dependence on welfare Morality Crime Single parenthood Breakup of families Intergenerational character traits Work ethic Racism and discrimination Commitment to achievement Spending habits Addiction, mental illness, domestic violence Planning skills Orientation to the future Language experience	*Sample topics:* Intellectual capital Social capital Availability of jobs Availability of well-paying jobs Racism and discrimination Availability and quality of education Adequate skill sets Childcare for working families Decline in neighborhoods Decline in social morality Urbanization Suburbanization of manufacturing Middle-class flight City and regional planning	*Sample topics:* Drug trade Racism and discrimination Payday lenders Subprime lenders Lease/purchase outlets Gambling Temp work Sweatshops Sex trade Internet scams	*Sample topics:* Globalization Equity and growth Corporate influence on legislators Declining middle class Deindustrialization Job loss Decline of unions Taxation patterns Salary ratio of CEO to line worker Immigration patterns Economic disparity Racism and discrimination

Note. From *Bridges Out of Poverty* (p. 267), by R. K. Payne, P. E. DeVol, and T. D. Smith, 2006, Highlands, TX: aha! Process. Copyright 2001 by aha! Process. Adapted with permission.

1. The first cluster of research on poverty holds that **individual initiative**—being on time, staying sober, becoming motivated—would reduce poverty. Indeed, voter research echoes this finding as 40% of voters said that poverty is due to lack of effort on the part of individuals in poverty (Bostrom, 2004).

   This area of research focuses on the individual as the cause of poverty and draws its conclusions primarily from correlative studies of choices and lifestyles of the poor. The research topics include intergenerational character traits, dependency, single parenthood, work ethic, breakup of families, violence, addiction and mental illness, and language experiences. In the past 60 years, considerable funding and time have been spent on these areas of research, with the focus on changing the thinking and behavior of the poor through such strategies as "work first," literacy education, treatment interventions, a cluster of abstinence issues, and programs that promote marriage. Overall, the intention of these strategies is to improve the choices, education, and internal resources of the poor. This cluster of research, however, does not take into account the influences of outside factors that tend to work against personal assets and choices.

2. The second area of research involves the **absence of human and social capital**—examining how communities provide resources and infrastructure so that individuals can achieve and maintain personal economic stability. In this cluster, topics of research include employment and education issues, declining neighborhoods and middle-class flight—all of which may lead to "donut cities" where suburbs thrive while the urban core from which people moved collapses, leaving a hole in the center.

   Local governments, service providers, and schools are held accountable for poverty through state audits, federal and state reviews of participation rates, and assessment scores. Therefore, the strategies often suggested for improving human and social capital include providing programming to enhance skills and build educational access (such as Head Start), growth in the labor market in order to offer full employment opportunities, antipoverty programs, and improved policing of communities. When individuals discuss how to end poverty from this perspective, the role of business and community development is crucial. Some businesses contribute by thinking not only of their "bottom line" but also about their contribution to their employees and to a sustainable local community.

3. **Exploitation,** the third area of the research continuum, involves abusing and taking advantage of dominated groups and markets for profit. Exploitation takes many forms. For example, people who cannot protest low wages for fear of losing their job work in slavery, sweatshops, and/or in migrant farming. Large corporations that hire employees for only 30 hours a week to avoid paying healthcare and other benefits also are preying on the people who need jobs and security. Exploitation of dominated groups for markets include drug trade, "buy here/pay here" car lots where the interest rate is 15.7%, as well as the "rent to own" stores that charge as much as 121% interest. The college student is particularly susceptible to predatory lending at cash-advance and payday lender storefronts in order to make financial ends meet.

Further, exploitation can happen to groups when geographic regions are plundered for their raw materials. Examples include the timber and coal being taken from Appalachian areas in the U.S. or oil being taken from the delta region of Nigeria, because the local people do not benefit from the local resources. Another example is the Native Americans who were driven onto reservations. These groups of people are out of the decision-making and profit-sharing loop. Unfortunately, dominant cultures are frequently reluctant to acknowledge exploitive practices. While half the states in the U.S. have passed antipredatory lending laws, the laws are in danger of being erased due to pressure from the lenders and lobbyists. Strategies to end exploitation found in the research include:

- Educating individuals and groups about exploitation
- Recognizing the role of government in sustaining or eradicating the exploitation
- Finding ways to make the system fair for getting money, products, services, and loans

4. Research topics relevant to how **social, economic, and political structures** contribute to poverty and prosperity examine why poverty exists from the standpoint of who benefits from it. For example:

- Deindustrialization and its toll on small communities across the United States
- The "race to the bottom" in which lower labor costs were meant to bring in new business but results in U.S. jobs moving overseas
- Increased productivity through high-tech equipment, which leads to job loss
- Corporate influence on legislators

Researchers who concentrate on this last category believe that studying poverty is not the same as studying the poor, noting that political/economic structures are a principal cause of poverty. Proponents believe in systemic change that enables people in middle class and poverty to influence the political and economic structures that affect them, just as the wealthy have done for generations if not centuries.

The following summarizes political and economic issues affecting public education in the United States (Gorski, 2005).

> A study from the National Commission on Teaching and America's Future (NCTAF, 2004) shows that high-poverty schools are more likely than low-poverty schools to have many teachers unlicensed in the subjects they teach, limited technology access, inadequate facilities, inoperative bathrooms, vermin infestation, insufficient materials, and multiple teacher vacancies. Other studies show that high-poverty schools implement less rigorous curricula (Barton, 2004), employ fewer experienced teachers (Barton, 2004; Rank, 2004), have higher student-to-teacher ratios (Barton, 2003; Karoly, 2001), offer lower teacher salaries (Karoly, 2001), have larger class sizes (Barton, 2003), and receive less funding (Carey, 2005; Kozol, 1992) than low-poverty schools. The study concludes: the most disadvantaged children attend schools that do not have basic facilities and conditions conducive to providing them with a quality education [NCTAF (2005), p. 7]. (p. 2)

A strategy for changing the political/economic structures includes creating a sustainable economy, with the intent of creating economic stability for all. Further suggestions include implementing measures of accountability beyond the shareholders' profits in business and government, as well as creating "whole-system planning," such as the Social Health Index (SHI) described by Miringoff and Miringoff (1999).

Other Areas of Research into Causes of Poverty: Race and Gender

Race and gender—more specifically, racism and sexism that involve the cultural dominance white males hold over people of color and women in America—are two additional areas of research into the causes of poverty. There are numerous other individual characteristics that intersect with economic class (disabilities, sexual orientation, age, religion), but none has as much impact on individuals, communities, and society as does race. Race/racism is so inextricably linked to economic class that it must be addressed directly as its own category.

As wealth is created over generations, it is estimated that 80% of assets come from transfers from the prior generations, not from income (Bucks, Kennickell, Mach, & Moore, 2009). Past policies and conditions clearly caused huge economic disparities between whites and people of color in the United States. The concepts of income and wealth are as fundamentally different as the concepts of situational poverty and generational poverty. In situational poverty, someone who once had economic stability becomes poor due to a circumstance—death, disease, disability, and so on. These individuals will react to the situation differently and have a greater chance of regaining economic stability than persons coming from two or more generations of poverty. Similarly, income—today's paycheck, lottery ticket, or stock dividend—is different from wealth. Income can change in the short term, but wealth changes over generations and is closely tied to policies that have historically benefited people (especially males) who are white. Wealth is far less dependent on daily income than most people imagine.

America's economic, social, and political policy and structures built and supported a white middle class. Slavery exponentially magnified racial disparities in income and wealth. Generations of African Americans were subjected to captivity, hard labor, and human rights controlled by slaveholders. The economic advantages slavery afforded to the slave owners is calculated in *The Color of Wealth* (Lui, Robles, Leondar-Wright, Brewer, & Adamson, 2006). During the mid to late 1800s U.S. government policy supported agriculture by giving lands taken from Mexico and Native Americans to white settlers (e.g., Manifest Destiny, the Gold Rush, and the Homestead Act). Land ownership was largely restricted to whites. U.S. policies continued to develop during the Industrial Revolution, which spawned the working class. Child labor was outlawed, tariffs made U.S. goods more desirable (hence more Americans could be employed), Ford mechanized production (and improved working conditions to a degree), unions developed to help protect workers, and some employers began to provide healthcare and pensions in order to compete for workers in a tight labor market. But segregation and discrimination limited employment opportunities. The white-collar middle class emerged and was supported by the GI Bill, mortgages, Social Security, and Medicare. Between 1930 and 1960, just 1% of all U.S. mortgages were issued to African Americans, and segregation in colleges meant there were not enough openings for black GIs to go to school on the GI Bill.

In 1994 the median net worth of whites was $94,500, compared with $19,000 for people of color. By 2005 white median income increased 48% (to $140,500), compared with nonwhite median income, which increased only 31% (to $24,900).

In 2006 the Minnesota Collaborative Anti-Racism Institute (MCARI) developed training materials on systemic racism for inclusion in the *Getting Ahead* (DeVol, 2006) workbook curriculum. MCARI (Valenzuela & Addington, 2006a) presents four features of racism that can validate the experience and intuition of people of color and shift the perspectives of whites so that they become intentionally aware of the daily advantages and disadvantages precipitated by racial identity.

FOUR FEATURES OF RACISM

1. Race matters. Compared with many countries in the world, the history of the United States is short. Though laws have been passed to change racial, economic, political, and social injustices, including segregation, racial identity still makes a difference, still "invoking mythological moral and intellectual superiority and inferiority."

2. Racism is more than the historical black-white dichotomy. This country's early laws and policies required definition of white and nonwhite. In the past, nonwhite primarily meant black. Today, the black/white dichotomy affects every community of color by paradoxically resulting in blindness to the issues of such other communities as Native Americans.

3. Racism and other oppressions interact. Race, gender, and economic class are so inter-related that some would argue one can't address one without accounting for the other two. Like economic class, "race shapes how we experience other socially defined identities." Race, gender, and class are relative to one another, such that the experience of one is inescapably connected to the experience of the other. "A white man's experience of gender is dramatically different [from] a black man's. Race is the most powerful factor … in how one experiences other systemic oppressions."

4. Identity formation, or racialization, "is the core feature of racism that reveals its forcefulness," according to MCARI. In the United States we're all assigned, for life, to a racial category that also holds social meaning. Even the national census every decade underscores the importance of identifying oneself by race. Racialization shapes individual, institutional, and cultural identity with cumulative and synergistic effects. Racism is enacted every day upon individuals—and broadly within communities and political and economic structures.

Payne's *A Framework for Understanding Poverty* (2005b)—referred to henceforth in the text as *Framework*—describes the patterns of behaviors seen in schoolchildren from poverty and their families. Its purpose is to help schoolteachers, drawn largely from the white middle class, understand their students better and teach more effectively. In *Framework* Payne does not present an analysis of the political and economic structures that perpetuate poverty—and does not outline strategies to address them. Nor does she deal in depth in *Framework* with racial, gender, and religious issues. Payne has been straightforward from the start that her focus is on the impact of economic class on issues related to poverty, middle class, and wealth. Nevertheless, by improving teaching and hence the educational system, the *Framework* approach does make important contributions to impacting systemic issues, particularly for students and families in the environment of poverty.

There are those who seem intent on translating Payne's descriptions of perceived patterns, hidden rules, and resources into negative stereotypes and indictments of individuals, as well as reinforcement of classist or racist attitudes. But such critics' focus tends to be on only one area of the research continuum (usually the political and economic structures *or* exploitation and racism), and this fuels polarizing arguments that oversimplify the problems of poverty and demand overarching societal reform from K–12 teachers who are only marginally equipped for the task. The critics offer little help to individuals themselves—or to those practitioners within the system who also seek change. Part of the thinking expressed in the research on exploitation and political/economic structures is that the individual is powerless and has little influence within the system. But many individuals do make it out of poverty, largely due to relationships and education. And most of them make it out *in spite of* the system. Society's systems are only as moral as the people who create and run them, and ignorance is a brutal form of oppression (Payne & DeVol, 2005). Payne, therefore, has offered a practical framework for helping teachers understand how to teach, build relationships, foster relational learning, and direct-teach skills for educational success. These strategies create awareness, build cognitive ability, and accelerate language acquisition to make up for the lags caused by growing up in a low-resource environment.

In this book the work is continued by addressing the specific needs of college students with the intention of creating highly effective faculty—and exploring the application of a process that engages learners and builds on their experience and expertise. In so doing, these students become able to effectively access the political/economic structures and address classism and racism as causes of poverty. In the process, colleges may discover new roles for supporting access and building community sustainability. Critiquing and challenging assumptions constitute the bread and butter of higher education, thereby driving deeper understanding and discovery. The expertise of scholars with research background in education, social activism, economic development, etc., will add to this work and its evolution. The expertise of under-resourced students, who understand how the system works *and* does not work, has as yet only the *potential* power to elevate instructional excellence of institutions of higher education. Indeed, there is room at the table for all opinions if the individuals who come together are supporting actions to end poverty and its devastating effects.

Under-Resourced Students in Postsecondary Education

The causes and effects of poverty on individuals, communities, and institutions are complex and multidimensional, and it is all too easy to grasp at numbers that point toward linear and absolute answers. With the preceding overview of the continuum of causes of poverty in mind, let's take a moment to review some of the research that documents the prevalence, associated characteristics, and effects of poverty on the college student population. More research is being produced, including longitudinal studies and control group studies, in an effort to increase data-driven, objective, decision making in higher education. Caution, however, must be exercised—and difficult questions posed—when examining the data and drawing conclusions from those statistics. The information presented here is intended to inform the reader about the effects of poverty on the educational outcomes of under-resourced students within the postsecondary system.

> Statistics are human beings with the tears wiped off.
>
> —Brodeur, 1985, p. 355

Representation of Students from Poverty in Higher Education

When attempting to quantify the percentages of students from poverty in higher education, one must rely on traditional measures of poverty, namely income as it relates to federal poverty guidelines.

- In 1995–96, twenty-six percent of all undergraduates were low income—from households at 125% of the federal poverty level or below (Choy, 2000).
- Working-poor adults have by far the hardest time going to school. In 2005 only 6% of poor adults ages 24–64 were enrolled in school, while 13% of nonworking-poor adults were going to school (Liebowitz & Taylor, 2004).

Risk factors reveal that students have many other things to worry about. The National Center on Education Statistics has distilled seven risk factors that negatively affect college academic performance:

- Part-time attendance
- Working full time
- Having dependent children
- Being a single parent
- Being financially independent
- Delaying enrollment after high school
- Having a GED (general educational development) diploma

Note that having a low income and being a first-generation college student are not risk factors in this national study—and that only "being a single parent" correlates directly with the causes of poverty just discussed. This shows that the resources introduced in Chapter 1 and discussed in detail in Chapters 3 and 4 are merely part of the equation that colleges must consider with regard to recruitment, along with retention and persistence of students, under-resourced or not, in order to meet standards essential to sustain funding. The more risk factors students have, the less likely they are to attain their educational goals (Horn, Peter, & Rooney, 2002). Risk factors can be found in students anywhere, for example:

- About half of students at public two-year institutions had two or more risk factors.
- Ninety-one percent of beginners at private for-profit schools had more than two risk factors, and 35% had four or more (Horn et al., 2002).
- Average first-generation, low-income students have three risk factors (Engle & Tinto, 2008).

Looking at the risk factors of working students, we find:

- Students who worked full time during their first year had the highest rates of attrition (52%) six years after matriculating (Berkner, He, Mason, & Wheeless, 2007).
- Fifty-six percent of low-income, first-generation students work, compared with 21% of students who are neither low income nor first generation (Engle & Tinto, 2008).
- About one quarter of students at two-year schools consider themselves to be "employees who enrolled in school" as opposed to "students who work" (Berkner et al., 2007).

The pressure to maintain one or more jobs often takes priority over education. This is compounded when employers are not willing to accommodate course schedules that change from semester to semester, provide time off for study during finals, or allow for extra hours to be worked during holidays and breaks.

Further, we can see that those who do not complete high school and/or delay the start of college are less likely to persist in postsecondary schooling.

Research on individuals with a GED reveals that:

- Sixty-five percent of those taking the GED test say they want to go to college.
- Thirty to 35% actually do enroll.
- Ten to 15% complete the first year.
- Four percent overall complete an associate degree (Liebowitz & Taylor, 2004).

Overall Goal Attainment

Most students entering two- and four-year institutions do so with a goal to obtain a degree. Specifically, 90% of beginning students at four-year schools plan to finish a degree program, while only half the beginning students at two-year schools intend to complete an associate degree (Berkner, He, & Cataldi, 2002). In general, retention and graduation rates of all students, across all types of institutions, are not impressive. More than a third of the students drop out, and six years after starting at a postsecondary institution, many still have not reached their goal.

Percentage Distribution of 1995–96 Beginning Postsecondary Students According to Initial Degree Goal in 1995–96 and Highest Degree Attainment as of June 2001

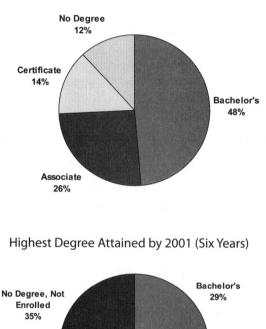

Initial Degree Goal in 1995–96

No Degree 12%

Certificate 14%

Bachelor's 48%

Associate 26%

Highest Degree Attained by 2001 (Six Years)

No Degree, Not Enrolled 35%

Bachelor's 29%

Associate 10%

No Degree, Still Enrolled 14%

Certificate 12%

Note. From *Descriptive Summary of 1995–1996 Beginning Post-Secondary Students: Six Years Later* (p. 11), by L. Berkner, S. He, and E. F. Cataldi, 2002, Washington, DC: U.S. Department of Education, National Center for Education Statistics. Copyright 2002 by U.S. Department of Education.

African-American students starting college in 2000 were 2½ times more likely to enroll at a school with a 70% chance of *not* graduating within six years than at a school with a 70% chance of earning a degree. Less than half of all black students who start college at a four-year institution graduate in six years or less, more than 20 percentage points less than the graduation rate for white students (Carey, 2008, p. 2). The data are even grimmer for Native Americans.

Although an increasing number of American Indians are enrolling at post-secondary institutions, the percentage of those attaining bachelor's degrees or higher remains relatively low—11 percent, compared with more than 25 percent for the general population—according to data from the U.S. Census Bureau.

American Indians have long had the highest college-dropout rate among minority groups in the United States. Many must overcome not only family pressures, poverty, and a weak high-school education to succeed in college, but also must assimilate to a campus culture much different from their own. (Hoover, 2004)

Income Has Multiple Effects on Educational Achievement

As noted in Chapter 1, students from poor or working-class backgrounds often lack the intergenerational transfer of knowledge regarding the skills necessary to navigate the system—and even the importance and relevance of college education. That social support, however, does not have to come from home. A strong "college-bound climate" in high school is at least as big a factor as even the presence of parents or other contacts with college experience.

Further, lack of access to income can preclude enrollment or affect the type of school the under-resourced student chooses. The College Board (2007) reports that nearly half of qualified low- to moderate-income students do not enroll in four-year institutions because of a combination of low expectations, poor preparation, and financial barriers. A Chicago study found that in choosing a college to attend, students tend not to consider qualitative differences in institutions or the meaning of credentials from different types of institutions. Rather, immediate cost, location, and accessibility are the primary criteria. Thus the researchers found only about one third of students from the Chicago public school system who wanted to go to college enrolled in a college with selection requirements commensurate with their ability. Nearly two thirds of the city's students attended schools with entrance requirements lower than their achievement level, safely securing access but not necessarily guaranteeing challenges and growth to their fullest potential. Only 41% of high school seniors who wanted to go to a four-year college completed the application and enrollment procedure to begin the process. Latino students were the least likely to apply to a four-year school, even when controlling for immigration and academic status (Roderick, Nagaoka, Coca, & Moeller, 2008).

Students from more affluent families understand the importance of ACT/SAT scores and usually have test preparation; some receive professional college admissions coaching. Although elite universities frequently offer large financial aid incentives, the application process requires the student to submit information about noncustodial parental income and employment—information that might be truly inaccessible (or the admission of which might have negative repercussions on government income or food subsidy programs for the rest of the family). For instance, only 12% of Stanford first-year students have Pell grants (Sturrock, 2008). The impact of the one resource of finances is crucial to students' perceived ability to succeed in postsecondary programs and, therefore, frequently keeps most of them from even considering the pursuit of such educational opportunities.

The Need for Remedial Education

Once enrolled, the under-resourced low-income student also is more likely to be under-prepared academically. This often includes lack of skills in oral communication and critical thinking. Many under-resourced students spend a good portion of their first few semesters in remedial courses that do not count toward degree attainment and frequently do not qualify for reimbursement through employer and government tuition programs. According to the National Center for Educational Statistics (Parsad & Lewis, 2003), 28% of entering freshmen are enrolled in at least one remedial course (reading, writing, mathematics). Urban community colleges serving low-income students place 70–80% of students in developmental courses (Liebowitz & Taylor, 2004). Another study found that only 30% of students assigned to introductory English and 20% to introductory math, the college-level courses required after completion of remedial courses, completed the course within three years (Brock et al., 2007), an indication that many students are not receiving the academic support they need to succeed in credit-bearing courses.

Percentage of Entering Freshmen Enrolled in Remedial Courses by Institution Type: Fall 2000

	Reading, Writing, or Math	Reading	Writing	Math
All institutions	28%	11%	14%	22%
Public two-year	42%	20%	23%	35%
Private two-year	24%	9%	17%	18%
Public four-year	20%	6%	9%	16%
Private four-year	12%	5%	7%	8%

Note. From *Remedial Education at Degree-Granting Postsecondary Institutions in Fall 2000* (p. 18), by B. Parsad and L. Lewis, 2003, Washington, DC: U.S. Department of Education, National Center for Education Statistics. Copyright 2003 by U.S. Department of Education.

Length of Time in Remediation by Institution Type: Fall 2000

	Less Than One Year	One Year	More Than One Year
All institutions	60%	35%	5%
Public two-year	37%	53%	10%
Private two-year	84%	11%	**
Public four-year	62%	35%	3%
Private four-year	83%	16%	**

Note. From *Remedial Education at Degree-Granting Postsecondary Institutions in Fall 2000* (p. 10), by B. Parsad and L. Lewis, 2003, Washington, DC: U.S. Department of Education, National Center for Education Statistics. Copyright 2003 by U.S. Department of Education.

'The Double Whammy of Disadvantage'—Low Income and First Generation

Jennifer Engle, interim assistant director of The Pell Institute for the Study of Opportunity in Higher Education, and Vincent Tinto compared low-income and first-generation college students to other students. The study found that under-resourced students tend to go to less selective schools than they are eligible to attend, as the Chicago study also revealed (Engle & Tinto, 2008).

Type of Institution Attended by Students Entering Postsecondary Education: 2003–04

	Public Two-Year	Public Four-Year	Private Four-Year	For-Profit	Other	More Than One Institution
Low-income and first-generation	52%	13%	6%	21%	2%	5%
Low-income or first-generation	53%	21%	10%	10%	1%	6%
Not low-income or first-generation	35%	35%	19%	4%	1%	6%

Note. From *Moving Beyond Access: College Success for Low-Income, First-Generation Students* (p. 10), by J. Engle and V. Tinto, 2008, Washington, DC: The Pell Institute for the Study of Opportunity in Higher Education. Copyright 2008 by The Pell Institute for the Study of Opportunity in Higher Education. Reprinted with permission.

Furthermore, low-income, first-generation students are the most likely to drop out of college after the first year, as shown in the table below.

Student Dropout Rate After Completing First Year: 1995–96

	Public Two-Year	Public Four-Year	Private Four-Year	For-Profit
Low-income and first-generation	32%	12%	26%	26%
Not low-income or first-generation	15%	4%	7%	18%

Note. From "Double Whammy of Disadvantage," by D. Lederman, June 16, 2008. Copyright 2009 by Inside Higher Ed. Reprinted with permission.

Once again, the combination of being both a low-income and first-generation student increases the risk of noncompletion. While low-income, first-generation students *are* more likely than their peers to attain certificates and associate degrees rather than complete four-year degrees, they also are more likely to drop out or not to have finished the coursework after six years. Among 27 community colleges participating in the *Achieving the Dream* project, it was found that only 36% of first-time college students entering a community college in 1995 earned a certificate or degree within six years (Brock et al., 2007).

Six-Year Outcomes by Type of Institution First Attended

	Low-Income and First-Generation	Low-Income or First-Generation	Not Low-Income or First-Generation
ALL INSTITUTIONS			
Attained certificate or associate degree	32%	21%	11%
Attained bachelor's	11%	26%	55%
Still enrolled	13%	16%	15%
Not enrolled	43%	38%	20%
Public Two-Year			
Attained certificate or associate degree	30%	23%	23%
Attained bachelor's	5%	9%	24%
Still enrolled	14%	19%	23%
Not enrolled	51%	49%	31%
Public Four-Year			
Attained certificate or associate degree	11%	7%	5%
Attained bachelor's	34%	50%	66%
Still enrolled	22%	18%	14%
Not enrolled	33%	25%	15%
Private Four-Year			
Attained certificate or associate degree	9%	6%	2%
Attained bachelor's	43%	64%	80%
Still enrolled	16%	9%	7%
Not enrolled	32%	21%	11%
For-Profit			
Attained certificate or associate degree	39%	62%	46%
Attained bachelor's	0%	3%	8%
Still enrolled	3%	4%	5%
Not enrolled	37%	31%	4%

Note. From *Moving Beyond Access: College Success for Low-Income, First-Generation Students* (p. 12), by J. Engle and V. Tinto, 2008, Washington, DC: The Pell Institute for the Study of Opportunity in Higher Education. Copyright 2008 by The Pell Institute for the Study of Opportunity in Higher Education. Reprinted with permission.

In the United States we believe in a level playing field and opportunity for all who are willing to work for it. Yet a 12-year longitudinal study of eighth-graders reveals that the best (academically speaking) eighth-graders from poverty have the same college graduation rates as the worst students from wealth. Stated differently, high-achieving (top 25% of eighth-grade math scores), low-income (bottom 25% of socioeconomic status) students completed college at the same rate as the lowest achieving students from the wealthiest backgrounds. The best wealthy students had a 74% graduation rate, but only one third of the brightest eighth-graders from poverty completed a bachelor's degree (Roy, 2005). The importance of truly leveling the postsecondary playing field—from matriculation to graduation—requires an in-depth examination of all the causes of poverty.

A summary of research from Pennsylvania State University found that of those students who struggled academically during the first semester of college, just 20% of the lowest income students graduated within six years. In the final analysis, there was no evidence of stronger academic skills among those who did graduate compared with those who did not, indicating that "skill deficiencies can be overcome." When compared with the nongraduate group, graduates were twice as likely to have parents who are married, and those at the main campus with higher admission placement scores were three times as likely to graduate. The student's level of poverty within the lowest quintile was not relevant to degree completion (Lederman & Heggen, 2008).

Research further indicates that students at four-year public and private institutions have the best chance of earning a bachelor's degree within six years of matriculation. For this reason, Chicago Public Schools focuses on and encourages its high school students to enroll in four-year schools (Roderick et al., 2008).

Finally, this research found that six years after starting at a two-year college:

- Twenty-six percent of first-generation, low-income students had transferred to four-year colleges.
- Forty percent of students who are *either* first-generation *or* low-income had transferred to four-year colleges.
- Sixty percent of students who are neither low-income nor first-generation had transferred to four-year colleges.

Some researchers have argued that six-year graduation rates, which measure the progress of freshmen five years after beginning, are based on the traditional-age college student and do not adequately reflect an institution's performance. Using "degree completion" as the analytical approach, which looks backward at the characteristics of students earning degrees, Kennesaw State University presents two very different pictures in 2006.

- Using the six-year model, of the 1,200 freshmen who began in the fall of 1999 and 2000, only 400 had graduated by 2006.
- Using degree completion as the analytical approach, Kennesaw awarded a grand total of 2,200 bachelor's degrees (Lederman & Heggen, 2008).

Some argue that part of the problem in collecting and analyzing data is that the national standard does not account for such variables as part-time student status, transfer students, and attainment of certificate rather than degree. In a study of Florida community colleges, however, data were examined for these typical criticisms of the national standard, and it was found that after adjusting for these variables, the results changed very little (Jaschik, 2007). A major factor in determining the ability of students to succeed is what the institution does, intentionally and unintentionally, that both supports and/or undermines achievement, particularly with regard to low-income and first-generation students.

In summary, then, it is important to be mindful that all this abstract information, all these statistics, relate to the complicated lives of people. Understanding something about the environment and lives of these students makes faculty and staff more competent. David Shipler's Pulitzer prize-winning book *The Working Poor: Invisible in America* (2004) brings home the concrete reality represented in the theory and data.

> For practically every family, then, the ingredients of poverty are part financial, part psychological, part personal and part societal, part past and part present. Every problem magnifies the impact of the others, and all are so tightly interlocked that one reversal can produce a chain reaction with results far distant from the original cause. A rundown apartment can exacerbate a child's asthma, which leads to a call for an ambulance, which creates a medical bill that cannot be paid, which ruins a credit record, which hikes the interest rate on an auto loan, which forces the purchase of an unreliable used car, which jeopardizes a mother's punctuality at work, which limits her promotions and earning capacity, which confines her to poor housing. If [any] impoverished working parents [or students] added up all of their individual problems, the whole would be equal to more than the sum of the parts. (p. 11)

Poverty traps people in the tyranny of the moment, making it … difficult to attend to abstract information or plan for the future— the very things needed to build [toward the attainment of a college degree].

—DeVol, 2006, p. 1

CHAPTER 3

Internal Resources

An individual's resources are unique personal qualities gained from family, friends, communities, experiences, and the environment in general. Understanding what these resources are and how they are acquired offers new perspectives of student behavior and can inform the myriad programs, pedagogies, and assessments performed both formally and informally by faculty and staff in numerous capacities.

> Resources can be defined as "quality-of-life indicators." Taking the 11 resources as a whole, it is better to have high resources than low resources. It would be fair to say that a high quality of life does not depend on having high financial resources, but it is also fair to say that being financially stable generally increases one's quality of life. (DeVol, 2006, p. 37)

Those qualities students bring with them both help and hinder their ability to succeed and their perception of what constitutes success.

The driving forces of poverty, middle class, and wealth shed light on differing definitions of success and how resources are used to realize those views of success. In many ways, this resembles the hierarchy of needs described by Abraham Maslow (1970). In poverty, a key driving force is relationships. Relationships with family and friends persist long after the low-wage job or the school day ends. This may be one reason that many college students from poverty seem to lack the academic focus that their instructors expect of them. On the other hand, students from the middle class with their driving force of achievement—and students from wealthy families motivated toward self-actualization and the cultivation of networks—behave in ways that are seen as "normal" or "expected" by their middle-class and upper-middle-class instructors.

Driving Forces	
Poverty	Survival, relationships, entertainment
Middle class	Work, achievement
Wealth	Financial, political, social connections

Note. From *Bridges Out of Poverty* (p. 44), by R. K. Payne, P. E. DeVol, and T. D. Smith, 2006, Highlands, TX: aha! Process. Copyright 2001 by aha! Process. Adapted with permission.

There are 11 resources individuals may identify as what they have, what can be developed, or what is lacking and out of reach (from that person's perspective). Payne (2008b, p. 2) believes that resources can be intentionally developed at any time in one's life relative to one's life experiences. The more resources individuals have, the more choices they have. And the more choices they have, the more stable, secure, and fulfilling their lives tend to be.

Further, from an academic standpoint, research shows that having the ability to actively control one's resources, both internal and external, is essential to college success. In fact, a commitment to academic success relies on students' ability to be self-regulating—that is to say, self-monitoring their learning, which may be driven by, yet also hindered by, their current set of resources (Pintrich, 1995; Perry, 1999). A student who is self-regulating is analogous to a thermostat monitoring and adjusting temperature. Paul Pintrich (1995) explains: "Students can monitor their own behavior, motivation, and cognition, and regulate and adjust these characteristics to fit the demands of a situation" (p. 5). As instructors and student services personnel build an awareness of these resources, they begin to create a meta-awareness in students of the roles these resources play in their academic success. Virtually all students could benefit from examining their reliance on and need for developing resources in order to achieve their goals.

Although there are fine lines between and among the 11 resources, for the sake of discussion they are treated separately and broken into two categories.

INTERNAL RESOURCES	EXTERNAL RESOURCES
1) **KNOWLEDGE OF HIDDEN RULES** Knowing the unspoken cues and habits of a group In college: Hidden rules of wealth, middle class, and poverty … 　Hidden rules of ethnic/racial groups 　Hidden rules of the institution 　Hidden rules of the classroom 　Hidden rules of the discipline/major field of study	8) **LANGUAGE** Having the vocabulary, language ability, and negotiation skills to succeed in work and/or school environment
2) **MENTAL/COGNITIVE** Having the mental ability to learn in order to gain an education and compete in the workforce; having acquired the "readiness" skills necessary for success in college, including organization, note taking, sorting, and planning	9) **RELATIONSHIPS/ROLE MODELS** Having frequent access to adult(s) who are appropriate, who are nurturing, and who do not engage in destructive (including self-destructive) behavior
3) **EMOTIONAL** Being able to choose and control emotional responses, particularly to negative situations, without engaging in self-destructive behavior	10) **SUPPORT SYSTEMS** Having friends, family, and backup resources available to access in times of need
	11) **FINANCIAL** Having the ability to earn and manage money to purchase needed goods and services
4) **MOTIVATION/PERSISTENCE** A mindset that includes having the energy and drive to prepare for, plan, and complete projects, jobs, and personal changes; having a willingness to learn from mistakes	
5) **INTEGRITY/TRUST** Related to predictability, reliability, and safety; having the desire to be accountable, to hold others accountable; trusting others and being trustworthy; having insight about people and situations that will contribute to well-being	
6) **PHYSICAL** Having physical health and mobility	
7) **SPIRITUAL** Believing in divine purpose and guidance; having optimism and hope for the future	

Note. From *Getting Ahead in a Just-Gettin'-By World* (p. 64), by P. E. DeVol, 2004, Highlands, TX: aha! Process. Copyright 2004 by aha! Process. Adapted with permission.

Notice that financial resources constitute just one of the resources—and that the other 10 may function independently of the amount of money individuals have or the economic background from which they come. It is the driving forces of the economic class with which a person identifies that influence how resources are perceived. Further, resources are interconnected; for instance, being in good physical health may influence one's emotional well-being, which in turn influences one's ability to be stable and hence impacts integrity and trust.

Assessing resources can be difficult, even painful. For students in poverty it can be reminiscent of the typical school and agency assessments in which they are eventually deemed "needy and deficient" and prescribed ways to remedy their "condition." In examining anyone's resources, therefore, it is important to look for individual strengths to build on and systemic barriers to remove in order to facilitate the increase of additional resources (see, e.g., DeVol, "The Additive Model" in *Bridges Out of Poverty,* 2006).

Internal Resources

In the following discussion, the first two internal resources—knowledge of hidden rules and mental/cognitive resources—are discussed at length, given their importance and relevance to college success. The other five internal resources are summarized, and discussion of external resources follows this chapter.

KNOWLEDGE OF HIDDEN RULES

Hidden rules exist in many aspects of life. They are the unspoken understandings that cue the members of any particular group concerning expectations and behaviors. There are hidden rules in religions, in fraternities and sororities, in families, in work settings, in ethnic cultures, and in numerous other places. A fascinating aspect of the 1990 movie "Pretty Woman" starring Julia Roberts and Richard Gere is the way in which the two main characters frequently stumble over the hidden rules between poverty and wealth. If there is a hidden-rules gap between poverty and middle class and between middle class and wealth, there's a veritable chasm between poverty and wealth!

Hidden rules are patterns. Patterns are not stereotypes. *All patterns have exceptions.* Therefore, no two families in any socioeconomic class will look the same. The intention in discussing patterns is not to assume or stereotype but to allow the reader to see and understand why such patterns are valid and important for the various classes—and how hidden rules might influence behaviors.

Most students, instructors, and staff know only the hidden rules of their own economic class and perhaps a few rules from another class. Being familiar with just one set of hidden rules restricts the array of choices and responses available, even possible, in a variety of situations. Because the hidden rules of the middle class have been normalized as the dominant culture in the United States, these rules govern most institutions (schools, agencies, and businesses). It is not uncommon for people who have been raised from infancy in middle-class environments to assume that everyone "should know how to act" according to the rules of their dominant group. Of course, this dynamic occurs in all groups in relation to other groups; it is one of the seedbeds of bias, prejudice, even racism. Recognizing the reality and purpose of hidden rules builds understanding and respect—and reduces judgmental and prejudicial attitudes.

Hidden Rules of Economic Class

	POVERTY	MIDDLE CLASS	WEALTH
DRIVING FORCES	Survival, relation-ships, entertainment	Work and achievement	Financial, political, social connections
POSSESSIONS	People	Things	"One of a kind" objects, legacies, pedigrees
MONEY	To be used, spent	To be managed	To be conserved, invested
PERSONALITY	Is for entertainment; sense of humor is highly valued	Is for acquisition and stability; achievement is highly valued	Is for connections; financial, political, social connections are highly valued
SOCIAL EMPHASIS	Social inclusion of the people they like	Emphasis is on self-governance and self-sufficiency	Emphasis is on social exclusion
FOOD	Key question: Did you have enough? Quantity important	Key question: Did you like it? Quality important	Key question: Was it presented well? Presentation important
CLOTHING	Clothing valued for individual style and expression of personality	Clothing valued for its quality and acceptance into the norms of middle class; label important	Clothing valued for its artistic sense and expression; designer important

continued on next page

continued from previous page

	POVERTY	MIDDLE CLASS	WEALTH
TIME	Present most important; decisions made for the moment based on feelings or survival	Future most important; decisions made against future ramifications	Traditions and past history most important; decisions made partially on basis of tradition decorum
EDUCATION	Valued and revered as abstract but not as reality; education is about facts	Crucial for climbing success ladder and making money	Necessary tradition for making and maintaining connections
DESTINY	Believes in fate; cannot do much to mitigate chance	Believes in choice; can change future with good choices now	*Noblesse oblige*
LANGUAGE	Casual register; language is about survival	Formal register; language is about negotiation	Formal register; language is about connection
FAMILY STRUCTURE	Tends to be matriarchal	Tends to be patriarchal	Depends on who has/ controls money
WORLD VIEW	Sees world in terms of local setting	Sees world in terms of national setting	Sees world in terms of an international view
LOVE	Love and acceptance conditional, based on whether individual is liked	Love and acceptance conditional, based largely on achievement	Love and acceptance conditional, related to social standing and connections
POWER	Power is linked to respect; must have the ability to fight; people respond to personal power; there is power in numbers; people from poverty cannot stop bad things from happening	Power is separated out from respect; must have an ability to negotiate; power is linked to taking responsibility for solutions; power is in institutions; people in middle class run the institutions	Power is linked to stability; must have influence and connections; people respond to expertise; power is information; people in wealth set the direction for business and public policy

Note. From *A Framework for Understanding Poverty* (pp. 42–43), by R. K. Payne, 2005, Highlands, TX: aha! Process. Copyright 1996 by aha! Process. Reprinted with permission.

The hidden rules of time, for example, influence decision making and problem solving. Under-resourced students often have very strong problem-solving skills, having had much practice in solving the problems and crises caused by a low-resourced environment. Their problem-solving skills concentrate most often in the present, in the moment, because the time horizon is the present, and immediate needs are the focus. As noted in

Chapter 1, people in poverty spend much of their time living in the tyranny of the moment. Although problem-solving skills are often well cultivated, life situations can be so intense that even problem solvers simply do not have the time or energy to plan. Time spent on planning is an investment, and many feel they do not have the time to invest or are opposed to spending needed resources pursuing dreams without the clear means of reaching them. In an environment with a chronic shortage of resources needed to carry a plan to fruition, planning can be considered a waste of time. Students may lack the future story to plan for long-term projects—or do not see the relevance of their present education to their future lives. Without planning skills, many under-resourced students simply do not know how to even start tasks that they consider to be complicated. Tasks that many would consider commonsensical can be overwhelming to those who have not succeeded in relation to similar challenges in the past.

Also, whenever something worthwhile is attempted there is some risk of failure. From the students' perspective, in some situations it seems better to do nothing than to risk trying to achieve, failing, and suffering negative consequences. A community college student writes about this experience as follows [verbatim from the student's paper]:

> I can relate to alot of the students when they say that asking alot of questions in class can make them feel "stupid" becaues of what some teacher might say or if the students might laugh. I have had plenty of teachers that could care less about what you needed help with and would be quick to say something to embarass u in front of everone in class. (DeWitt, 2007b)

For many from generational poverty, the hidden rule of "fate as destiny" reinforces the feeling of being controlled by forces beyond their control. Indeed, their choices are often limited, and unavailable resources keep many options outside of the realm of possibility. Thus they feel there is little point in trying. Further, some may have had previous negative experiences with plans from agencies and other "helping organizations," while still others avoid planning tasks because they lack commitment, are resistant to change, believe things are OK the way they are, or don't know where to start. Theories of learned helplessness (Abramson, Seligman, & Teasdale, 1978) support the concept of the hidden rules regarding power ("One cannot stop bad things from happening") and destiny ("One cannot do much to mitigate fate").

According to social psychologist Raymond Perry (1999), achievement-driven students respond differently from "students prone to the feeling of helplessness (p. 17). The feeling of helplessness affects their willingness to try and the reasons they perceive to be causing their failure or success. "Maladaptive attributional profiles" (reasons for behaving helplessly) are evident as early as elementary schools (Diener & Dweck, 1978) and stem from such characteristics as students' self-esteem, gender, and cultural backgrounds. Thus Perry and his many associates recommend that professionals model "adaptive attributions"—behaviors and beliefs that promote adapting to the task and completing it (e.g., Menec, Perry, Struthers, Schonwetter, Hechter, & Eichholz, 1994)—and carefully examine their motivational strategies for the consequences they might have on under-resourced learners (Menec & Perry, 1995).

Another example of the differing hidden rules in wealth, middle class, and poverty relates to possessions. Middle-class students who have a history of owning and caring for "things" place more value on possessions—and are then very concerned about keeping up with their books and other school materials. Therefore, they will put their name on their textbooks, so that if the textbook is lost, it can be returned. Students from poverty are less likely to put identification on their belongings because in their experience "things" come and go with the situations and circumstances of life. Most have learned to find happiness outside of material possessions. The consequence, then, is that the student who does not put any identification on his or her book is less likely to get it returned—and it might be this same student who was least able to afford the book in the first place, let alone a replacement.

Knowledge about hidden rules is often mistakenly equated with intelligence, thereby playing a vital role in prompting success within, or alienation from, a group. Such knowledge is related to "a sense of knowing" or what is perceived as "common sense" within the group in which the rules are found. When seeking entrance into a group (in college that might mean classmates in an extracurricular sport, club, or honor society—or simply students who "hang out" in a certain study area or specific places on campus) it is necessary for students to adjust their behavior, at least to some extent, to be compatible with the group's culture. Those who do not make adjustments can expect to be "expelled" from the group (Harris, 1998). Much has been written about the consequences of social exclusion—the lack of opportunities to participate in mainstream activities (Glennerster, 2002) and the devastating effects of life devoid of bridging capital (Mosse, 2005):

> [P]eople become empowered not in themselves, but through relationships with outsiders, and not through the validation of their existing knowledge and actions, but by seeking out and acknowledging modern technology and lifestyles, and by aligning themselves with dominant cultural forms. (p. 58)

For young adults the effects of growing up in poverty and not knowing the hidden rules of middle class are intensified as they "may be at a significant disadvantage in terms of their ability to compete effectively within the labor market" (Rank, 2005, p. 47). The effects of poverty also include "reduced participation in civic activities, as well as in other aspects of life" (Rank, p. 47). In a chapter titled "Group Savvy: Interpreting the Situation and/or Network of an Organization" from the book *Emotionally Intelligent Leadership: A Guide for College Students,* Marcy Shankman and Scott Allen (2008) liken the process of understanding group culture to that of peeling away the layers of an onion. On the outside are the brown protective layers of skin, but each layer after that moves from something fragile and paper-like to something stronger, including the pungent and powerful center from which new growth occurs. The outer layers, Shankman and Allen explain, are the written rules of the group, but as you get to know a group, you find out who is really in charge and what really matters to the group … even who is the "in" group and who are the outsiders. Within one's own economic class, many are proficient at using group savvy by "seeking out the questions that reveal the center." There are plenty of opportunities once students set foot on campus to practice using their "group savvy" skills to identify hidden rules of this new culture. The key is that college instructors and support staff build students' understanding of the concept of hidden rules in general and their awareness of opportunities to learn the rules that exist on campus.

Hidden Rules of College

Think of any college campus and the routines, traditions, and culture created by students, faculty, student organizations, and stakeholders of the institution. There may be hidden rules about how to contact instructors between classes or how to inquire about a grade. There may be hidden rules about what types of classrooms allow food and drink or where different groups of students sit in the cafeteria or what goes on during hazing and "freshman rush." Under-resourced students, as well as others, may never have heard of a provost, bursar, or ombudsman. They might not realize the "Center for Student Progress" provides tutoring and is not a political action group.

There were hidden rules for students in high school that they may continue to act on in college. For instance, many students are passed on from grade to grade without meeting class requirements. Some graduate from high school and come to college not realizing that one must actually *pass the course* (generally inclusive of meeting the course requirements) in order to proceed. Or, if one is upset with an instructor, the first step is not to go to the college president. Indeed, that's not even the *fourth* step at some schools. Rather, one is expected to meet first with the instructor. Similarly, staff persons involved in recruitment, admissions, and placement testing offices might share with students the fact that the college placement test is taken seriously and determines what level of coursework the student will be required to take. Consider how many standardized tests the average student from a public school system has taken and how rarely the tests have any impact on actual course of study. But "blowing off" the placement exam might result in semesters lost to developmental education. Directly teaching students about this, coupled with brush-up courses, can reduce the number of students mistakenly placed into noncredit-bearing coursework.

Many students, whether deemed "at risk" or "honors," treat learning as a largely passive task. When they are not immediately successful, perhaps getting a low score on a quiz or a first paper, they see themselves as "not college material" because they expect learning and good grades to be largely effortless (Singham, 2005). They expect to enter a classroom, be quiet, and let the instructor teach, forgetting, if they ever realized otherwise, that teaching is done for the sake of their learning. Some students have a great fear of failure and, therefore, avoid taking risks in the classroom, so "class discussions" frequently involve only a few courageous or extroverted students and the instructor. If students have any prior knowledge of the course materials, most tend to leave it at the door—where it does little good for making connections in the process of learning. Studying outside of class time usually means rote memorization of notes and possibly textbook materials. In the consumer model for college learning, students are the customers. Because tuition was paid for their seat in the classroom and they participated in the curriculum in some minimal way, they expect a good grade. Here the product (the grade) takes precedence over cognitive and behavioral change (the learning), a philosophy quite at odds with the perspectives of most instructors.

The college scene tends to be intimidating to new students—and even more so to under-resourced students who may lack the self-confidence to withstand the risk of ridicule. Many under-resourced students, lacking in planning behaviors and an understanding of consequences, do not consider asking for help—in order to avoid making mistakes in connection with hidden rules. It simply does not occur to them to ask. Since many under-resourced students are first generation, they likely lack the social capital of family members or mentors with college experience to share. That intergenerational transfer of knowledge allows students to learn about the hidden rules of college either through shared stories or direct-teaching. Such information helps adequately resourced students feel more prepared for the joys and demands of college. As a result, they are more likely to feel connected and to persist in their educational efforts. Many under-resourced students, on the other hand, need intentional infusions of such information and social capital once they arrive on campus.

Students should not be criticized or ridiculed for their lack of knowledge of hidden rules any more than they could be expected to know calculus before taking the course. The rules they know have been learned for the sake of survival and inclusion within their group. To be successful at school and in technical and professional positions, students from poverty need to learn the middle-class hidden rules, which govern most institutions. These rules, therefore, need to be explicitly taught. In other words, instructors may find it helpful, even necessary, to discreetly teach certain hidden rules. Middle-class instructors who participate in discussions with students about hidden rules often become more informed about the hidden rules of poverty in the process, thereby becoming essentially "bilingual" themselves. As a result, working from more than one set of rules can help both students and staff put positive actions into practice—and perhaps keep problematic things from happening when rules are broken.

Given that many students from poverty value relationships more than possessions, it is important for instructors and other postsecondary educators to build relationships of trust and mutual respect with students. Within the safety of such relationships, instructors can teach and students can learn from very personal lessons related to hidden rules. It is also within the context of these relationships that accommodations can be made. For example, even when it is understood that cell phones are prohibited in the classroom, it may be a good idea for a teacher to counsel students that if an emergency call is anticipated, they may notify the instructor at the beginning of class, put their phones on vibrate, sit near the door, and answer the call *outside* the classroom. And suppose a student missed an exam because her driving force of relationships and hidden rule of seeing people as possessions motivated her to attend to her sister's need for a ride to work instead of taking the test. In this case, the instructor might conference with the student to explain the hidden rules of middle class about keeping appointments and obligations, as well as to brainstorm options that could be considered in the future. Could the sister arrive at work early? Could the student enter into a contract with the instructor to negotiate missed tests in the future? The instructor might consider coaching the student in the importance of talking to the instructor about missed classes—and in how to tell a story (provide an explanation) using the language of negotiation that addresses the *instructor's* driving force of achievement, along with hidden rules about time management, education, and responsibility. In this way students learn to translate their needs and experience into language acceptable to the instructor, such that perhaps some compromise about how to handle the missed test can be arranged.

Instructors have reported a change in their opinions about and attitudes toward students after learning about the hidden rules of poverty. Many report that they no longer interpret certain behaviors—such as students laughing in the face of discipline—as a personal affront. Rather, they recognize it as a teachable moment. Others have reported that learning about hidden rules has helped them better understand not only their students but also themselves and their life partners.

Hidden Rules Self-Assessments

The following self-inventory surveys provide a sense of how strongly one identifies with an economic class and what triggers positive and negative reactions. The surveys also illustrate that successful movement between economic classes is a function of much more than having (or not having) money.

Could You Cope with a Spouse/Partner Who Came from Generational Poverty (or Had That Mindset)?

It would bother me if my spouse or partner:

____ Repeatedly gave money to a relative who would not work.
____ Left household bills unpaid in order to give money to a relative.
____ Loaned the car to a relative who doesn't have insurance and cannot be insured.
____ Allowed a relative to move in and stay with us.
____ Didn't pay attention to time (e.g., missed dates, was extremely late, didn't show).
____ Quit jobs without having another one because he/she didn't like the boss.
____ Cursed at his/her boss in public.
____ Physically fought—fairly frequently.
____ Didn't think education was important.
____ Left items in the house unrepaired.
____ Used physical punishment on the children as part of discipline.
____ Viewed himself as a "fighter" or a "lover" who works hard physically.
____ Served food from the stove—and ate most meals in front of the TV.
____ Almost always had the TV and/or radio on … and often loudly.
____ Kept the house dark on the inside—poorly lit and with window coverings closed.

____ Kept organizational patterns of household chaotic.
____ Bought clothing from secondhand stores, garage sales, and so on.
____ Bought designer clothing or shoes for our children, but didn't pay an urgent household bill.
____ Made a big deal about the quantity of food.
____ Viewed me as a possession.
____ Had family members who made fun of me for having a college degree.
____ Bragged about me by talking badly about me.
____ Chose to spend time with relatives, rather than spending time with me.
____ Purchased alcoholic beverages for entertainment before paying for necessities (e.g., car insurance, utilities, rent).

Could You Cope with a Spouse/Partner Who Came from Middle Class (or Had That Mindset)?

It would bother me if my spouse or partner:

____ Spent long hours at the office.
____ Required our household to run on a budget.
____ Planned out our week in advance.
____ Started a college fund at the birth of our child.
____ Hired a plumber to do a needed repair.
____ Fixed the plumbing himself/herself.
____ Played golf every weekend with his buddies.
____ Kept a job that he/she hates for financial reasons.
____ Rigidly adhered to time demands–and was often early.
____ Was organized, keeping a paper trail on everything.
____ Refused to give money to relatives who weren't working.
____ Refused to allow a relative to come live with us.
____ Planned vacations a year in advance.
____ Spent evenings taking graduate courses.
____ Devoted considerable time to a community charitable event.
____ Shopped for high-quality clothing/shoes/accessories, then charged those items.
____ Withdrew TV, computer, and other privileges from the children as part of discipline.
____ Paid for our child's college expenses and tuition.
____ Paid for tennis, golf, dance, swimming, and other types of lessons for our child.
____ Often made a big issue over the quality of food.
____ Bought reprints and numbered artwork as part of our home's décor.
____ Purchased furniture for its practicality and match to the décor.
____ Had family members who discounted me because of my lack of education or achievement.

Could You Cope with a Spouse/Partner Who Came from Old Money (or Had That Mindset)?

It would bother me if my spouse or partner:

_____ Spent money on private club memberships.

_____ Had a trust fund from birth.

_____ Insisted on the artistic quality and merit of household items, clothing, accessories, and so on.

_____ Had a personal assistant to assist with purchases of clothing and accessories.

_____ Spent money on a personal tailor and physical trainer.

_____ Spent a great deal of time on charitable activities and did not make or take money for that time.

_____ Placed our children in the care of a nanny.

_____ Insisted that our children be placed in private boarding schools at the age of 6.

_____ Talked a lot about the presentation of food.

_____ Staffed and maintained homes in more than one country.

_____ Spent money on a private airplane and/or yacht.

_____ Established trust funds for our children at birth.

_____ Maintained social and financial connections with individuals whom I didn't like.

_____ Had family members who looked down on me because of my bloodline or pedigree (or lack thereof).

_____ Kept an accountant, lawyer, domestic service agency, and investment broker on retainer.

_____ Was adamant about details, insisting on perfection in virtually everything.

_____ Wanted to have nothing further to do with a decent individual who didn't have a suitable connection.

_____ Spent $1 million-plus on an original piece of art, and would only purchase original works of art.

_____ Attended an Ivy League college or university.

_____ Valued me largely for my social connections.

_____ Reviewed family assets and liabilities on a monthly basis.

_____ Purchased furniture and furnishings for their artistic merit or designer designation.

_____ Kept almost no food in the house.

Note. From *Crossing the Tracks for Love* (pp. 13–17), by R. K. Payne, 2005, Highlands, TX: aha! Process. Copyright 2005 by aha! Process. Reprinted with permission.

Identifying what we cannot cope with or tolerate helps us determine the hidden rules that we ourselves live by. These surveys illustrate that the middle class and wealthy are not very well equipped to cope with daily realities in poverty—and that money does not make "poor people" able to meet mainstream expectations. The eye-opening truth for many middle-class readers is that more money will not really help most individuals in poverty function successfully among the middle class any more than money helps the middle class function successfully among the wealthy.

Characteristics, attributes, and behaviors of students with knowledge of and practice in the hidden rules of middle class, as well as high levels of emotional intelligence, include:

- Able to adapt to social situations outside one's comfort zone
- Can identify at school or work what will actually get you into trouble versus what the rules say will get you into trouble
- Can identify and avoid "pet peeves" of persons in charge—that is, boss, teacher, adviser, et al.
- Is successful with different teachers, students, bosses
- Knows who the "real authority" is in a given situation versus the "stated authority"
- Can work/learn from others, even if he or she does not like them
- Can appropriately use humor or avoid using humor as is appropriate to the situation

Note. From *Under-Resourced Learners* (p. 13), by R. K. Payne, 2008, Highlands, TX: aha! Process. Copyright 2008 by aha! Process. Adapted with permission.

When talking about hidden rules, it is important to note that students may actually need to learn several sets of rules. In college alone these rules may include:

- Hidden rules of wealth, middle class, and poverty
- Hidden rules of ethnic/racial groups
- Hidden rules of the institution
- Hidden rules of the classroom
- Hidden rules of the discipline/major field of study

Also, patience and perseverance are needed by those who assume the role of teaching hidden rules to students, as the rules by which both parties are living have been acquired over their lifetimes. Students will need many opportunities to practice new rules before they become automatic.

MENTAL/COGNITIVE

Mental resources encompass the cognitive skills and ability to process information and use it in daily living. The individual's ability to read, write, compute, and access information from a variety of sources (lectures, textbooks, periodicals, online materials, media, etc.) will influence success in college. Hundreds of studies indicate that a wide range of circumstances affect, both negatively and positively, cognitive development and student achievement, including:

- Birth weight
- Being read to as a child
- Television watching
- Student mobility (moving to new school districts)
- Rigor of curriculum
- Teacher experience and preparation
- Class size
- Technology-assisted instruction
- Safety

Most colleges and universities require some entry-level assessments that report a student's likelihood for success based on academic performance. While there are limitations to these assessments, they are helpful in identifying students who need academic remediation. Nonetheless, instructors commonly find that some students are taking college-level courses without college-level skills.

Just as hidden rules are acquired first through the modeling and reinforcement by caretakers in the child's home, so too are cognitive skills developed. The family provides the primary environment within which the physical structures of the brain and the cognitive structures of the mind are developed. Reuven Feuerstein (as cited in Sharron & Coulter, 2004, p. 37) researched and quantified the development of cognitive structures in childhood, as well as the resulting problems in processing information (thinking) that manifest themselves when a child does not have sufficient opportunities to acquire these skills. The complicated stressors associated with poverty and low-resource environments can have profound effects on a child's exposure to experiences that facilitate development of learning structures. The summary of research that follows might inform the design and development of college syllabi because, fortunately, missed childhood opportunities to build cognitive structures can be overcome.

Feuerstein, who had studied with Jean Piaget, believed that "the Piagetian concept of development could not explain the very large differences in learning abilities between individuals and within groups, classes, and cultures. It could not, for example, explain the poor performance of [children from poverty] compared to … working-class children generally" (Sharron & Coulter, 2004, p. 37).

Feuerstein (as cited in Sharron & Coulter, 2004) explained that parents, caretakers, or teachers "mediate" experiences. Mediation means helping to construct the child's world by selecting, ordering, emphasizing, and explaining selected stimuli (things, events) at the expense of other stimuli. Mediation supplies the *why,* which forms the foundation for cognitive skill development. The mediation of meaning occurs when adults bring significance to things, events, or situations, thereby transferring values to the child. For example, note how values about books are shared when a parent says, "What do you ever see in those books? Go outside and play!" versus "This was my favorite book when I was your age; I think you will love it too." Mediated learning experiences (as opposed to direct physical experiences) necessitate a "human mediator" between the child and the environment. The mediator interprets and prepares experiences for the child "so that the child builds up strategies for how to focus, how to observe and how to differentiate" (Sharron & Coulter, p. 350), according to a shared system of cultural meaning and values.

"Intentionality" is Feuerstein's term (as cited in Sharron & Coulter, 2004) for a complex process in which an adult shows the child a new function of an object, different from what the child already knows. For example, when showing a baby that a ball not only rolls but bounces, the intentional teaching behavior of the adult engages the child and teaches him or her to focus and to perceive the connection between object, function, and action. In the long term, this is critical to goal setting and planning. The cognitive processes that are used when perceiving a goal include representation, analysis, comparison, sequencing, ordering in terms of magnitude, and thinking hypothetically and inferentially (Feuerstein, 1985).

Another critical feature in mediated learning experiences is "transcendence"—the extent to which adult-child interactions transcend the immediate experience and move into life lessons. According to Howard Sharron and Martha Coulter (2004), transcendence can be demonstrated in a family outing when the

> opportunity for conveying planning behavior and aspects of time relations before, during, [and] after are grasped. In response to simple questions parents often provide much more than they were asked for and, by so doing, transcend the original need that provoked the question or request. (p. 45)

Sharron and Coulter (2004) further report Feuerstein's summary of the importance of the family dynamic to cognitive development:

> Family structures arise from the environment and meet the survival needs of the people in the family—often dictating the types of interactions and life lessons a person will have to build on as they grow older. The root of cognitive deficiencies lies in the quality of children's relationships within their families. Parents who completely lack routine, drag their children around behind them, and impose restrictions that are not explained, or parents who fail to instill the habit of picturing the future or of precision in gathering and expressing information, could impair the development of thinking skills in their children. Mediated interactions between parents and children can be very subtle, and may be accomplished in non-linguistic codes that convey immense information but are very difficult to spot. It is rare to find a complete absence of routine, or an absence of any reciprocal communication between parents or caretakers and children. The success or failure of parents to mediate effectively to children is a question of degree. (p. 73)

In order for observers to pinpoint children's cognitive difficulties, the act of thinking may be separated into three theoretical parts or stages:

1. The input of information, concerned with gathering data necessary for task completion
2. The elaboration phase where the data are manipulated and processed
3. The output phase where application and expression through writing, talking, or some physical action take place. (Sharron & Coulter, 2004, p. 60)

Each stage in the mediated learning experience can be understood as processing the thinking by first asking *what* at the input stage, then *why* at the elaboration stage, and finally *how* at the output stage. It is important to note that the thinking components are separated for theoretical purposes into these three stages, but they rarely occur separately in real life.

The types and degrees of cognitive skill gaps demonstrated by college students (and all adults) range far and wide, with equally diverse implications for student success and the design of programs and pedagogy. Though our emphasis remains on students' strengths, the language of the day for Feuerstein and Dorothy Merchant focused on "deficiencies." The following table defines the intellectual processing challenges, as well as diagnostic language describing observable behaviors and examples of student behavior in the classroom.

Student Characteristic Resulting from Missing or Lacking Input, Elaboration, and Output Skills	Classroom Behaviors That Demonstrate These Characteristics
Input Phase Impairments concerning the quantity and quality of data gathered by the individual	
▪ Blurred and sweeping perceptions	▪ Misses seeing salient features of an object or event ▪ Has difficulty concentrating ▪ Cannot relate parts of information to a whole structure
▪ Unplanned, impulsive, and unsystematic exploratory behavior	▪ Does not care where they start or move to next in solving a problem ▪ Does not have a need to do things sequentially
▪ Impaired receptive verbal tools and concepts that affect discrimination	▪ Does not fully understand concepts
▪ Impaired spatial organization, including the lack of stable systems of reference, which impairs the establishment of topological and Euclidian organization of space	▪ Has difficulty organizing space
▪ Impaired temporal orientation	▪ Does not "fully comprehend sequences of events or the concept of succession" (p. 64) ▪ Fails to "use past experience or anticipations of the future to control themselves" (p. 64) ▪ Has difficulty organizing time effectively ▪ Is unable to read question completely before starting a task because "time during periods of excitement, danger, depression or great anticipation can burst far beyond its 'real' barriers" (p. 64) ▪ Spending too much time on one question
▪ Lack of or impaired conservation of constancies	▪ Has difficulty remembering shapes, colors, and orientation of an object in order to compare it with another
▪ Lack of or deficient precision and accuracy in data gathering	▪ Considers "accuracy in what they do as a waste of time and energy" (p. 66)
▪ Lack of or impaired capacity for considering two sources of information at once, reflected in dealing with data in a piecemeal fashion rather than as a unit of organized facts	▪ Misses some clues when several clues present themselves for use in solving a problem ▪ Lacks need or ability to impose order on information
Elaboration Phase Impairments concerning the efficient use of data available to the individual	
▪ Inadequacy in experiencing the existence of problems and subsequently defining actual problems	▪ Misses clues or alarms that indicate that a problem exists
▪ Inability to select relevant, as opposed to irrelevant, cues in defining a problem	▪ Has difficulty summarizing
▪ Lack of spontaneous comparative behavior or limitation of its appearance to a restricted field of needs	▪ Demonstrates judgmental and "iffy" thinking ▪ When asked to compare two objects or events, first describes one at a time, without referring to the other

continued on next page

continued from previous page

Student Characteristic Resulting from Missing or Lacking Input, Elaboration, and Output Skills	Classroom Behaviors That Demonstrate These Characteristics
Elaboration Phase *(continued)* Impairments concerning the efficient use of data available to the individual	
▪ Narrowness of the psychological field	▪ Cannot process much information at one time ▪ Has poor short-term memory
▪ Lack of or impaired need for summative behavior	▪ Is unable to measure progress toward goals
▪ Difficulties in projecting virtual relationships	▪ Lacks need to provide logical reasons for their opinions ▪ Has no need to pursue logical evidence when confronting a problem
▪ Lack of orientation toward the need for logical evidence as an interactional modality with one's objectal and social environment	▪ Is unable to construct strategies for solving a problem
▪ Lack of or limited interiorization of one's behavior	▪ Is unable to construct hypotheses of possibly correct solutions
▪ Lack of or restricted inferential/hypothetical thinking	▪ Cannot generate information from given information
▪ Lack of or impaired strategies for hypothesis testing	▪ Becomes committed to hypotheses before testing them
Output Phase Impairments concerning the communication of the outcome of elaborative processes	
▪ Egocentric communicational modalities	▪ Has impaired need to express thoughts clearly
▪ Blocking	▪ Has impaired or lack of ability to express ideas
▪ Trial-and-error responses	▪ Is unable to learn a route to a successful answer again
▪ Lack of or impaired verbal tools for communicating adequately elaborated responses	▪ Is unable to communicate problem solutions that the student has solved mentally
▪ Impulsive acting-out behavior, affecting the nature of the communication process	▪ Says the first thing that comes to mind

Note. From *Changing Children's Minds: Feuerstein's Revolution in the Teaching of Intelligence* (pp. 60–74), by H. Sharron and M. Coulter, 2004, Highlands, TX: aha! Process. Copyright 2004 by aha! Process. Adapted with permission.

Merchant's 1986 study shows that indeed most students placed into developmental education (DE) classes see themselves as needing to improve in certain areas. In Merchant's study, community college students in DE courses were asked to rank the characteristics identified in the preceding chart in terms of how often they experience them and the impact of these deficiencies on their academic performance. DE students identified 13 deficiencies as "frequent problems" compared with only two for the nondevelopmental education group (Merchant, 1986). Frequent problem areas for students in developmental education classes included a "limited need for spontaneous comparative behavior"

(p. 122) being experienced by most of the students and "poor strategies for hypothesis testing" (p. 122) identified by 30% or more for both groups. "Blocking," described by Merchant as giving up when frustrated, was the problem DE students identified as having the greatest impact. Further, Merchant found that

> DE students felt especially handicapped by their lack of command of the language; inability to communicate verbal response, lack of precision and accuracy of verbal tools, and egocentric communication were all cited as having a major impact on academic performance by developmental education students. (p. 122)

When faculty in Merchant's (1986) study ranked the characteristics for frequency and impact, DE faculty observed more deficiencies than nondevelopmental faculty. For DE students and faculty, there was considerable overlap in the deficiencies identified. Merchant concluded that cognitive skill training and language enrichment activities were clearly indicated as necessary to addressing the limitations identified by both students and faculty.

Interestingly, however, a significant disparity existed between faculty and student perceptions of the impact of these limitations on academic performance—suggesting, according to Merchant (1986), "a need to increase student awareness of the fact that these deficiencies may be the basis of their academic difficulties" (p. 124). Thus Merchant points out that while the students identified deficiencies from the output and elaboration phases as having the greatest impact, students may need to focus on input strategies to strengthen their overall skills. Payne observes that most K–12 teachers "begin teaching at the elaboration level (i.e., use of the data). When students do not understand, we reteach these strategies, but we do not revisit the quality and quantity of the data gathered" (Payne, 2005b, p. 95). Thus teaching occurs with the assumption that the input strategies are already in place. Without the *what* (input strategies), many learners are at a disadvantage, leaving any reference to *why* and *how* irrelevant to them. Essentially, Merchant urges that "students must be encouraged to be more active learners and taught how" (p. 126).

While many postsecondary staff and instructors have some knowledge of the above theories, many others do not. Expert faculty in their discipline may have limited exposure to educational theory. At times, instructors and academic support staff alike might misinterpret common behaviors that many under-resourced students exhibit as meaning the student is "unintelligent" or "not college material." However, when student behavior is interpreted as less than adequate input, elaboration, and/or output strategies, accommodations are more easily identified and accurately implemented. These could range from the "macro" (curricular changes to facilitate greater learning success) to the "micro" (perhaps one-on-one assistance to help overcome the frustration of filling out a form). For students in general, behaviors that might interfere with college success may result from one or a combination of missing and/or lacking input, elaboration, and output skills as illustrated below.

Concrete vs. Abstract Thinking

Understanding involves two perceptual qualities: concrete and abstract. Students whose early years are enriched with opportunities for dealing with abstract thought, along with the vocabulary with which to express abstract thoughts, typically have acquired the foundation for both abstract and concrete levels of understanding. For other students, however, a focus on the concrete is, in part, a survival skill stemming from the fact that their lives are so often lived in the moment. To survive in poverty, one must be very sensory based and nonverbal. To survive in school, one must be very verbal and abstract, conversant with both the paper and, increasingly, computer worlds. The inability to think abstractly can be detrimental to the type of learning expected at the college level.

In its simplest form, concrete understanding deals with real or actual things about which people can gather information through their five senses. Abstract understandings include ideas, visualizations, and concepts that one cannot actually see or sense tangibly. Brophy (1998) points out that "definitions, principles, and other abstract information may have little meaning for students unless made more concrete" (p. 180). Such definitions largely comprise the *what* of the mediated learning experience. If the definitions and principles are missing or not connected to the concepts to be learned in a college classroom—or to the process necessary to get admitted, access tuition support, and so on—many students will be left behind, feeling frustrated and inadequate from the start.

An example of an abstraction that can pose a variety of problems for under-resourced students is the emphasis in higher education on the abstract nature of the world of paper and the computer (Payne, 2008b, p. 53). A different set of skills is required for interpreting the sensory information represented on paper or screen. For example, a blueprint represents a house but is not the house. More abstractly, numbers written on a piece of paper represent an amount, but they are not the actual items being counted. At the foundation of this phenomenon with the abstract representation of paper is the fact that paper, as well as most information on a computer screen, does not have nonverbal cues (e.g., hand gestures, facial features, body language), emotions, or human interaction, which are crucial to effective communication within the casual register. Rather, a shared understanding of vocabulary is necessary in order to communicate meanings for abstract concepts.

The number and type of paper documents in a household reveals to some extent the family's familiarity and comfort with the paper world. The volume of paper increases, as well as the level of abstraction, as a person's financial situation improves. The continuum below demonstrates three levels of documents a family acquires as income and wealth accumulate.

Continuum of Paper Documents

birth certificates
immunization records
driver's license
rental agreements
money orders
paycheck stubs
bills

wills
magazines/newspapers
payment records
credit-card and bank statements
mortgage papers
calendars
planners
to-do lists
tax returns
books
coupons
passports

corporate financial statements
prenuptial agreement
stock certificates/personal investments
provenance
property deeds
charity events/invitations
board of directors minutes/records
club memberships
trusts

Note. From *Under-Resourced Learners* (p. 55), by R. K. Payne, 2008, Highlands, TX: aha! Process. Copyright 2008 by aha! Process. Reprinted with permission.

For students low in resources, application to college can seem daunting, even prohibitive—because words, symbols, etc., are used to convey meanings on paper. Some examples of abstract items that are represented on paper are included in the following chart:

ABSTRACT ITEM	REPRESENTS
Grades/transcripts/GED/ certificate of completion	The ticket to get out of high school, into college, a better job, more money
House deed	The physical property
Social Security number	The person (way to keep track of people on paper)
Daily to-do list	Daily tasks, the day's work ahead
Calendar	Abstract time—past, present, future
Placement tests	Academic qualifications
Homework, assignments	Ability to complete a task in a given time frame, to prove understandings
Insurance papers	Protection from or support during unusual circumstances, safety
Musical notations	Symbols that represent sounds, timing
Student handbook	Appropriate behaviors, processes on campus
Add/drop forms	Permission to be in class or not
Online/library book loan systems	Library stacks, books, check-out desk, librarian
Financial aid forms, scholarship applications	Tuition
Virtual learning environments, such as WebCT and Blackboard	Classrooms, instructors, study groups, assignments
Syllabus	Teaching, learning in any given course
E-mail, attachments	Conversations, documents
Licenses, continuing education units	Technical, professional proficiency

Note. From *Under-Resourced Learners* (p. 54), by R. K. Payne, 2008, Highlands, TX: aha! Process. Copyright 2008 by aha! Process. Adapted with permission.

Characteristics, skills, attributes, and behaviors that indicate high levels of mental/cognitive resources generally necessary for college-level work include:

- Can read at a rate that does not interfere with meaning and comprehension
- Can read material required for the college-level course
- Can read at a rate that allows for completion of reading assignments
- Can operate in the "paper world" (and technology world) of school and work
- Can type/keyboard well enough to do word processing
- Can write to communicate sufficiently for assignments required in and out of class
- Can use specific vocabulary related to the content or the task
- Can prioritize important information for a task or in a text
- Can explain how concepts are alike or different
- Can develop questions over content or tasks on the job

continued on next page

continued from previous page

- Is organized and can find materials when they are needed
- Can add, subtract, multiply, and divide without a calculator
- Can do the math as required for the entry-level courses
- Can operate a calculator
- Can understand money as represented on paper—that is, checkbooks, bank statements, etc.
- Can solve problems by trial and error
- Knows how to prepare for and take tests
- Is able to write a formal paper with appropriate language skills
- Can read a map
- Can follow written directions
- Can use a calendar
- Can divide tasks into parts, setting goals for accomplishing the task
- Is generally on time to class and appointments
- Is able to engage in procedural self-talk
- Can make decisions based on future needs, not just immediate needs
- Can get tasks or projects done on time (paper representation of time)
- Can represent an idea in a visual or a story (using mental models)
- Enjoys using artistic or creative skills

Note. From *Under-Resourced Learners* (pp. 7–8), by R. K. Payne, 2008, Highlands, TX: aha! Process. Copyright 2008 by aha! Process. Adapted with permission.

This list of cognitive-based abilities is indeed lengthy—but in its length we see the variety of mental operations needed to function in most college classrooms and to pass most college courses. Understanding how to build these skills into college assignments, class discussions, and individual discussions with under-resourced students can significantly increase students' ability and motivation to accomplish their higher education goals. The first step in helping students develop cognitive skills is to understand why such skills may be missing in the first place for some students.

EMOTIONAL

Emotional health has been defined as the "state of mind" that determines the way we think, feel, and behave at any given moment. It also includes interpersonal skills, such as teamwork, teaching, leadership, negotiation, and working with people from a variety of backgrounds. Emotional resources provide the stamina to withstand difficult and uncomfortable situations. Strong emotional resources allow people to take risks, assimilate new thoughts and behaviors, and avoid old and often destructive patterns if challenged.

> Poverty, addiction, abuse, and other dangerous situations can create in us reactions and patterns of behavior that work against us. They can create thoughts, feelings, and behaviors that are weak. For example, we might think, I can't do this, I'm no good, It's all my fault, or It's all someone else's fault. We might feel sorry for ourselves, useless, ashamed, angry, or self-destructive. We might blame others, whine, waste time, manipulate others, give up, hurt ourselves, or hurt others. If this is our way of looking at the world and ourselves, it will be hard to complete our plans and take the action steps necessary to get out of the trap of poverty. (DeVol, 2004, p. 65)

In order for under-resourced students to cope with the college environment of challenge, stress, anxiety, and change, they must suspend the "emotional memory bank" of the past, which includes or is a result of myriad external factors:

- Instability (frequent moves)
- Fewer household routines
- Greater incidence of family disruptions, violence, and separations
- Child-rearing patterns that are associated with stricter and harsher discipline
- Less emphasis on self-directedness
- Greater exposure to aggressive peers and deviance
- Less interpersonal trust
- Less likelihood to subscribe to norms of reciprocity
- Less of a sense of belonging (connectedness) to school. (Evans, 2004, pp. 77–92)

Daniel Goleman (1995) is known for coining the term "emotional intelligence." Drawing on the relatively recent research of Gardner, Sternberg, and Salovey, as well as the earlier works of Thorndike, Goleman writes:

> An inability to notice our true feelings leaves us at their mercy. People with greater certainty about their feelings are better pilots of their lives, having a surer sense of how they really feel about personal decisions, from whom they marry to what job to take. (p. 43)

In his book *Emotional Intelligence,* Goleman examines the five domains of emotional intelligence. They include:

1. Knowing one's emotions
2. Managing emotions
3. Motivating oneself
4. Recognizing emotions in others
5. Handling relationships. (p. 43)

The under-resourced student is likely to have significant strengths and weaknesses in Goleman's five domains. The emotional environment in poverty is often intense, unpredictable, even hostile, and many decisions are based on the driving force of relationships. It is through an understanding of this driving force that educators can better gauge the reactions and the needs of the under-resourced student so that situations can be created in which change is possible. The stress of college is reflected in these statements from two students in a community college in California:

> I could really relate to the student who said she felt like she was sinking. I am often overwhelmed due to my learning disability, and reading takes me much longer … sometimes makes me wish I could just give up on school.

> Sometimes school gets depressing. Sometimes when you try to keep up with your work and understand everything, it just doesn't click. You sit in the class or in your room trying to figure out how to do something … then you feel nobody can help you and you feel like you're hopeless. (DeWitt, 2007c)

Characteristics, attributes, and behaviors that indicate high levels of emotional resources include:

- Controls impulsivity most of the time
- Can plan behavior and assignments
- Manages anger
- Generally has a positive attitude
- Uses positive self-talk
- Sees the relationship between choice and consequence
- Refrains from fighting with and/or threatening others
- Can predict outcomes based on cause and effect
- Can use words to resolve problems
- Uses formal register during arguments
- Can separate criticism from the person giving it
- Accepts and considers constructive criticism
- Has the words to name feelings
- Can use the adult voice
- Actively seeks to improve emotional/mental health in self and others

Note. From *Under-Resourced Learners* (p. 6), by R. K. Payne, 2008, Highlands, TX: aha! Process. Copyright 2008 by aha! Process. Adapted with permission.

Emotional resources are complicated and heavily influence all the other resources. Indeed, emotions are the hardest part of our "total behavior" to control (Glasser, 1998). While we can change what we do, say, and even think, our emotions run all the way to our physiology—and are frequently revealed when we attempt to change a behavior or thought pattern. Therefore, it is incumbent upon all who plan to guide others, whether as counselors, advisers, mentors, or teachers, to have "emotional intelligence" of their own.

MOTIVATION/PERSISTENCE

Motivation is a function of the extent to which students believe they are capable of attaining a goal, as well as the degree to which the setting promotes it (Pintrich, 1995, p. 76); persistence is the ability to continue even when adverse circumstances appear to be insurmountable. These resources could easily be subsumed into several of the others, especially emotional, spiritual, and mental. However, both high school and college students who have assessed their own resources have found it meaningful to consider motivation/persistence as a separate resource because there is often peer and family pressure to forsake the accomplishment of goals in favor of maintaining family and community relations. Energy and drive can be hard to summon, but knowing that these resources are key to one's success can help students validate, measure, and intentionally develop them for themselves. Students also report that it was easier to identify the people in their lives who supported their dreams and future stories when the motivation/persistence resource was considered separately from the others. This, in turn, helps under-resourced students build their important support systems.

Further, students who are pursuing a degree and adapting to the hidden rules of middle class sometimes must sever ties with their worlds—leaving behind people in their lives who are not accepting of the changes they observe in the students. Payne (2005b) says it this way: "To move from poverty to middle class or from middle class to wealth, an individual must give up relationships for achievement (at least for some period of time)" (p. 3). Thus understanding and developing motivation and persistence make such loss more comprehensible and even acceptable to the under-resourced student.

Characteristics, attributes, and behaviors that indicate high levels of motivation/persistence resources include:

- Works hard most of the time
- Usually has a high level of energy
- Belongs to at least one club or organization that promotes personal and/or community development
- Can set short-term and long-term goals (future story)
- Seeks to do the right thing for self, others, and organizations
- Can work with others to set goals and accomplish them
- Recognizes and/or seeks out opportunities for personal development
- Enjoys learning new things for the sake of learning, not just for a class or designated purpose
- Talks about and/or applies newly learned concepts outside the classroom
- Accepts responsibilities without reluctance or reservation
- Is flexible and adaptable as situations warrant
- Is willing to risk failure and to take risks to succeed

Note. From *Getting Ahead in a Just-Gettin'-By World* (p. 95), by P. E. DeVol, 2004, Highlands, TX: aha! Process. Copyright 2004 by aha! Process. Adapted with permission.

The issue of motivation is not new to the educational world. Instructors have implemented "motivational techniques" as long as teaching has existed as a profession. Indeed, parents also employ motivational techniques, which then affect the way students react to classroom motivational techniques. These strategies range from guaranteeing students that there will be more work if the present tasks are not appropriately completed (sometimes viewed as a threat) to making such statements as "This test will separate the sheep from the goats" to rewarding expected behaviors with a treat—be it food or a preferred privilege, such as computer time or playing a game. Motivational strategies can be analyzed from the perspective of the under-resourced learner. Menec and Perry (1995) explain that a statement such as "Any idiot could understand this"—intended to convey that the material is easy enough for anyone to learn—might be received very differently by an under-resourced student. Such a thoughtless remark might be interpreted as "I must be even dumber than an idiot" or "I'll really look stupid if I ask for help now." Motivation, in the world of instructional designers, "refers to the magnitude and direction of behavior ... to the choices people make as to what experiences and goals they will approach or avoid, and the degree of effort they will exert in that respect" (Keller, 1983, p. 389). Thus instructors are encouraged to model effort and persistence indirectly through sharing their personal stories of how they became experts or how they mastered difficult materials (Menec & Perry, p. 111).

Karen Pellino, in her article "The Effects of Poverty on Teaching and Learning," states: "Emotional draining and negative self-status can literally zap the motivation to learn out of children" (2007). She cites "agency and conation" as keys to understanding motivation as it relates to children from poverty. The concept of "learner agency" relates to students' locus of control. This underlying concept in social learning and social cognitive theory reminds instructors and academic advisers that they can enable students to engage in their own learning process, personal development, and achievement (Brophy, 1998; Bandura, 2001). "Conation," Pellino explains, "refers to the connection between knowledge, affect and behavior. It is the intentional, goal-oriented component of motivation that explains how knowledge and emotion are translated into behavior" and is closely related to volition or will.

Hidden rules about destiny and power can influence motivation/persistence as well. Students from generational poverty are apt to believe in fate—that they can do little to mitigate chance and that they have little personal power within the system, often feeling acted upon rather than in control. The middle class, on the other hand, believes that individuals can change the future by making good choices now. For educators and staff in postsecondary institutions, it is essential to build awareness of how one's background can affect motivation, so that they not only understand "where their students are coming from" but the struggles they face in navigating the middle-class rules of college. Listening for the language students use to describe the reasons for their success or failure is a starting point in illuminating how their personal belief system affects their feelings and behavior. Making such a statement as "You all have the ability to succeed in this course" is motivational to students and provides hope when they are doubting themselves (Perry, 1999).

INTEGRITY/TRUST

Like motivation/persistence, integrity/trust was added to the original list of resources from DeVol's (2006) work with adults in poverty. Integrity and trust merit their own category due to the issues many people in poverty have with authority figures, as well as issues many authority figures have with people from poverty—even the idea of their receiving an education.

Characteristics, attributes, and behaviors that indicate high levels of integrity/trust resources include:

- Can be trusted to keep his or her word
- Can accomplish tasks as assigned
- Models and inspires others to obey laws and rules
- When laws and rules do not make sense, is willing to seek answers to questions from appropriate sources
- Keeps self accountable to others
- Accepts responsibility for self and does not blame others
- Is willing to do more than is required in some situations
- Trusts others
- Can verbalize why a person is to be trusted or safe
- Seeks help from others
- Includes a variety of people as his or her social capital
- Takes risks and does not assume bad things will happen at every turn
- Recognizes the value of honesty

Note. From *Getting Ahead in a Just-Gettin'-By World* (p. 94), by P. E. DeVol, 2004, Highlands, TX: aha! Process. Copyright 2004 by aha! Process. Adapted with permission.

Misunderstandings and mistrust between/among economic classes about their driving forces and hidden rules can be mitigated if not eliminated through education for students and teaching/professional staff. Once this is accomplished, mutually respectful relationships based on integrity can evolve and be tested. These relationships are more likely to develop and be maintained when the higher education professional models positive thinking and motivating attributes. The multitude of issues students bring to or develop in the classroom might be reduced when students are supported in this way, thereby benefiting the instructor as well.

PHYSICAL

As a resource for students, physical health is probably one of the first things that come to mind when we think of wellness and well-being. In fact, in a college textbook (Donnelly, Eburne, & Kittleson, 2001) for a mental health and wellness class, physical health is described as complex and multifaceted, including

> levels of nutrition, rest, exercise, growth and development, aging, as well as
> freedom from infectious, communicable, and chronic disease ... [involving] all
> of the body systems—the nervous system, the skeletal system, the muscular

system, the integumentary system (skin), the endocrine system (hormones), and the circulatory system. (pp. 3–4)

The importance of physical resources is underscored by research finding that individuals base 80% of their expectations of a person on his or her appearance. Appearance is dramatically affected by physical health, including dental health. For the college student, physical resources enable students to remain healthy throughout the term, despite the number of people one comes in contact with during the day who may be sick or carrying a virus. The ability to stay healthy frequently falls prey to high levels of stress experienced by under-resourced students in the college environment. Stress levels related to students living in the tyranny of the moment are often greater than those of more fortunate students not struggling with self-esteem, time management, family issues, work, and culture shock between the college and home environments.

Characteristics, attributes, and behaviors that indicate strong physical resources include:

- Is usually free of illnesses
- Clothes, hair, and body are clean and presentable in accordance with social/cultural norms
- Is within the healthy weight/height range for his or her age
- Can see and hear well
- Can move around without assistance
- Can stay awake during class and study time
- Has health insurance and/or access to preventive healthcare
- Engages in regular exercise
- Does not abuse substances
- Is free from physical and sexual abuse
- If a biochemical issue is present, it is addressed either with medication or a series of interventions
- Eats a balanced diet on a daily basis
- Is generally free of dental problems

Note. From *Under-Resourced Learners* (pp. 9–10), by R. K. Payne, 2008, Highlands, TX: aha! Process. Copyright 2008 by aha! Process. Adapted with permission.

Most campuses contribute to students' physical health through their health services, food services, and fitness centers. But within the classroom and/or mentoring context, understanding the under-resourced students' levels of resiliency—and the juxtaposition of students' current resources with those available on campus—is helpful. Serving as an ally, the instructor or staff person can then point out specific resources available on campus. Such resources might include access to nutrition, healthcare and dental care, birth control, transportation, or childcare. Given the fact that many under-resourced students lack the intergenerational transfer of knowledge, they may not even know that such resources could be free or at a discounted rate.

SPIRITUAL

Most societies throughout history have held to or developed a belief system that involves something beyond the human experience. Whether based on precise practices and beliefs or free of organization, these systems incorporate such practices as attending a place of worship, praying, meditating, singing, communing with nature, enjoying fellowship with others, and perhaps providing service to others. The broader perspective may include guidance or a divine purpose but also may include (or be limited to) a rich cultural connection. In any case, the focus here is on what offers direction and support to the student. Spirituality generally is a source of optimism and hope and may be a basis for one's value system. A necessary component in overcoming the tyranny of the moment is having a future story—that is, plans and hopes for the coming months and years—beyond today. For many, surviving the day is all they can hope for; thinking of tomorrow, let alone long-term goal setting, requires resources they do not have. This reality becomes a barrier at many levels to achieving, both personally and academically. For some, this barrier is lessened through the spiritual resource.

"Hope," "optimism," "divine guidance," and "values" are not foreign to study in many college courses, be it a world religion course or a course on societal and personal wellness—or even an orientation course where personal development is a goal. According to a college text used to assist students with transitions, "Values serve as a kind of internal decision compass, helping us steer our way through confusing and conflicting situations" (DiMarco, 2000, p. 111). In the same college text cited above for a mental health and wellness class, Donnelly et al. (2001) state:

> Spiritually healthy individuals are able to hold firmly to a belief system, have faith in and gain strength from a belief in something beyond themselves, yet do not need to belittle, demean, or interfere with the spiritual focus of others. (p. 7)

In her 2005 dissertation for Azusa Pacific University, Kimberly Greenway conducted a path analysis of 531 surveys of juniors and seniors at the University of North Alabama. Her research results show that spirituality has positive effects on purpose, which predicts academic engagement. Greenway (as cited in Council for Christian Colleges and Universities, 2005) summarizes her findings as follows:

> The findings in this study indicate that students are searching for meaning and purpose, that faculty interaction and spirituality predict purpose in life, that purpose in life and faculty interaction predict academic engagement, and that academic engagement predicts academic success. Based on these findings, the implications for higher education are to cultivate the search for meaning, to assist students in finding purpose in life, and to promote the types of faculty-student interaction that lead to academic engagement.

Characteristics, attributes, and behaviors that indicate high levels of spiritual resources include:

- Is open-minded
- Shows a caring, thoughtful spirit
- Has and appreciates a sense of community
- Values life and not just oneself
- Lives life with a purpose
- Views self as part of a whole
- Remains positive even with failure
- Can delay gratification
- Has a personal sense of destiny about his or her life

Note. From *Under-Resourced Learners* (p. 8), by R. K. Payne, 2008, Highlands, TX: aha! Process. Copyright 2008 by aha! Process. Adapted with permission.

Spiritual resources can build a sense of empowerment and resiliency; both traits are necessary for college students—and especially under-resourced students. Research analysis by Andrews, Guadalupe, and Bolden (2003), grounded in the participants' perspectives, yielded a definition of empowerment that highlights faith as a spiritual power. Many faculty and staff at postsecondary institutions may feel awkward considering the private idea of "spirituality" as part of their curriculum. However, Pingree (2009) points out that it is time to retire the traditional spirituality framework that keeps people from attending to this development and instead see it from the two sides that usually conflate the issue: religion and psychosocial development. In so doing, the psychosocial development that is indeed part of a college student's development will be enhanced so that the whole student might be educated.

According to a research project by UCLA's Higher Education Research Institute (2005) on spirituality in higher education, 56% of students reported never being given the opportunity to discuss, within the college or university context, the meaning and purpose of life, and only 55% surveyed were satisfied with the opportunity given in college courses to reflect on spirituality or religion. Thus Pingree (2009) suggests:

- Incorporating discussions of meaning and purpose
- Cultivating student-focused pedagogies that allow for multiple forms of exploration (including journals in registers other than those usually seen in academe)
- Engaging students' knowledge and experiences and applying them beyond the campus
- Creating a method to assess this development
- Safeguarding time for reflection for faculty, staff, and students. (pp. 8–9)

Each person's spiritual journey will be different, but when honored, it is beneficial to the individual and the community, especially in the complex and diverse environment of postsecondary institutions.

CHAPTER 4

External Resources

Having discussed some of the origins of mental/cognitive resources, as well as how varying levels of other internal resources impact individuals, it becomes apparent that there is a great deal of interrelationship among the resources. A holistic investigation reveals that each student's unique attributes, behaviors, characteristics, and personality create a tapestry representing the interwoven and interdependent nature of each individual's resources, external forces, and life journey.

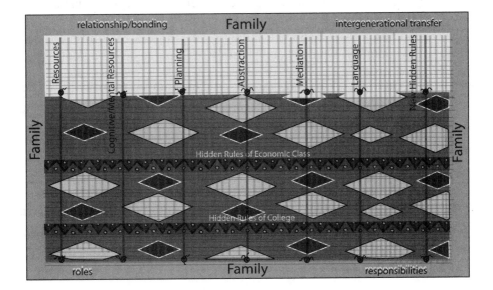

Using the metaphor of creating a tapestry, the mental/cognitive resources might be seen as the warp of the tapestry of their lives, an underlying foundation that strengthens the fabric and holds it together. The range and intensity of hidden rules at their disposal can represent the weave, the colorful woven material that makes the students who they uniquely are. Finally, language is the weft, or weaver's knots, which ties the weave in place. The loom for this piece of art is the foundation of family and community—the student's first learning environment where mediated learning and intergenerational transfer of knowledge took place.

The ongoing interweaving among the resources is complex. For example, there may be any number of combinations of mediation, intergenerational transfer of knowledge, and language acquisition that influence a student's understanding of the hidden rules of college—including those in the classroom, campus, or discipline. However, since many under-resourced students may be overlooked as "college material" by high school counselors, as discussed in *Removing the Mask: Giftedness in Poverty* (Slocumb & Payne, 2000), these students may be more prone to be misdirected to less rigorous majors. Consequently, they would carry with them misconceptions about the academic or cognitive skills needed to succeed in particular fields of study. Once students discover that a field requires a series of math courses, they may change majors or drop out, feeling inadequate and uncertain. Having mentors or bridging relationships could assist them with the transition to college and could mitigate their lack of intergenerational transfer of knowledge, thereby lessening the likelihood of the kinds of events that impede progress. For example:

- Late registration that leads to filling one's schedule with classes that do not count toward a degree (and add to the cost and length of their education)
- Late withdrawals that precipitate failing grades or loss of full-time status, ultimately disrupting financial aid and possibly resulting in dropping out.

These examples could go on and on; the reader is encouraged to make his or her own observations regarding the concepts in this chapter. The following discussion is intended to add additional information to that knowledge base.

External Resources

This chapter continues the discussion of 11 resources by investigating the external resources of language, relationships/role models, support systems, and finances. Language and relationships are areas of focus that are particularly important to the postsecondary student.

LANGUAGE

While the acquisition and learning of language are very much an internal process, the source and use of the language acquired or learned are external and have wide-ranging effects on the individual. Indeed, language is used not only to express oneself but to define oneself. Many key issues in education and work are centered in five aspects of language:

- Registers of language
- Discourse patterns
- Story structure
- Vocabulary
- Voice

Understanding language as having hidden rules means understanding it as a resource—and vice versa (understanding language as a resource also means understanding the hidden rules of language). The way language is used in poverty is different from middle class, which, in turn, is different from wealth. In higher education, students are required to read formal language in their textbooks, as well as to communicate orally and in written form using formal register. Further, they may be challenged by listening to lectures that are in formal register and use abstract vocabulary. The tests that students take to gain entrance and establish placement in many college settings employ vocabulary that is challenging to all students—and nearly overwhelming to those for whom the concrete vocabulary of casual register represents their primary experience with language. As students advance toward career interviews, an inability to adeptly use language will lower their chances of gaining many positions.

According to Joos (1967), every language in the world has five registers. They are:

REGISTER	EXPLANATION
FROZEN	Language that is always the same. For example: Lord's Prayer, wedding vows, etc.
FORMAL	The standard sentence syntax and word choice of work and school. Has complete sentences and specific word choice.
CONSULTATIVE	Formal register when used in conversation. Discourse pattern not quite as direct as formal register.
CASUAL	Language between friends, characterized by a 400- to 800-word vocabulary. Word choice general and not specific. Conversation dependent upon nonverbal assists. Sentence syntax often incomplete
INTIMATE	Language between lovers or twins. Language of sexual harassment.

Note. From *Under-Resourced Learners* (p. 40), by R. K. Payne, 2008, Highlands, TX: aha! Process. Copyright 2008 by aha! Process. Reprinted with permission.

Formal register also might be called Standard American English (SAE), and using it in combination with the consultative register in most circumstances is one of the hidden rules of middle class. Extending the idea of hidden rules of language, Joos (1967) found that it is socially acceptable for a person to go one register down in a conversation, but to drop two registers or more in the same conversation is usually considered socially offensive. Another key point about register is that students' conversations in casual register are often heavily supported by "nonverbal assists," thus making communicating through writing without such nonverbal assists a task to be avoided if possible.

Direct-teaching of formal/consultative register typically takes place in institutions of higher learning when SAE was not part of the student's original language acquisition. The transition from casual register or a non-English native language is difficult. Montano-Harmon (1991) reported that, in order to move from casual register English to formal register English, students must actually translate word choice, syntax, and discourse patterns—skills that are rarely taught directly at any level. Some who teach college composition or grade writing assignments in other courses often simply point out errors in punctuation and usage, with little additional feedback to the students. Such a superficial examination of the act of writing does little to help students develop understanding and meaning—or learn new ways of expression.

Discourse patterns are linked to how an individual gains access to language. Gee (1987) refers to "primary discourse" as the language a person first acquires and "secondary discourse" as the language necessary to function in the larger, or dominant, society. For example, while numerous dialects constitute people's original languages in the Caucasus Mountains, Russian is the national language. In the Ivory Coast, it is French that brings many tribes together in a national dialogue. Gee breaks down discourse into "acquired" and "learned." Acquisition is the most natural manner of learning a language and usually involves "immersion"—that is, living in the environment in which the language is used for constant interaction. Learning a language involves direct-teaching and requires metacognition of language components and uses on the part of the student.

Patterns of discourse—how information is organized for conversation—also relate to language registers. The discourse pattern in the formal and consultative registers of English is to linearly and logically get straight to the point. This is what is expected in the middle-class educational environment on campus. In casual register, on the other hand, the pattern is circular and less direct. When under-resourced students attempt to explain a position, get help or direction, or express an opinion but can only do so in the casual circular fashion, they are often perceived as inarticulate at best and ignorant at worst. Similarly, when a person accustomed to the circular, casual register discourse is cut short by someone using the formal register fashion of getting to the point, there can be misconceptions of rudeness or a lack of concern about the details of the longer version.

Similar to patterns of discourse, formal register and casual register carry their own story structures. The formal register story structure is delivered very much like the familiar story line in a storybook or situation comedy on television—that is, commonly accepted narrative pattern.

Formal register story structure

Note. From *Under-Resourced Learners* (p. 51), by R. K. Payne, 2008, Highlands, TX: aha! Process. Copyright 2008 by aha! Process. Reprinted with permission.

For example, in formal register a story in a financial aid office would be told like this:

Student to cashier: "I need to speak with someone about my monthly textbook payment."

"You can talk with me."

"Great. Thank you. I do not have my payment at this time because, unfortunately, my mother's check was mailed to our former address, where it was received and cashed by the current resident at that address. The bank is attempting to fix the situation, but the process will require approximately two weeks."

"I'll make a note on your records that your payment will be two weeks late."

"Thank you so much. I'll see you in two weeks."

Those who teach language arts-oriented courses will recognize formal register as including setting, rising action, conflict, turning point, *denouement* (or lowering action), and finally resolution, incorporating sequence, as well as cause and effect. The formal register story structure chronologically goes from beginning to end and emphasizes plot. The casual register story structure, however, generally begins either at the end of the story or at the part of the story with the greatest emotional intensity. This is followed by "vignettes" of information that are best conveyed with audience participation in between. This version is usually more entertaining (and more participatory) and displays richness of character development, along with use of humor and feeling, than formal story structure. The emphasis in the casual register story structure is on the characterizations—the people—a factor that correlates with the driving force of relationships.

Casual register story structure

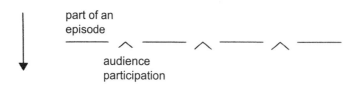

Note. From *Under-Resourced Learners* (p. 51), by R. K. Payne, 2008, Highlands, TX: aha! Process. Copyright 2008 by aha! Process. Reprinted with permission.

In casual register the same story would be told like this:

Student to cashier: "Some man cashed my mom's check, so I can't pay for my books yet."

"What man?"

"Where we used to stay. He got it and cashed it and didn't care. Mama's so mad."

"How did the man get your mother's check?"

"Told you. He's where I used to stay. Mama left a message on the message box."

"Voice mail?"

"Yeah, where she works. To tell them she didn't get her check. They said they mailed it, but we don't stay there no more" (shrugs shoulders).

"Oh, I see. Your mother's check was mailed to a previous address and the person who now lives there received and cashed her check."

"That's what I've been tryin' to tell you" (looks at others standing in line and laughs).

It is not hard to see how the differences in register, discourse, and story structure can impact classroom discussions and students' ability to address writing assignments in college. Feuerstein (as cited in Sharron & Coulter, 2004) found that story structure affects more than just communication. Cognitive and brain research shows that story structure is related to the way information is stored in the brain (Zull, 2002). Thus the episodic casual version can impede information processing for students who did not acquire linear formal patterns.

Vocabulary is the fourth part of the language resource and an essential tool for thinking. The mind uses vocabulary—including jargon and specialized terms from a discipline—to categorize, sort, and communicate information.

In a long-term study of stable, healthy families from professional, working-class, and welfare homes, Betty Hart and Todd Risley (1995) studied children soon after they were born. In tracking the language experience of young children, they found that in all the homes the children learned to talk, but there were significant differences in the language experience and development by economic class. The following findings from their book *Meaningful Differences in the Everyday Experience of Young American Children* illustrate the main differences.

Research About Language in Children, Ages 1 to 4, in Stable Households by Economic Group

Number of words exposed to	Economic group	Affirmations (strokes)	Prohibitions (discounts)
13 million words	Welfare	1 for every	2
26 million words	Working class	2 for every	1
45 million words	Professional	6 for every	1

Note. From *Meaningful Differences in the Everyday Experience of Young American Children* (p. 198), by B. Hart and T. R. Risley, 1995, Baltimore: Paul H. Brookes. Copyright 1995 by Paul H. Brookes. Adapted with permission.

This research tells us that the more words children are exposed to from their parents in the first four years, the more neural pathways are developed in the brain (but the *nature* of those words is important). The research did not include words heard on TV or radio but rather from persons with whom the children had significant relationships. Further, the more encouragements a child receives, the more words he or she has and the more learning structures are built. An affirmation (or encouragement) is when an adult responds to something the child has interest in and encourages the child to explore and talk about it, whereas a prohibition is when an adult stops a child from an idea or a behavior with words such as "Shut up" or "Don't do that." Overall, then, the more words children acquire in their first four years, the easier and faster it is for them to learn more words.

College of the Ouachitas

More than any other single factor, a student's vocabulary will determine how successful he or she will be in college and later in life (Pikulski & Templeton, 2004).

> It seems almost impossible to overstate the power of words; they literally have changed and will continue to change the course of world history. Perhaps the greatest tools we can give students for succeeding not only in their education but more generally in life, is a large, rich vocabulary and the skills for using those words. (p. 1)

In fact, Bors and Stokes (1998) determined that among college students:

- Those who have large vocabularies make better grades.
- Those with large vocabularies do better on writing assignments.
- Having a large vocabulary actually helps students "think faster."

A detailed analysis of the Bors and Stokes study, which focused mainly on first-year psychology students, revealed that every student in the study with a better vocabulary made better grades than those with a command of fewer words.

Students who come to college with a small vocabulary lack the prior knowledge on which to build shared meaning. When considering the expectations of a college classroom, students are likely to struggle if they are oriented toward casual register; circular, random, episodic story structure; and concrete thinking. In constructivist theory, value is placed on students' points of view and their need to attach relevance to coursework. Constructivists promote student learning based on their construction of knowledge around current suppositions (Brooks & Brooks, 1993). Beyond this theory, Payne (2008b) believes that

> One of the misunderstandings of constructivism was that as long as a student made meaning inside his/her head, he/she was OK. But meaning only has value to the extent that it can be shared and communicated. This requires a shared understanding of what a word means. (p. 67)

Abstract vocabulary is found most in formal register. Therefore, to "bridge" into the abstract representational world of paper and technology, the integration of formal register into the students' repertoire of speaking, listening, and writing skills is essential.

How students and staff speak, how they are spoken to, and how they are perceived also is influenced by the concept of "voices" originated by Eric Berne in the early 1960s. Berne (1996) contends that inside virtually everyone's head are three internal voices that guide the individual, and when people interact they normally do so in one of these voices.

Berne labels these as follows:

1. A child voice (in conflict) who is whining
2. A parent voice (telling)
3. An adult voice (in conflict) who is asking questions for understanding.

There are two kinds of parent voices—a positive and a negative (Payne, 2005b, p. 84). The positive voice is firm and insistent, as well as supportive, but the negative parent voice has a judgmental, evaluative, bossy, and sometimes threatening tone. One might imagine negative, overbearing gestures—for example, finger pointing, hands on hips, frowning, etc., that accompany this voice. The punitive parent voice often includes "should" and "ought" messages.

THE CHILD VOICE

(defensive, victimized, emotional, whining, losing attitude, strongly negative nonverbal)

- Quit picking on me.
- Nobody likes (loves) me.
- You make me sick.
- He or she _____ did it.
- You don't love me.
- I hate you.
- It's your fault.
- You make me mad.
- You want me to leave.
- You're ugly.
- Don't blame me.
- You made me do it.

The child voice is also playful, spontaneous, curious, etc. The phrases listed often occur in conflictual or manipulative situations and impede resolution.

THE PARENT VOICE

(authoritative, directive, judgmental, evaluative, win-lose mentality, demanding, punitive, sometimes threatening)

- You shouldn't (should) do that.
- That's wrong (right) to do _____ .
- That's stupid, immature, out of line, ridiculous.
- Life's not fair. Get busy.
- You are good, bad, worthless, beautiful (any judgmental, evaluative comment).
- You do as I say.
- If you weren't so _____ , this wouldn't happen to you.
- Why can't you be like _____ ?

The parent voice also can be very loving and supportive. The phrases above usually occur during conflict and hinder resolution. The internal parent voice can create shame and guilt.

THE ADULT VOICE

(nonjudgmental, free of negative nonverbal, factual, often in question format, attitude of win-win)

- In what ways could this be resolved?
- What factors will be used to determine the effectiveness, quality of _____ ?
- I would like to recommend _____ .
- What are choices in this situation?
- I am comfortable (uncomfortable) with _____ .
- Options that could be considered are _____ .
- For me to be comfortable, I need the following things to occur _____ .
- These are the consequences of that choice/action _____ .
- We agree to disagree.

While the phrases listed in the child and the parent voices impede resolution, an adult voice provides the language of negotiation and allows issues to be examined in a nonthreatening way.

Note. From *A Framework for Understanding Poverty* (pp. 83–84), by R. K. Payne, 2005, Highlands, TX: aha! Process. Copyright 1996 by aha! Process. Adapted with permission.

College students who have not learned to use the adult voice, which is the voice of negotiation, have access only to the child and parent voices. Payne (2005b) states, "It has been my observation that individuals who have [in effect] become their own parents quite young do not have an internal adult voice. They have a child voice and a parent voice, but not an adult voice" (p. 82). This can be problematic in the college setting when students who do not know or use the adult voice are confronted—and respond in either the child or the parent voice. Instructors and staff might interpret the parent voice as argumentative or combative, whereas the student who responds in the child voice appears manipulative, immature, or irrational. In either case, little negotiation takes place, and respect can be diminished or lost. Faculty and staff are ideally placed to model the appropriate voice for college classrooms and offices, as well as remaining sensitive to comments and suggestions that inadvertently cast doubts on students' abilities (Perry, 1999).

In order to navigate their way through college and later their careers, students must learn to use the adult voice, formal and consultative register, linear discourse, sequenced story structure, and additional vocabulary—all components of the language of negotiation. Acquiring these skills is particularly crucial for students whose primary discourse is casual register and who rely heavily on nonverbal assists in communication. Speaking and understanding the spoken word may be the easiest modes of language to adjust to formal register; reading and writing are more difficult because the nonverbal assists common in casual register are missing. To write without these is a formidable task—and to read without them often seems boring to those who have relied on nonverbal assists throughout their lives. When talking about textbooks versus lectures, students at Chabot College again commented:

Jennifer: The textbook was "Here it is." And expecting you to already know it.

Liz: Lectures are really cool because you get examples, and you get all the cool stuff.

Matt: I'm always most comfortable with lectures; you know it's coming out of the teacher's mouth, and I always feel more comfortable. Like, hey that's gonna be on the test.

Bio student #4: I mean, I'm not in elementary school anymore, but I still would like to feel engaged. (DeWitt, 2007a)

Characteristics, skills, attributes, and behaviors that indicate high levels of language resources include:

- Can use the formal register of the language of the dominant culture
- Can tell a story in chronological order
- Can get to the point in a discussion
- Can resolve conflict using formal register, avoiding offensive and confrontational tone
- Is aware of and is able to use current "politically correct" terminology (understands this as a hidden rule)
- Can ask questions syntactically
- Can use formal organizational patterns for written discourse
- Can use specific vocabulary in speech and writing
- Can sort what is and is not important in nonfiction text
- Can write a persuasive argument using support and logic
- Can appropriately use "voices" (especially adult and positive parent voice)
- Can share personal experiences using formal story structure
- Can relate concerns succinctly—both orally and in writing

Note. From *Under-Resourced Learners* (p. 5), by R. K. Payne, 2008, Highlands, TX: aha! Process. Copyright 2008 by aha! Process. Adapted with permission.

It is difficult to overstate the importance of language skills to student success and student-faculty-staff interactions. Finding ways to engage students in the language experience of reading, writing, and oral discourse is highly dependent on relationships with people who are able to impart their own enthusiasm for this work—and are willing to support the students' efforts.

RELATIONSHIPS/ROLE MODELS

Most people draw strength, knowledge, and energy from interactions with other people. Students who arrive on campus already knowing hidden rules, the questions to ask, and the expectations of college probably have role models who conveyed this information to them either directly as advisers, mentors, or instructors—or indirectly through parents or other relatives, such as a sibling or cousin who recently graduated from college or is currently attending college. Positive role models are nurturing, supportive, insistent, and even demanding. Mike Rose is the associate director of the UCLA Writing Programs and originally from an under-resourced background. He describes a mentor who helped him fit in with traditional, exclusive, and highbrow academic clubs when Rose was an undergraduate: "What Father Albertson did was bring us inside the circle, nudging us out into the center, always just behind us, whispering to try this step, then this one, encouraging us to feel the moves for ourselves" (1989, p. 38).

While not all instructors will choose to enter into a mentoring relationship, most will likely be seen as role models within their discipline and possibly beyond. Instructors model thinking, as well as the hidden rules, vocabulary, language register, and story structure in their discipline. Many college graduates credit an instructor on campus for building the bridge they needed to make the transition from high school and succeed in college. It is helpful to be aware of the major significance placed on relationships by under-resourced students. With this as a driving force, they may tend to respond on a more personal level than students from middle class. They also are more likely than their peers with adequate relationships in other contexts to be motivated by their relationships with faculty. First-generation students from under-resourced backgrounds generally need connections with other people who understand their hidden rules, are supportive, and are interested in helping them build their resources. An adage to remember is "No significant learning occurs without a significant relationship" (Comer, 1995). Respect and trust are essential to building these relationships. These qualities are vital when planning for student services or considering one's interaction with students during class and conference time. As keen observers of the behavior of others, under-resourced students are sensitive to how they are perceived and what is expected of them. When staff and faculty are aware of their own expectations and even prejudices, they are more likely to be accepted as genuine and trustworthy. Indeed, maintaining high expectations for all students is an essential characteristic of relationships of mutual respect.

Beginning with *Pygmalion in the Classroom: Teacher Expectations and Pupils' Intellectual Development* (Rosenthal & Jacobson, 1968), an extensive body of research describes how instructors' expectations can affect student performance—and how the relationship between student/teacher interactions and students' academic performance influences their behavior toward their students (Brophy, 1998; Douglas, 1964; Rowe, 1969; Mackler, 1969). Brookover & Lezotte (1979), Cooper (1984), Good (1987), and others have identified numerous factors that can lead teachers to hold lower expectations for some students than others. These include:

- GENDER. Lower expectations are often held for older girls—particularly in scientific and technical areas—because of sex/role stereotyping.
- SOCIOECONOMIC STATUS (SES). Teachers sometimes hold lower expectations of students from lower SES backgrounds.
- RACE/ETHNICITY. Students from minority races or ethnic groups are sometimes viewed as less capable than Anglo students.
- TYPE OF SCHOOL. Students from either inner-city schools or rural schools are sometimes presumed to be less capable than students from suburban schools.
- APPEARANCE. The expense or style of students' clothes and students' grooming habits can influence teachers' expectations.
- ORAL LANGUAGE PATTERNS. The presence of any nonstandard English speaking pattern can sometimes lead teachers to hold lower expectations.
- MESSINESS/DISORGANIZATION. Students whose assignments are messy are sometimes perceived as having lower ability.
- READINESS. Immaturity or lack of experience may be confused with learning ability, leading to inappropriately low expectations.
- HALO EFFECT. Some teachers generalize from one characteristic a student may have, thereby making unfounded assumptions about the student's overall ability or behavior.
- SIBLING CONNECTIONS. Teachers sometimes expect too much or too little of later siblings, based at least in part on prior knowledge of an earlier child (or children) from a family.
- SEATING POSITION. If students seat themselves at the sides or back of the classroom, some teachers perceive this as a sign of lower learning motivation and/or ability and treat students accordingly.
- OUTDATED THEORIES. Educational theories that stress the limitations of learners can lead to lowered expectations.

Note. Adapted from *Expectations and Student Outcomes,* by K. Cotton, 1989.

Too often under-resourced students are seen as "needy and deficient" and are not given the opportunity to experiment and develop the confidence needed to become higher level thinkers.

The following quotes from college students reflect their perceptions and expectations of faculty, including the desire to be supported by teachers who have high expectations of them.

Liz: … A lot of people don't understand: They think you're being lazy, and you're not taking the time to *(heavy breath in, holds tears)* … People don't understand how hard it is. It really is. And everybody's telling you that, "You're so lazy, 'cause you're not trying."

Lydia: I think every teacher, whether or not they see the student, and they think that they don't want to do it, they should treat them like they do. Even if they're 100% sure the student is slacking off and doesn't care, I think that they should treat them like they do.

Kalif: 'Cause most teachers I don't have a good student/teacher relationship with, so if I talk to them, they'll be like, "What, are you serious? This is college, you're asking me how to read? I can't help you, you should have learned that in eighth grade. Sorry, I can't really help you out there."

Nicole: … They don't understand like, if I ask them, that I don't know what the assignment means. They'll be like, "It's easy; you can do it." And then they just send me out.

Shawn: And when you have a student/teacher relationship, when you don't read the book you feel bad when you come to class. (DeWitt, 2007a)

Positive relationships with instructors and staff not only support learning, they actually enhance it. This is reinforced in *The Growth of the Mind and the Endangered Origins of Intelligence* (1997), in which Stanley Greenspan and Beryl Benderly state that all learning is double-coded—both mentally and emotionally. Further, if we look at the dimensions of William Perry's (1970) scheme for college-age male students and the perspectives of the Belenky, Clinchy, Goldberger, and Tarule (1986) study of women, we see that students learn by making meaning, which is best made when there is that double-coded connection. This finding also is correlated with those of Mezirow (1981), Habermas, (1971), and Caine and Caine (1991). If instructors and student services officials proceed unaware of the under-resourced students' need for mutual respect and intellectually concrete learning strategies, students will learn at a "surface level" (Caine & Caine, 1991) at best. If we realize, however, that students' problem-solving spirit and skills could be ignited in the classroom through the use of specific learning strategies and confidently built and maintained through student experience, deeper (both cognitive and emotion-based) learning will take place.

Characteristics, attributes, and behaviors that indicate strong resources in the area of relationships/role models include:

- Has at least two friends his or her own age who are eager to change and succeed
- Has at least two adults outside of school who care about him or her
- Has at least one positive/upstanding person he or she admires who is not a sports figure or entertainer
- Can identify positive traits he or she admires in a role model
- Can identify the kind of person he or she want to be
- Manages friendship and relationships that are not destructive
- Can give and accept a compliment with appropriate etiquette
- Has access to and maintains interaction with individuals who have succeeded in the dominant culture but who also have retained their cultural/racial roots
- Knows the history and examples of successful individuals in his or her family or racial/cultural past
- Believes that the choices individuals make create their future
- Has appropriate role identity

Note. From *Under-Resourced Learners* (p. 12), by R. K. Payne, 2008, Highlands, TX: aha! Process. Copyright 2008 by aha! Process. Adapted with permission.

SUPPORT SYSTEMS

In *Bowling Alone,* Robert Putnam (2000) describes support systems as social capital and states that they are just as important as financial capital. Social capital is our connections, networks, and what we do for each other out of trust, with the knowledge that the favor may be returned. Putnam describes two types of social capital: bonding and bridging. Both are important to survival, as long as the relationships are not destructive or sabotaging. Positive bonding relationships occur with one's family and closest friends and serve the need to belong. These people generally have resources and connections similar to what we have. Bridging relationships, on the other hand, are with people outside one's regular circle who usually have a different background. These individuals may not be considered close friends, but when one develops bridging social capital, it is good to have many acquaintances, as they provide leads for jobs, write references, and give advice about hidden rules within new venues of opportunities. They are the people who will help us rise out of places in our lives in which we may be stuck. Putnam explains that "bridging social capital can generate broader identities and reciprocity, whereas bonding social capital bolsters our narrower selves" (p. 23). He goes on to point out that urban sociologist Xavier de Souza Briggs emphasizes that bonding capital is good for "getting by" while bridging capital is good for "getting ahead" (p. 23).

Rose (1989) once again speaks from his personal experience:

> We live, in America, with so many platitudes about motivation and self-reliance and individualism—and myths spur from them. Like those of Horatio Alger—that we find it hard to accept the fact that they are serious nonsense. To live your daily life … in any one of hundreds of depressed communities—and to journey up through the top levels of the American education system will call for support and guidance at many, many points along the way. You'll need people to guide you into conversations that seem foreign and threatening. You'll need models, lots of them, to show you how to get at what you don't know. You'll need people to help you center yourself in your own developing ideas. You'll need people to watch out for you. (p. 48)

College students may find that formerly positive bonding relationships become negative as family members and friends react to changes they see in the students. Within the context of the close relational ties common to the under-resourced student's family and community, attending college and/or perhaps succeeding in college and the world of work can be threatening. Since the student is perceived by the family to be a possession, when a student is successful and perhaps decides to "go away" to school or to complete a further degree, the family may fight the whole idea. The tug of war between the reality of the family's poverty and the future story of the student can be intense. It's a common dilemma that many students from poverty find themselves caught in as they attempt to further their education and go on to a career. Richard Rodriguez (2005), son of Mexican immigrants and now an educator, consultant, and author of several works, describes the dilemma:

> [The student] must move between environments, his home and the classroom, which are at cultural extremes, opposed. With his family, the boy has the intense pleasure of intimacy, the family's consolation in feeling public alienation. Lavish emotions texture home life. *Then* at school the instructor bids him to trust only reason primarily. Immediate needs set the pace of his parents' lives. From his mother and father the boy learns to trust spontaneity and nonrational ways of knowing. *Then* at school there is mental calm. Teachers emphasize the value of a reflectiveness that opens a space between thinking and immediate action. (pp. 564–565)

A mental model for defining one's bonding and bridging social capital might look like this:

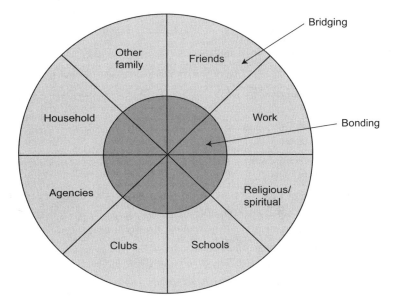

Note. From *Getting Ahead in a Just-Gettin'-By World* (p. 68), by P. E. DeVol, 2004, Highlands, TX: aha! Process. Copyright 2004 by aha! Process. Adapted with permission.

The physical home environment is another aspect of support systems and an example of how the family influences students' performance at a postsecondary institution. In poverty, the physical space is usually crowded with people. The rooms in the house are sometimes used for multiple purposes, ranging from entertaining and eating to sleeping. A lack of order in the house can be compounded by other hidden rules of poverty—including the emphasis on entertainment. There may be a TV and music going loudly at the same time, several dogs barking, children playing, and adults talking. Because people have to move frequently, belongings and possessions generally are few and are shared. Books, awards, and other school mementos may be left behind or lost in a move. What appears to be chaos to a person from middle class is viewed as normal in the household from generational poverty; likewise the quiet and orderly zones generally associated with studying by the middle class are seldom comfortable or familiar to students from generational poverty. In fact, there is hardly ever a *place* for a student to study or a way to organize. Thus filing systems, planners, and other devices for organizing materials are largely absent. All this has implications for students in community colleges who still live at home, as well as for life in the residence hall where under-resourced students tend to replicate their home environment in the dorm room.

Characteristics, attributes, and behaviors that indicate strong resources in the area of support systems include:

- Can make new friends (social capital)
- Is willing to initiate conversations
- Understands nonverbals of various registers and groups
- Has and can seek out at least two adults who care about and nurture him or her
- Has and can seek out at least two friends (peers) who are nurturing and not destructive
- Belongs to a peer group; can be racial, cultural, religious, activity-based (e.g., sports, music, academic)
- Has at least two friends who are different from self (by race, culture, interest, academics, religion, etc.)
- Has and can seek out at least two people who will advocate for him or her
- Can locate, identify with and participate in a larger social network (bridging social capital)—for example, church, 4-H, sports league, country club, Boys and Girls Club, chat rooms and other virtual friends
- Is a mentor or friend to whom others come for advice
- Seeks to be challenged by others

Note. From *Under-Resourced Learners* (pp. 10–11), by R. K. Payne, 2008, Highlands, TX: aha! Process. Copyright 2008 by aha! Process. Adapted with permission.

FINANCIAL

In poverty, money is to be spent, lent, and given away to friends and family in need. In middle class, money is to be managed and used to get the things (possessions) or the information (achievement) desired. In wealth, money is invested, conserved, and cultivated (Payne, 2005b). However, being taught middle-class rules about money without consideration of poverty's driving forces or the other 10 resources seldom results in significant changes in generational poverty. Moreover, when people from generational poverty acquire a windfall, it is not at all uncommon for them to go through it fairly rapidly and soon be right back where they started.

As an external resource, this probably is not one that most instructors would directly teach in a classroom, except perhaps as a review in an economics class. The assumption tends to be that everyone already is in the know—or just too careless or lazy to "do the right thing." For the instructor, understanding the hidden rules behind money for under-resourced students does shed light on some of their decisions, which in turn affect their education. In middle class, if your car breaks down, you call AAA. In poverty, you call

"Uncle Ray," a friend or relative who can help (DeVol, 2006). A student may be the friend who is called upon and therefore skips class to help. The student who decides to help may either owe this person a favor or knows that he or she might later need a favor from this person, so therefore finds it wise to oblige. Many under-resourced students make decisions based on their lack of financial resources; this can be the underlying cause of much stress in the person's life, which can lead to other major stressors, such as illness, divorce, or family violence.

Characteristics, attributes, and behaviors that indicate high levels of financial resources include:

- Has funds or scholarships for necessary school supplies
- Has funds or scholarships that pay for textbooks
- Has funds or scholarships for fees and other incidental charges
- Manages credit card use for minimal to no debt
- Has food every evening and twice a day on weekend/holidays
- Wears different clothing at least five days a week
- Has more than one pair of shoes
- Can "defer gratification" and not spend money right away
- Has a stable place to live (not a motor vehicle or shelter; doesn't move every three months)
- Has his or her own books
- Has a place to study that includes good lighting and a table/desk
- Has had the opportunity to participate in educational activities outside of school (e.g., camps, museums, travel)
- Has access to transportation (e.g., bus, subway, household vehicle)
- If owns a car, has insurance
- Has healthcare insurance
- Understands and maintains a "credit report"
- Puts a portion of money away for the future

Note. From *Under-Resourced Learners* (pp. 3–4), by R. K. Payne, 2008, Highlands, TX: aha! Process. Copyright 2008 by aha! Process. Adapted with permission.

Financial resources are being discussed last in order to emphasize that they are only one of many resources. Some students who lack money nonetheless possess other resources that compensate, thereby creating opportunities for a stable and fulfilling life. A college degree is not a guarantee of stability or income, but it certainly provides opportunity to develop many resources throughout the graduate's lifetime.

It is important to keep in mind how much financial resources influence the availability of other resources. Without adequate financial resources to pay for childcare—and without familial or community support for assistance—it would be difficult indeed for a parent to pursue higher education and persist in it. It is paramount for institutions of higher education to analyze the needs of all students and work not only to supply financial assistance as necessary but also to eliminate such barriers to education as unavailable or unaffordable childcare.

Building Resources in Higher Education

Rose (1989) makes the following observation about the challenge of connecting campus personnel with students who need their guidance:

> The way schools are set up, however—the loads teachers carry, the ways they're trained to deal with difference, the vast patchwork of diagnostics and specialists—[makes] it very hard for [students] to get what they need: a guide sitting down on the steps … and building a relationship through the words on a printed page. (p. 125)

There are those in higher education who feel it is "not my job" to address student issues outside of their teaching of content and process—or the particular student services they provide. Understanding a bit more about the causes and effects of poverty, along with the resources and hidden rules of economic class, offers the opportunity for faculty and staff to essentially increase their cultural competence and be able to better serve a more diverse array of students. It is not necessary to become close friends with a student in order to foster a relationship of mutual respect, nor does it necessarily require hours of additional work. The shifts in behavior might be subtle, yet they can make all the difference in the world. It is necessary to be sensitive, empathic, and to seek to understand. Rose (1989) speaks of one of his students:

> I began to think about how many pieces had to fall into place for her to be a student. The baby couldn't wake up sick, no rashes, no colic, the cousin or neighbor had to be available to watch him, the three buses she took from East L.A. had to be on time—no accidents or breakdowns or strikes. Her travel alone took almost three hours of her school day. Only if all these pieces dropped [into] smooth alignment could her full attention shift to the complex and elusive prose of Thomas Szasz. (p. 185)

For those who feel that postsecondary institutions need to focus on education and not the development of a full set of resources, there is compelling evidence to the contrary.

In fact, the 36 national organizations that comprise The Council for the Advancement of Standards in Higher Education (CAS) recognize that:

> Both educational and developmental needs brought to campus by students may change over time, requiring new and different approaches for those needs to be met effectively. As institutions and their constituents change, so too must the vehicles that guide practice within the shifting culture. As new developments occur that result in previously unrecognized and newly identified student needs, programs and services must change as well. (Dean, 2006, p. 168)

CAS has worked to overcome the "silo effect" in which "autonomous administrative units, programs, and services function independently and sometimes inconsistently" (p. 3). CAS standards also speak to the need for academic programs and services that support holistic development of students. The premise of seeking to meet students "where they are" indeed must include approaches that focus on the shifting culture of the students' community, the institution(s) they attend, and the places where students currently and prospectively are employed.

The majority of CAS's (Dean, 2006) efforts to continually assess and develop standards for postsecondary programs are applauded and in sync with the evolving landscape of higher education. The following five (of eight) presuppositions from CAS's Guiding Principles are aligned with today's growing population of under-resourced students:

- The student must be considered as a whole person.
- Each student is a unique person and must be treated as such.
- The student's total environment is educational and must be used to achieve full development.
- The primary responsibility for learning and development rests with the student.
- Institutions are responsible for creating learning environments that provide a choice of educational opportunities and challenge students to learn and develop while providing support to nurture their development. (Dean, pp. 7–8)

The "increasingly complex and shrinking global environment" is seen by CAS as a significant rationale for students' learning "to function effectively and justly when exposed to ideas, beliefs, values, physical and mental abilities, sexual orientation, lifestyles, and cultures that differ from their own" (Dean, 2006, p. 8). Dialogues that include people from all classes transform the work of faculty and staff from "doing to" and "doing for" students to "doing with." The model for educating under-resourced students that is presented in this book follows CAS's assertion that "Theory without practice is empty, and practice without theory is blind" (Dean, 2006, p. 8). A true application of student development theory becomes best practice when all players in the academic scene—students, staff, administrators, advisers, and faculty—become consciously aware of hidden rules and patterns of behavior associated with economic class.

Essential to educating and empowering the under-resourced learner is finding practices that follow the CAS guidelines of:

- Realistically linking the student to the institution
- Affirming and teaching about diversity and multiculturalism so that students can become change agents for themselves and their community
- Promoting change for individuals and their society in truly "benevolent environments" conducive to student learning and development
- Creating mentoring relationships between students and "those who facilitate their learning and development" (p. 9) that are founded on humane, ethical practices. (Dean, 2006)

From these guidelines, CAS (Dean, 2006) offers 16 Student Learning and Development Outcome Domains, a list of developmental domains that help college officials assess student achievement. These outcome domains are directly related to each of the 11 resources just discussed. Therefore, it is the responsibility of everyone in higher education to seriously consider his or her role is supporting this type of student development. The 16 outcome domains adapted from CAS are:

1. **Intellectual growth:** Produces personal and educational goal statements; exercises critical thinking in problem solving; applies previously understood information *(mental/cognitive resource)*

2. **Effective communication:** Writes and speaks coherently and effectively, after reflection; effectively articulates abstract ideas; uses appropriate syntax *(language resource)*

3. **Enhanced self-esteem:** Shows self-respect and respect for others; takes reasonable risks; engages in assertive behavior as appropriate *(emotional resource)*

4. **Realistic self-appraisal:** Acknowledges strengths and weaknesses; seeks feedback; learns from past experiences *(mental/cognitive and motivation/persistence resources)*

5. **Clarified values:** Makes decisions that reflect personal values; explains how values influence decision making *(mental/cognitive and integrity/trust resources)*

6. **Career choices:** Articulates career choices based on assessment of interests, skills, values, and abilities; makes connection between classroom and out-of-classroom learning; can articulate preferred work environment *(knowledge of hidden rules resource)*

7. **Leadership development:** Serves as leader; understands group dynamics; can visualize group purpose and desired outcomes *(emotional, relationships, and support systems resources)*

8. **Healthy behavior:** Chooses behaviors that promote health and reduce risk, as well as advance a healthy community *(physical resource)*

9. **Meaningful interpersonal relationships:** Develops and maintains satisfying interpersonal relationships, establishes mutually rewarding relationships with friends and colleagues; listens to others' points of view; treats others with respect *(emotional, integrity/trust, and relationships resources)*

10. **Independence:** Exhibits self-reliant behavior; functions autonomously; accepts supervision; manages time effectively *(motivation/persistence, emotional, and relationships resources)*

11. **Collaboration:** Works cooperatively with others; seeks involvement and feedback; works toward group goal(s) *(knowledge of hidden rules, relationships, and support systems resources)*

12. **Social responsibility:** Understands and participates in governance systems; challenges unjust behavior; participates in service/volunteer activities, as well as takes part in orderly change of community, social, and legal standards or norms *(knowledge of hidden rules resource)*

13. **Satisfying and productive lifestyle:** Achieves balance among education, work, and leisure; meets goals; overcomes obstacles; functions on the basis of personal identity and ethical, spiritual, and moral values *(all resources)*

14. **Appreciation for diversity:** Understands own identity and culture; seeks involvement with people different from self and with diverse interests; challenges stereotypes; understands impact of diversity on society *(knowledge of hidden rules resource)*

15. **Spiritual awareness:** Develops and articulates personal belief system; understands roles of spirituality in personal and group values and behaviors *(spiritual resource)*

16. **Personal and educational goals:** Sets, articulates, and pursues individual goals; uses personal and educational goals to guide decisions; understands effects of one's personal and educational goals on others. (Dean, 2006, pp. 23–24) *(mental/cognitive resource)*

The Student Learning and Development Outcome Domains can be addressed through building the 11 resources and assessed in light of the degree to which a student has these resources. Further, the outcome domains speak to strategies that help end poverty. For example, "Realistic self-appraisal" addresses individual choices, "Meaningful interpersonal relationships" relates to the presence of human and social capital in the community, and "Social responsibility" speaks to the role of the individual in shaping the sociopolitical and economic structures that govern wealth. Thus we see a wide range of expertise supporting holistic and even systemic approaches to teaching, learning, and the development of students into civically engaged citizens.

CHAPTER 5

In Action—the *Why* and the *How* of Learning Strategies

Both the internal and external resources—especially the cognitive strategies that under-resourced students need—can be developed at most postsecondary institutions. Due to the impact of faculty and staff on educational outcomes, it is vital for them to intentionally engage in building resources as appropriate in all categories, particularly the following:

- Hidden Rules of Class and College
- Relationships of Mutual Respect
- Mental/Cognitive Resources
- Language Resources

There is overlap not only among resources but also among related topics as well.

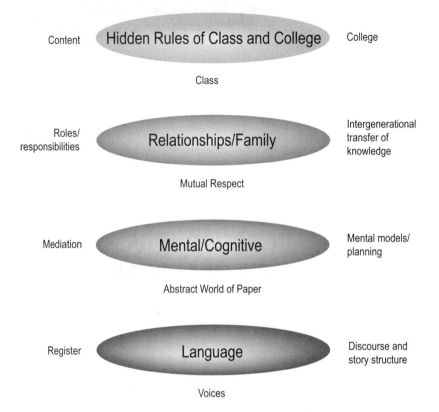

Earlier chapters explored why some students seem to lack the cognitive processes, behaviors, and skills necessary for effective academic progress. Institutions at the postsecondary level cannot immediately change the effects of growing up in communities with under-resourced public schools, sporadic access to healthcare, limited employment opportunities, etc. It is important, however, that these influences are recognized, and staff persons strive to empower students to develop the "weft and weave" of their strengths. Indeed, personnel at postsecondary institutions can do a great deal to validate students' backgrounds and be cognizant of how personal experiences affect students' ability to learn, prioritize, and survive on a daily basis.

The focus of this chapter is what happens in the classroom—or during programs sponsored by student services—to mediate and contextualize the learning experience. What does the instructor or facilitator see in students? And what can be done to (1) make up for the gaps in prior learning and (2) accelerate learning to make up for the learning lag, all within the limited amount of available time? As instruction occurs the focus can be on:

- Strengthening the warp of the tapestry—the mental and cognitive resources that already include strong problem-solving skills
- Bringing new color and texture by teaching hidden rules, not only of economic class and college but also of language
- Reinforcing the weave through the weft—tying off the knots with bridging relationships built on mutual respect.

When students arrive at college without needed strategies in their repertoire or skill set, instructors and student services personnel can help them acquire these tools. The strategies presented in this chapter draw on both adult learning theories and practical instructional techniques, including many designed specifically to fill in cognitive gaps due to inadequate mediation. The correlations between the needs of under-resourced students and adult learners are significant. Under-resourced students, many of whom have years of experience raising younger siblings or helping their family to survive on a daily basis, typically share more characteristics with nontraditional students (generally 24 years of age and above) who return to or even start college after raising a family and/or holding down a job than with typical first-year students. Therefore, because of these diverse and often intense life experiences, adult learning theories and strategies will be explored as well.

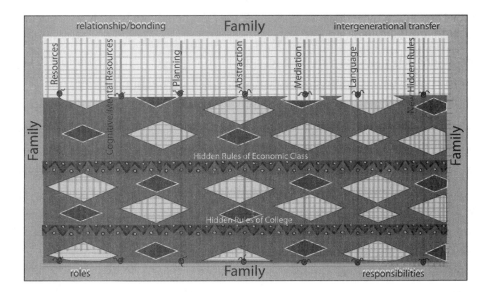

The challenge is to make college (and especially the initial experience) positive, personally relevant, and meaningful to all students. Otherwise, the well-meaning instructor's admonition of "You *should* _____ " or "*Everybody* knows _____ " is received at best as middle-class "noise" to be filtered out in order to attend to what is seen as important and at worst as insults, thereby eliminating the likelihood of a mutually respectful relationship with that student. Perry (1999) points out that negative comments to under-resourced students imply that their "performance is a product of uncontrollable factors (e.g., intelligence) beyond the students' capacity to change" (p. 19). To under-resourced students such comments confirm that whatever success they have is based on fate and that they are incapable of changing. As a result, this negative message and how it is received by under-resourced students perpetuates the frustration of faculty and staff who believe that students will not or cannot change—or that it is not "my job" to invest time and energy in building students' self-esteem, motivation, and persistence.

Many students become better learners if immersed in activities—particularly activities that interest them. Similarly, students engaged in learning experiences relevant and similar to those of a nurse or engineer will learn to be better nurses or engineers. Jean Lave and Etienne Wenger's (1991) stipulation, though, is that the situation must be as similar to or as embedded in "real life" as possible. Otherwise, the student is learning to do math as a *student,* rather than learning to do the thinking about math that a *nurse* or *engineer* will use. David Conley (2008) in *College Knowledge* challenges high school curricula for even well-prepared students by asking "how high school math or science courses prepare students for studies that lead to careers in engineering, for example. They are often unprepared for the more conceptually oriented curriculum they encounter" even though they received good grades in high school (p. 75). Elementary and middle school English curricula are oriented almost entirely toward grammatical analysis, missing opportunities to improve actual literacy. To illustrate, being literate involves being able to convey something meaningful, "creating narratives, shaping what we see and feel into written language, listening to and reading stories, playing with the sounds of words" (Rose, 1989, p. 109). Therefore, situating under-resourced students in experiences that develop their language skills, their learning skills, their thinking skills, their problem-solving skills, and their communication skills—as well as their motivation and internal locus of control (willingness to take responsibility for one's performance)—will benefit them both as students and eventual practitioners in their chosen careers. The expectation is that students begin to weave new patterns for themselves and finally design a whole new tapestry—that is, create a future story based on what is possible in addition to what is known.

Merchant's (1986) research on cognitive deficiencies can form the basis for discussion of how the mental/cognitive resources that under-resourced learners lack might be developed. Merchant suggests three areas in which change is needed; these areas coincide with the philosophy described in this book:

- Change in attitude about what learners are capable of doing—even those with a long history of low achievement
- Assessment [focusing] on the processes of learning and less on the product or manifestation of prior learning
- Changes in the curriculum and in instructional practices that will promote the development of underlying cognitive functions. (p. 126)

Merchant (1986) further states that "students must be encouraged to be more active learners and taught how" (p. 126). William McKeachie (2002) echoes what is being said here by referring to a familiar Talmudic expression that translates "If you give people a fish, you have fed them for a day, but if you teach them how to fish, you have fed them for a lifetime." He continues with this analogy: "As college instructors our task is to provide edible fish (content knowledge), but our task is also to teach our students how to fish (learning how to become strategic learners in our field)" (p. 283). These goals can be accomplished by staff and instructors through introducing students to specific learning strategies. In addition, helping them understand and believe that "performance is modifiable and under their control" is crucial for a lifetime of learning (Perry, 1999, p. 17). We begin the discussion with teaching students the hidden rules of college and coursework.

Hidden Rules of Class and College

Payne (2008b) summarizes some of the differences between a "situated learning" environment comfortable to under-resourced students and the formal educational environment.

"Situated" learning in an environment where there is not much formal schooling	Formal school learning environment
Language is oral and uses many nonverbals.	Language is written, with specific word choice and sentence structure.
Math skills are related to trading, bartering, specific tasks, money.	Math tasks/skills are written and involve generic, unrelated story problems, formulas, and patterns.
Teaching/learning is very relational; respect may or may not be given to learning and/or teaching.	The relationship between teacher and learner is much more formalized; respect is expected by teacher from learner.

continued on next page

continued from previous page

"Situated" learning in an environment where there is not much formal schooling	Formal school learning environment
Learning environment is often unpredictable; reactive skills are important.	Planning is required in formal learning; both teacher and learner are expected to be able to plan.
Information is conveyed through story or media.	Information is conveyed through textbook and/or lecture.
Laughter is used to lessen conflict.	Laughter during conflict is viewed as disrespectful.
Paper (decontextualized) information is not valued.	Decontextualized information is what is tested and valued.

Note. From *Under-Resourced Learners* (p. 57), by R. K. Payne, 2008, Highlands, TX: aha! Process. Copyright 2008 by aha! Process. Reprinted with permission.

Teaching the hidden rules of the college or university setting means teaching students how to survive, function, and thrive in this "other" environment. Learning from a vastly different landscape results in "decontextualized" learning. When learning becomes decontextualized, the amount of support a student needs in order to make the transition to that actual environment increases.

Adult learners want their life experiences to matter, but they also expect to change and grow as a result of their learning experience. Jack Mezirow (1981) says that at the heart of adult learning is critical reflection in which learners test their assumptions and beliefs in order to transform them. Teaching can be difficult for some instructors when many students come to the institution lacking in life experiences that directly or easily apply to the course content and college success. These life experiences sometimes include learned helplessness (Perry, 1999) and internalized stereotypes regarding what it takes to succeed in various academic disciplines (Menec & Perry, 1995). The challenge, then, is to find those connections and address faulty, undesirable, maladaptive definitions of success and failure (Perry).

Some connections may be discovered through the relationships between under-resourced students and college staff. In these relationships, reciprocal learning about hidden rules can be quite beneficial, even symbiotic, with each party learning more about the other in order to better understand and work toward student success. For college staff, such relationships will likely shed light on a landscape quite different from middle-class experience.

Instructors and academic support personnel who wish to serve under-resourced learners must "consider ways of thinking not only as results of instruction but also as a prerequisite for instruction, [including providing] direct instruction concerning strategic approaches to the tasks specific to their content area" (McKeachie, 2002, p. 275). Teaching under-resourced students entails teaching them about content *and* about how to learn. In postsecondary contexts, two principal areas assist in focusing the discussion:

- The integrated, contextualized world of the content—that is, how to think like (e.g.) an engineer or a nurse
- The integrated, contextualized world of instruction and learning—how to read the text, listen to lectures, and do assignments.

Without these being made explicit, students are likely to approach all classes with their under-developed skills and their own hidden rules and assumptions, seldom or never associating the courses with the future story they could help create. Instructors and academic support personnel who wish to serve under-resourced learners must "consider ways of thinking not only as results of instruction but also as a prerequisite for instruction, [including providing] direct instruction concerning strategic approaches to the tasks specific to their content area" (McKeachie, 2002, p. 275). Faculty and staff are "ideally situated to engage in some rudimentary attributional retraining" (Perry, 1999, p. 18), which is shown to be effective across many disciplines in which some students are particularly at risk (Menec & Perry, 1995).

MOVING TOWARD A CONTEXTUALIZED WORLD OF CONTENT

Under-resourced learners, most of whom need support in their learning and adapting processes, are best served by learning experiences that are engaging, relevant, and meaningful. Lave and Wenger (1991) focus attention on "situated learning" and emphasize that "no activity is not situated" (p. 33). In other words, "learning is an integral part of generative social practice in the lived-in world" (p. 35). Therefore, in order to bridge the cognitive processes of learning with the social practices of the context of the discipline, the instructor in this "expert/novice paradigm" must model and share the dimensions of an expert:

- Knowledge of organization and structure
- Depth of problem representation
- Quality of mental models
- Efficiency of procedures
- Automaticity

- Procedures for theory change
- Proceduralized knowledge
- Metacognitive skills for learning. (Glaser, Lesgold, & Lajoie, 1987)

Instructors can more fully share their expertise in their discipline by shifting from being "content driven" to being "pedagogy driven" (Saroyan, 2000, p. 93). Techniques include establishing instructional routines, using additional process-oriented handouts, being alert to students' cues regarding their interpretation and misconceptions of the material, and being flexible regarding students' needs (Bess, 2000; McKeachie, 2002).

Toward a contextualized classroom

The strategies presented in the mental/cognitive and language portions of this chapter can help students develop their classroom and study habits. Learning involves repetition, organization of information, and elaboration on materials through mediated learning experiences that make it meaningful and memorable. The instructor as expert can model thinking and learning practices, such as paraphrasing, so that students make the "transition from existing knowledge structures in their minds to more accurate or advanced knowledge structures" (McKeachie, 2002, p. 275).

The following activities can help bridge the novices' thinking to that of the expert (McKeachie, 2002) and the under-resourced students' skills to those of adequately resourced adults:

1. Preview the textbook and its text structures [pointing out how they supplement lecture, lab, and course assignments].
2. Provide anonymous student work as examples of dos and don'ts.
3. Provide sample items from previous tests for students to practice [and learn about testing styles].
4. Be clear about terminology that has domain-specific meaning. (p. 276)

In order to help students better understand instructional approaches common to the domain, a faculty member might consider providing notes for his or her first lecture, even creating the notes "live" during the class via an LCD projection. Explicitly demonstrating other pedagogical approaches, such as laboratory procedures or working with case studies, helps students experience process, understand how to learn within a specific academic discipline, and understand the instructor's expectations. These and other strategies build students' self-regulated learning.

It must be noted, however, that directly teaching these hidden rules also requires self-awareness of one's own predilections and proclivities in relation to the material.

TEACHING ABOUT THE CAMPUS CONTEXT

It is helpful to show students where to go on campus to build specific resources necessary to meet their goals. Often campus resources (the clubs, medical assistance, and academic support centers) are the "best-kept secrets"—and are, in a sense, a set of hidden rules or resources worth learning about. The following chart shows the 11 resources in relation to where they might be addressed within a campus environment.

Internal Resources	Source of Resource at College
Knowledge of hidden rules	Individual discussion, advising, or classroom discussion regarding domain-specific rules; may need to focus specifically on those who lack transfer of knowledge or are first-generation college students
Mental/cognitive	Classroom primarily College environment in general Support services
Emotional	Support services primarily Classroom/college environment in general
Motivation/persistence	Classroom primarily College environment in general Support services
Integrity/trust	Classroom primarily College environment in general Support services
Physical	Support services primarily PE courses College organizations
Spiritual	Support services Psychology, religion, and philosophy courses Wellness course

External Resources	Source of Resource at College
Language	Classroom (ranging from register to domain-specific jargon) College environment Support services; direct-teach formal register in orientation course and/or intro composition course
Relationships/role models	Classroom College environment College organizations Support services
Support systems	Support services College organizations
Financial	Support services College organizations (through scholarships)

Finding ways to guide students toward accessing these services might seem simple at first. However, successfully doing so requires sensitivity to experiences that can result in some students' feelings of ignorance or not fitting in. It is helpful to follow up on such suggestions by encouraging the student to describe his or her experience and explore where these feelings might have originated. For example, was the attendant at the student center rude, or did the student feel uncomfortable having never gone to a research center like that before? Were the students in the club intentionally being hurtful, or were they completely unaware of the fact that some students do not have the money to go to Florida for Spring Break? Suggesting and encouraging students to try new approaches, then processing their experiences with them, builds their confidence and can help them keep things in perspective as they find their way.

Relationships of Mutual Respect

Since a key driving force in poverty is relationships, it follows that success for under-resourced students can be enhanced through the connections they make. Connections built on trust, high expectations, and a common understanding of hidden rules form positive bridging relationships. According to Stephen Brookfield (1990), a leader in the field of adult and higher education, "Trust between teachers and students is the affective glue binding educational relationships together" (p. 163). Citing the earlier work of Moustakas (1966) on "authentic teachers," Brookfield makes the following suggestions for modeling authenticity and building trust (adapted from *The Skillful Teacher*):

- **Don't deny your credibility.** In an effort to affirm the validity of the students' experiences, do not undermine your own credibility in their eyes.
- **Be explicit about your organizing vision.** As instructors introduce the syllabus, the assignments, the class proceedings (such as labs), and even how to read the textbook, it's helpful to make explicit the expectations and organizing principles of the classroom, the content area, and the department at the institution.
- **Make sure your words and actions are congruent.** If instructors are explicit with teaching and learning agendas and then break their own rules and codes of conduct, trust will be reduced or even lost.
- **Reveal aspects of yourself unrelated to teaching.** Tarule (1988) calls this the use of autobiographical metaphors that show the sources of the instructor's passions that led to interest in the field.
- **Show that you take students seriously.** This can be done by listening to their concerns and issues—and reinforcing their motivation for success. Be open to change if it will help students learn, and be explicit why activities, projects, and readings are included in the class and curriculum.
- **Don't play favorites.** Relationships will be broken if one student or group of students is regarded more favorably than others, and that bias is shown against others' failing efforts.
- **Realize the power of your own role modeling.** This is a key to transformative teaching, as humans have symbolic significance for students. Instructors start to make the concrete abstract and vice versa. (pp. 164–175)

Establishing trust can take time if an individual is not comfortable with believing in another person from the start, but along the way the demonstration of mutual respect through understanding and appreciating each others' hidden rules will enhance this process. While "bonding relationships" are important for unconditional support, "bridging social capital" (Putnam, 2000; Bourdieu, 1984) can offer a link to new resources, as well as a bridge between the world of poverty and middle class. Those who form bridging relationships act as coaches or mentors who in turn advocate for under-resourced individuals and "translate" for them the language and hidden rules of the dominant culture. The true bridging relationship is safe and moves toward the provision of missing resources.

In *The 7 Habits of Highly Effective People,* Stephen Covey (1989) states that relationships of mutual respect are like bank accounts. You make emotional deposits to those relationships, and you make emotional withdrawals from the same relationships. Under-resourced students are sensitive to these "withdrawals" and will distance themselves from instructors and staff they perceive as untrustworthy, rude, condescending, and so on. The following items are of particular importance to under-resourced students:

Deposits	Withdrawals
Seeking first to understand	Seeking first to be understood
Keeping promises	Breaking promises
Kindness, courtesies	Unkindness, discourtesies
Clarifying expectations	Violating expectations
Loyalty to the absent	Disloyalty, duplicity
Apologies	Pride, conceit, arrogance
Openness to feedback	Rejecting feedback

Note. From *A Framework for Understanding Poverty* (p. 111), by R. K. Payne, 2005, Highlands, TX: aha! Process. Copyright 1996 by aha! Process. Adapted with permission.

BUILDING MUTUAL RESPECT IN THE CLASSROOM AND ON CAMPUS

Teaching and learning can be much more rewarding and meaningful when the learning environment includes mutual respect. In *The Art and Science of Teaching* (2007), Robert Marzano identifies the following action steps that communicate an appropriate level of concern and cooperation—two important components of support:

    a.   Attempt to learn something unique or interesting (positive) about each student.
    b.   Engage in behaviors that indicate concern for each student.
    c.   Bring student interests into content, and personalize learning activities.
    d.   Use humor when appropriate.
    e.   Consistently reinforce positive and negative consequences.

Some instructors will feel that building relationships with students is not "part of the job." Parker Palmer (1998), in the book *The Courage to Teach,* refers to a "complex and interactive community of truth," stating that "good teachers do more than deliver the news from that community to their students" (p. 115) and "conventional pedagogy emerges from a principle that is hardly communal" but instead basically "delivers conclusions to students" (p. 116). Palmer reminds his readers that it is the "subject-centered classroom" in which this community happens. He cites everything from the kindergarten classroom, service learning programs, and learning through digital technology as examples of scenarios for community building—where the instructor's central task is to give an independent voice to the course content. Building mutual respect, therefore, also can build respect for the subject matter—really a three-way interaction in any learning environment.

The following (adapted from Payne, 2005b) can serve as a starting point for creating an interactive community in which content-specific learning occurs while bridging relationships are fostered.

1. Create a safe environment (emotionally, verbally, and physically)

Learning levels are much higher when there is safety. Sarcasm and verbal abuse, particularly when they involve authority, create latent hostility. Robert Boice (1996) refers to these incidents as "classroom incivilities" (CIs) in his book *First-Order Principles for College Teachers*. In Boice's personal study of CIs, he found that faculty and students commonly identified three kinds of strongly disturbing classroom distracters, and they named different distracters at lesser levels. Congruent with most college classrooms, both instructors and students consider the following to be problems:

1. Students conversing so loudly that one third or more of the classroom lecture and resulting discussion were hard to hear.
2. Students confronting instructors with sarcasm and groans.
3. "Classroom terrorists" whose unpredictable and emotional outbursts made the entire class tense. (p. 11)

With regard to instructors' abuse of authority and students' behaviors, Payne (2008b, pp. 35–37) adapted the following chart from *The Verbally Abusive Relationship* (Evans, 1992).

TYPE	DEFINITION	EXAMPLE
Withholding	To remain cool and indifferent, to be silent and aloof, to reveal as little as possible	"What do you want me to say?" "I shouldn't have to tell you how to do it."
Countering	To express the opposite of what the person says	"This assignment isn't hard. It's easy."
Disguising as a joke	To make disparaging comments disguised as a joke	"How did you get into college?"
Blocking and diverting	To prevent the conversation from continuing, often by switching the topic	"You're just trying to have the last word." "You heard me. I shouldn't have to repeat myself."
Accusing and blaming	To blame the other person for one's own anger, irritation, or insecurity	"You're looking for trouble."
Judging and criticizing	To judge and express the judgment in a negative, critical way	"You're lazy." "You can't keep anything straight."

continued on next page

continued from previous page

TYPE	DEFINITION	EXAMPLE
Trivializing	To diminish and make insignificant the work or contribution of the other person	"Who helped you with this? I know someone did."
Undermining	To dampen interest and enthusiasm by eroding confidence	"Couldn't you find a more boring topic?" "Who are you trying to impress?"
Threatening	To manipulate by threatening loss or pain	"Do that again, and I'll kick you out."
Name calling	To call the other person names, including terms of endearment that are said sarcastically	"Well, darling …" "Why, you little squirt …"
Forgetting	To forget incidents, promises, and agreements for the purpose of manipulation	"I never agreed to that!"
Ordering	To give orders instead of asking respectfully	"Just do your work and stop asking questions."
Denying	To deny the reality of the other person	"You made that up." "Where did you get that?"
Abusive anger	Includes verbal rage, snapping at person, and shouting (often is part of the anger addiction cycle in which the person releases inner tension)	"You never understand." "Why are you in this class anyway?"

Note. Adapted from *The Verbally Abusive Relationship* (p. 85), by P. Evans, 1992, Avon, MA: Adams Media. Copyright 1992 by Adams Media.

The goal in creating an engaging environment is to be sure that both students and instructor are safe. If a student does use abusive language, the instructor's response may be as simple as saying, "You may not do that here"—and then reinforcing that this is a rule of the classroom that will be upheld. Given that under-resourced students may feel uncertain and sensitive to appearing weak or "looking dumb" in front of their classmates, instructors can establish ground rules (such as those in the Appendix: "Giving Empowering Feedback" and "Receiving Empowering Feedback"). Beyond providing these guidelines, though, the class can be encouraged to recognize empowering feedback with applause—and to prohibit disempowering reactions or abusive criticism.

2. Pay attention to nonverbal communication

As we communicate with others we send hundreds (some say thousands) of nonverbal messages at any given moment. These messages can be communicated through our facial expressions, hand gestures, stance, voice tone, and body positioning. Nonverbals are based on intent, and it is nearly impossible for us to conceal the unspoken messages we are sending out. So whether it is the student or the authority figure who enters a conversation with the intent to dominate, it will be reflected in the nonverbals, and the responder is likely to be on the defensive. Entering into a conversation with the intent to understand, however, will be reflected as well in the nonverbals. Therefore, it is important to examine one's intentions prior to beginning a conference or discussion. Tone of voice is also a major issue in conversations. For instance, the phrase "Help me understand" can be stated with sarcasm or with caring. Even though the words are the same, the meanings can be very different and so will the result be in building mutually respectful relationships.

3. Hold students accountable

What good instructors, facilitators, administrators, and parents know is that it is far more difficult to hold young people accountable than it is to simply let them do as they please. Accountability can be a positive facet of both teaching and learning, especially when it arises naturally and personally from a learning situation. One way to develop students' accountability is to extend to them opportunities for power and choice. For many under-resourced students, power and choice have largely been missing from their lives. Thus "accountability" is equated with predetermined expectations when people from the middle class set requirements that rule out the individual's power to choose—and administer punishment when those expectations are not met (DeVol, 2004). Accountability that fosters mutual respect also is reflected in the way student evaluations are carried out. Students whose lives have been devoid of power and choice are keenly concerned about fairness, particularly with regard to how grades are assigned. Therefore, it is recommended that instructors implement rubrics to show what is expected in an assignment and how objective grading decisions are made, as well as to give students a choice about how much effort to invest. Using grading rubrics helps to create an atmosphere of fairness, objectivity, and ownership in the grading process, along with accountability in the classroom (see Appendix for sample grading rubric).

In order for students to experience accountability, they must have choices with logical consequences. When consequences are applied to a situation, it is best to do so face to face, so the experience can be mediated. Then, even in light of negative consequences, learning and growth still occur (DeVol, 2004). Pfarr (2009) suggests using the following statement when discussing needed changes and awareness of a situation that requires students being held accountable: If you choose _____, then you have chosen _____ (p. 65). She reminds the user of this phrase to apply it twice in any situation—once for the bad choice and once for the better choice. To paraphrase Pfarr, if you choose not to attend class, then you've chosen to lose 10% of your grade for each two classes missed and possibly flunking the course. But, if you choose to come to class regularly, you choose to pass the course and keep your financial aid coming, thus eventually getting a degree and helping your family. The application of this phrase in similar situations may open students' eyes not only to the choices and consequences (and ultimately future orientation) they may have but also that power lies with each individual to make the choice.

ORGANIZATIONAL STRUCTURES FOR CREATING FEELINGS OF CONNECTEDNESS

Within a college classroom, organization, work environment, or learning community, developing a sense of "belonging" is central to many retention strategies. Frank Smith (1985, 1986), an educational/cognitive psychologist, uses psycholinguistic theories to advance the idea that "learning clubs" allow students to perceive themselves as having "mutual acceptance." The impact of this inclusive feeling for students builds self-concept (Knowles, 1990), empowerment (Mezirow, 1981), and the ability to commit to relativism (Perry, 1970, 1981). The opposite also is true. Exclusionary attitudes and practices in the classroom tend to induce rote, disconnected learning, or, even worse, reluctance to persist at the college level. Think about the satisfaction gained when learning something and having the opportunity to use it again in a meaningful way; this feeling is what students need in order to understand the impact of the deeper learning tactics they can develop with effort. Such "connectedness," like Palmer's "community," is present not only between the student and the instructor or facilitator but also among students, as well as between the individual student and the content. In short, it is the best of all worlds for teaching and learning.

Students are more likely to succeed when they feel connected to campus life. Connection is the belief by students that adults on campus care about their learning, as well as about them as individuals. The key requirements for feeling connected include students' experiencing:

- High academic expectations and rigor coupled with support for learning
- Positive adult/student relationships
- Safety: both physical and emotional

Strong scientific evidence demonstrates that increased student connection to school promotes:

- Educational motivation
- Improved attendance

Note. Adapted from "Wingspread Declaration on School Connections," 2004, *The Journal of School Health, 74,* pp. 233–234. Copyright 2004 by Blackwell.

A student's feeling of being part of campus life and cared for is reflected in student achievement—and is believed to be a strong factor in helping students cope with stress, both inside and outside the college setting. Unfortunately, there are students who go through a complete day on campus and speak with virtually no one. Several U.S. campus shootings in recent years and many behavioral issues have to do with students who are "isolates." This isolation from others often leads to a sense of not belonging—when belonging is a basic human need, as Maslow (1970) identified years ago in his "hierarchy of needs."

As noted, both bonding and bridging social capital enhance a sense of belonging and connectedness. One way to build bridging capital is with mentors and internships. Mentoring a younger student by the college student himself or herself is another way and can be a powerful experience for both. Following are ways in which faculty, staff, and students can engage in mentoring and coaching on a college campus.

Personal adviser programs

Based on current research evidence, the most effective strategy for increasing the likelihood that students will be connected to campus life is ensuring that every student feels close to at least one supportive adult. This is a difficult task when the number of students greatly exceeds that of the adults on campus. One way of meeting this goal for the students deemed most at risk is a personal adviser program, which calls for each student to be assigned to both an academic and a personal adviser. Academic advisers are assigned as usual, and responsibilities continue to be those of typical academic advisers.

The assignment process for a personal adviser, however, should begin by identifying the 20% of first-year students deemed likely to be in greatest need of interventions. Faculty members who are willing to serve in this capacity may request to work with students on the list whom they know and with whom they would particularly like to work. Remaining students are then distributed equally among personal advisers.

Faculty members can notify a student's personal adviser when the student consistently breaks hidden rules, fails to complete projects, or demonstrates other needs. The personal adviser can then schedule a meeting with the individual student or a group of students to discuss campus policies, hidden rules, cognitive strategies, etc.

Campus clubs

Campus clubs can help create feelings of belonging, but many students do not have the time or other resources to invest (figuratively or financially) in membership. One approach would be to expect all students to participate in one or two clubs upon entry into college. Club membership should require no dues or significant dedication of time, but membership should be recognized periodically through friendly competitions, campus publicity, etc. The question to ask in the orientation of all first-year students is not: "Do you want to join a club?" Rather, the approach is: "As a student at this college, you are automatically a member of Club X or Club Y. Which additional campus club or clubs on this list do you want to join?" Most students are not aware of the wide variety of active clubs on a campus, so simply showing students a list could well spark interest in membership.

Group work in classrooms

In classes and in on-campus programs students should regularly be assigned to work in pairs. Assignments can be designed so that each student would be responsible for his or her own work, but groups must interact with each other (collaborative learning) in order to get the assignment done. Not only will this mitigate the isolationist tendencies of some students, it will begin preparing them for the workplace where collaboration is the norm.

There are many methods of assessing group work and individual participation that can keep these processes fair and functioning.

As previously discussed, one of the best gifts that instructors and academic support staff can give students is an understanding of the hidden rules of class, along with the skills they need in order to negotiate the language and cognitive challenges they will face. But further, the hidden rules of the classroom, including the content domain, also are essential for students to discover in order to enhance their learning at higher (or deeper) levels. As Palmer (1998) reminds us:

> A subject-centered classroom is not one in which students are ignored. Such a classroom honors one of the most vital needs our students have: to be introduced to a world larger than their own experience and egos, a world that expands their personal boundaries and enlarges their sense of community. (p. 120)

While entering under-resourced students may have only their present situations in mind, it will become important for them—as they engage in situated classroom experiences and form bridging relationships—to continue to learn and use the hidden rules of the middle class, the college, and the classroom, which includes the content area of the course.

Brain research shows that "emotions give a sense of reality to what we do and think" (Caine & Caine, 1991, p. 57). Since all learning is double-coded, both emotionally and mentally (Greenspan & Benderly, 1997), how one feels about something is part of the learning experience (Payne, 2008b, p. 25). Both learning *and* memory are strengthened when there is an emotional impact in connection with a situation. For instance, when students become aware that a strategy can focus their fuzzy thinking about how to comprehend an assignment and complete it on time, they are more likely to try it in the first place and use it again in the future, both in classroom assignments and in familial or community projects and obligations. This is particularly true when students have a personal investment in the class and the grade they receive, so that they can continue in a program they find meaningful.

Philip Candy (1991), in discussing how the learner approaches learning situations, offers the following series of questions from Biggs (1986) that individuals deliberately trying to learn something might ask about their *intent* and *process* (not about the content).

Motives	"What do I want?"
Goals	"What will it look like when I've gotten there?"
Task demands	"What do I need to get there?"
Context	"What resources do I have to use?"
	"What constraints must I contend with?"
Abilities	"What am I capable of doing?"
Strategies	"Well, then. How do I go about it?"

Once again, the stages in the mediation of the learning experience are easily seen in this list of questions focusing on *what, why,* and *how* the task will get done, including the individual's motivation and resources. For adults and/or under-resourced learners to become self-directed, the learning situation must include opportunities for them to develop their own repertoire of learning skills and to deepen their understanding of the knowledge, as well as their self-awareness (Candy, 1991). Through relationships of mutual respect, students are more likely to accept, try, and adopt strategies for improving resources in which they are low.

Mental/Cognitive Resources

BUILDING COGNITIVE STRUCTURES: METACOGNITION

According to research on adult learning (Lindemann, 1961; Knowles, 1990), students at the college level value and want validation for their life experiences (the *what*); they seek to know the rationale for what they are being taught (the *why*); and they prefer to be guided toward self-direction or self-efficacy (the *how*). McKeachie (2002) explains this process by referring to "metacognition"—defined as "thinking about thinking, or knowing about knowing"; the concept of metacognition is attributed to research by Flavell (1979); Pintrich, Walters, and Baxter (2000); and Zimmerman and Paulsen (1995). Reflecting Feuerstein's mediated learning model (as cited in Sharron & Coulter, 2004), along with adult learning theories, metacognitive processes include knowledge about:

- Oneself as a learner
- Academic tasks
- Strategies to use to accomplish the academic tasks

These are the mediated steps in learning—the *what,* the *why,* and the *how.* Therefore, essential strategies for under-resourced students include:

- Planning so they can attend to both the world of survival and to the college agenda that lies before them
- Sorting more important from less important information
- Organizing space
- Focusing on essential stimuli
- Utilizing data

Strategies also must include how to learn the academic materials that may not yet be emotionally interesting to students. Strategies may need to give attention to the more basic issue of how under-resourced students best learn. Meaningful learning requires moving students along in their learning process by attaching meaning, adding mutual respect to promote motivation, and then being certain that the purpose for learning or the activity is made clear to the learner.

In relation to the following diagram, the under-resourced learner, who may be operating primarily at the "body" level, relies first on sensory data. When people are processing mostly at the body level, they act primarily on their feelings: "I was embarrassed when you asked me that question and I didn't know the answer. I'm leaving." Moving to the "mind" level, processing uses language. When individuals are processing at this level, they tend to feel the feelings and express them in language: "I didn't understand your question, and I was embarrassed in class today." By second and third grade, most students should be capable of functioning at the third level, metacognition—using mental constructs and representing the feelings involved; individuals of all ages, however, revert to lower levels in times of stress or great uncertainty. The level above metacognition is called "epistemic cognition," which is the ability to analyze the framework or the theoretical structure of thinking. Therefore, the individual has the ability to use words and phrases to represent feelings like "This incident really made me angry," or "I felt like David in front of Goliath."

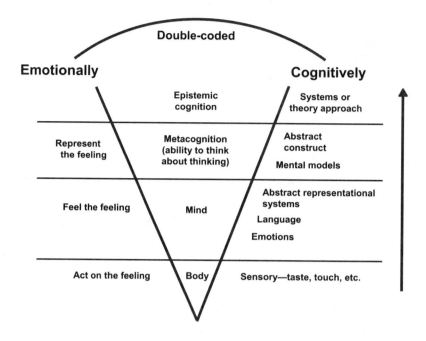

Note. From PowerPoint presentation on preventing dropouts, by R. K. Payne, 2008, Highlands, TX: aha! Process. Copyright 2008 by aha! Process. Adapted with permission.

Payne (2005c) elaborates using the example of a welder. At the body level, he or she welds. This level involves the senses—vision and touch, in this example—and the person acts on his or her senses/feelings. At the next level, the mind, the welder can talk about welding and feel the feeling that comes with a job well done. At the mind level, the welder uses language to express feelings and thoughts, and at metacognition he or she welds against a blueprint. At the level of epistemic cognition, the welder can assess blueprints for structural strength. A systems approach or theory approach is involved (p. 116).

Payne (2005c, 2008a) points out that abstract thinking is found at the mind, metacognitive, and epistemic levels. Dee Fink (2003) highlights three types of thinking based on Sternberg's (1989) "triarchic" view of the thought process: critical thinking, creative thinking, and practical thinking. Fink's interpretations exemplify the types of thinking under-resourced students need to develop, as follows:

106

Critical thinking: to learn how to analyze and evaluate, requiring relevant conceptual understanding

Creative thinking:

In humanities—finding new forms of expression or new interpretations of existing work

In social sciences and natural sciences—developing new perspectives on phenomena being studied; devising new solutions to old problems

Practical thinking: learning how to answer questions, make decisions, and solve problems. (pp. 41–42)

Sternberg's (1989) examples are included in Fink's (2003) book to help illustrate the content-specific questions designed to prompt these three types of thinking. A few examples include:

Field	Critical Thinking	Creative Thinking	Practical Thinking
Biology	Evaluate the validity of the bacterial theory of ulcers.	Design an experiment to test the bacterial theory of ulcers.	How would the bacterial theory of ulcers change conventional treatment regimens?
History	How did events in post-WWI Germany lead to the rise of Nazism?	How might Truman have encouraged the surrender of Japan without A-bombing Hiroshima and Nagasaki?	What lessons does Nazism hold for the events in Bosnia today?
Art	Compare and contrast how Rembrandt and Van Gogh used light in [specific paintings].	Draw a beam of light.	How could we reproduce the lighting in this painting in an actual room?

Note. From *The Triarchic Mind: A New Theory of Human Intelligence,* by R. J. Sternberg, 1989, New York: Penguin. Copyright 1989 by Penguin. Adapted with permission.

While all of these are valuable ways of thinking, practical-thinking questions help to answer the under-resourced student's question, "Why is this important to me now?" by bringing the learner into the present for analyzing content. These needs of the adult learner will build the cognitive strategies for taking an abstract concept, like ulcer bacteria, and making it meaningful and concrete so that the learner begins to make sense of it—thus eventually becoming comfortable enough with the material to connect further abstract concepts for more concrete learning.

APPROACHES TO DEVELOPING THINKING SKILLS

The development of content-specific thinking skills requires an understanding of the purpose, structure, and patterns of the discipline being studied. Payne (2005b, 2005c) recommends being explicit about the purpose of the discipline and why the content information—particularly its structure and patterns—is connected to the discipline at large. A pattern in social studies is the causes of war: territory, religion, etc. If wars discussed in class are examined in light of their causes and compared and contrasted with other wars, students can better understand the discipline than if they study details in isolation.

The ability to identify and teach the purpose, structure, and patterns of a discipline requires a clear understanding and in-depth knowledge of that discipline. The difference between good teachers and excellent teachers is the depth and breadth of their knowledge of their discipline (Shulman, 1986). Excellent instructors can deliver the "big picture" of the course to their students in such a way as to make the information relevant and meaningful. Using mental models is a strategy instructors can use to convey big picture ideas, processes, and specific content.

Teaching *using mental models*

The term "mental models" is believed to have originated in Kenneth Craik's 1943 book *The Nature of Explanation,* in which he suggested that the mind constructs "small-scale models" of reality that it uses to anticipate events. Payne (2002) advances the concept of mental models by explaining that "Mental models are how the mind holds abstract information, i.e., information that has no sensory representation" (p. 44). For the college student whose language and experiences are rooted in concrete needs and concerns, mental models are a crucial tool for dealing with abstractions and developing higher level thinking skills. Students whose experiential base intersects with course content have developed detailed mental models of many of the topics discussed. Under-resourced students' understanding of many disciplines, however, tends to be sketchy at best. Therefore, these students are not sure how to sort and mentally store new information and are often reluctant to share opinions or ask questions related to the discussion, for fear of revealing their lack of knowledge or insecurity about the topic at hand.

Instructional mental models are shared understandings of the constructs (structure, purpose, and patterns) of the content in a discipline. All subject areas have their own mental models—that is, structures for representing and communicating information. The mental models of each college discipline are found within the course objectives, individual units within a course, and the desired outcome or objectives for the student. The ensuing chart outlines the analysis of the purpose, structure, patterns, and processes within the discipline of music.

Structure of Discipline of Music

PURPOSE	To use sound and instruments to make meaning
STRUCTURE	Voice Time Instruments Written notation Sounds (keys, notes, etc.)
PATTERNS (partial listing)	Groups of instruments Patterns of time (rhythm, beat, half notes, etc.) Patterns of sounds (keys, notes, sharps, flats, etc.) Patterns of notations Voice ranges Voice quality Interpretation Group patterns (orchestra, band, choir, duet, solo, etc.)
PROCESSES	Practice/repetition (music performance skills) Analysis/synthesis (music theory skills) Composition/arrangement (music production skills)

Note. From *Learning Structures* (p. 112), by R. K. Payne, 2005, Highlands, TX: aha! Process. Copyright 1998 by aha! Process. Adapted with permission.

Mental models—as presented by instructors to students—tell us what is and is not important in the discipline. They help the mind sort. Students with some understanding of ancient cultures, for example, can recognize information that is relevant to a discussion of Greek history and will know that when the instructor digresses to a remotely related topic about his adventures in an athletic event, this sidebar discussion does not require note taking. Under-resourced students, however, are less able to sort this from essential facts and will likely take notes on all that is said. If a mental model of the topic were presented prior to the discussion, however, the under-resourced student would be better able to sort important from unimportant information.

Mental models are held in the mind as drawings (visual or pictorial representations), stories, movements, or analogies. A major benefit of mental models is that they "collapse" the amount of time it takes to teach or learn information (Payne, 2002, p. 46). The following pictorial mental model, for example, clarifies the concept behind the Pythagorean Theorem concretely and immediately for most observers.

Pythagorean Theorem: $a^2 + b^2 = c^2$

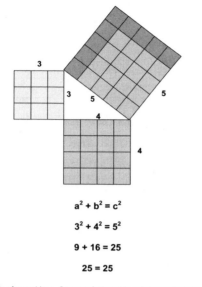

$$a^2 + b^2 = c^2$$

$$3^2 + 4^2 = 5^2$$

$$9 + 16 = 25$$

$$25 = 25$$

Square of one side + Square of other side = Square of hypotenuse

Therefore, the use of mental models to guide instruction is crucial for helping under-resourced students who lag behind their more adequately resourced peers in cognitive skill development—and need to accelerate their learning processes in order to bridge the gap.

The first step in mental model development is for the instructor to create an analogy, visual representation, movement, or story that succinctly and clearly explains the purpose of the discipline. The question to be asked is "If the purpose of social studies, for instance, is to examine human interaction throughout history, what simple visual representation can reflect this purpose and serve as a focal point for students taking the course?" The resulting mental model might be embedded boxes showing how individuals relate to families, then communities, then governments, etc.

This step is then repeated for each of the structures and patterns within the discipline. A pattern in language arts, for example, is genres. A mental model depicting genres and how they interface with other patterns within the discipline can help students sort information and quickly grasp related abstract concepts. Next, mental models are developed for individual skills. The following pictorial mental model clearly and quickly explains multiplication of positive and negative numbers. It is important to note that the mental model goes beyond mere recall; it reflects the *reasons* for the results achieved.

Multiplying Positive and Negative Numbers

+ = Good guys − = Bad guys	+ = Coming to town − = Leaving town	+ = Positive results − = Negative results
+	+	+
+	−	−
−	+	−
−	−	+

When good guys come to town, the results are positive. Translated into math, this would read: A positive number (+) multiplied by a positive number (+) yields a positive number (+), and so on.

Examples: When 10 good guys come to town and each performs 5 good deeds, the positive results are +50.

When 10 good guys (each of whom would have performed 5 good deeds) leave town, the impact is -50.

Note. From *Learning Structures* (p. 17), by R. K. Payne, 2005, Highlands, TX: aha! Process. Copyright 1998 by aha! Process. Adapted with permission.

In addition to illuminating the purpose, structure, and patterns of a discipline, mental models can assist students in understanding process skills—the *how* component. Unless the *how* is directly taught, a student may not have the tools necessary to understand a process or complete a task. The following folder activity, which has been used effectively with students in elementary school through college, is a mental model for the process of writing research papers.

Research Folder

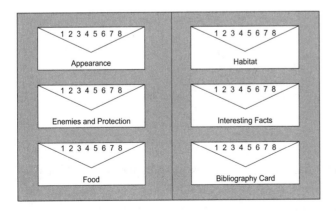

Directions: Each student glues six envelopes to the inside of a manila folder. Each envelope is labeled with a subtopic related to the broad topic. On the outside of each envelope the numbers 6, 5, 4, 3, 2, 1 (or the number of sources that the student needs to find about that topic) are written. As the student records data on a 3x5 card, he or she puts it in the appropriate envelope and then crosses off a number. Once the student has collected the required number of cards for each subtopic, he or she is ready to write the paper.

Mental models offer a way for instructors and students alike to gain control over massive amounts of course materials. While the construction and use of mental models may require considerable planning, the benefits to overall student understanding and cognition are worth the effort. The more that instructors or student services staff share these units of curriculum through visual representations, stories, analogies, and hands-on activities with under-resourced learners, the more the students will understand and make connections with the materials being explained. (Additional examples of mental models appear in the Appendix.)

Teaching *using graphic organizers*

For decades if not centuries educators have sought to identify and develop tools for helping students grasp abstract concepts. Research shows that the use of visual knowledge representation techniques can be one approach to helping students understand abstractions and communicate ideas and concepts succinctly and clearly (MacEachren, 1995; Hyerle, 1996). In addition to mental models, visual knowledge representation tools that have proven beneficial include mind mapping, concept mapping, and process mapping.

Mind maps

Mind maps can help students associate ideas and make connections they might not otherwise make. A mind map usually starts with one main topic or idea, then expands with other relevant ideas and notes added to branches extending from the main topic.

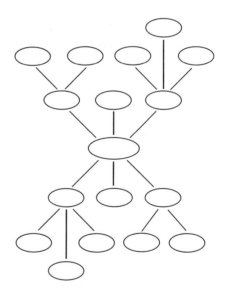

Concept (or semantic) maps

In contrast to mind maps, a concept map typically frames the perspectives and ideas of a group. It is usually based on a number of principles placed at the top of the map, with other secondary concepts arranged in hierarchical fashion below, linked by lines or arrows showing the relationships between and among the concepts. Concept or semantic mapping can be used as a learning tool—or as an evaluation instrument to assess the knowledge level of a group. It is also an effective technique for group brainstorming and activities planning. The semantic vocabulary map at right illustrates key components of a definition grouped around the term in order to answer three questions:

- What is it?
- What is it like?
- What are some examples?

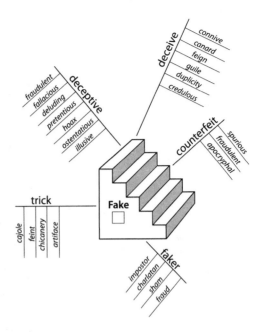

Note. From *Word Atlas: Mapping Your Way to SAT Success.* Copyright 1981 by Townsend Learning Center. Reprinted with permission.

Process maps

Process maps are similar to mind maps and concept maps, but they include such information as process complexity, steps, people to be involved, time, and costs. A process map (usually consisting of flow charts) is a graphical representation of a procedure, showing the starting point, inputs, outputs, and ending points. The following flow chart maps the process for the nomination and swearing in of a member of the U.S. Supreme Court.

Process Map for U.S. Supreme Court Nomination and Confirmation

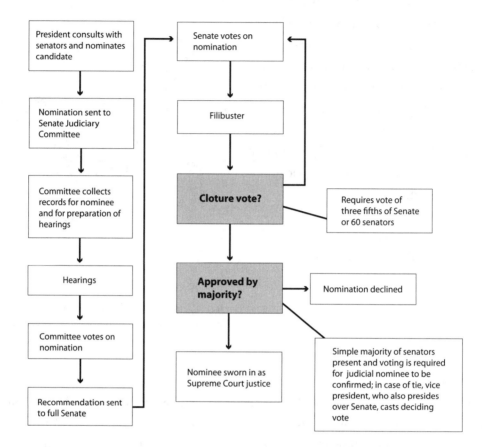

Note. From "Flowchart: Nomination and Confirmation." Copyright 2009 by SmartDraw.com. Adapted with permission.

David Ausubel (1960) suggested using graphic organizers before presenting new information. Through the use of "advance organizers," students are exposed to a higher level of abstraction and generality regarding the new topic, but then the framework or cognitive structure for the new learning also is introduced. The visual capacity of the graphic organizer will facilitate learning for students who may have difficulty with the written or spoken words describing the concept to be learned. At the same time, students are provided with placeholders for the information to be elucidated as their understanding grows. Research supporting the use of graphic organizers shows that these tools are reasonably effective for students of all abilities when learning unfamiliar or extremely difficult material (Williams & Butterfield, 1992). Advance organizers, such as flow charts, can assist students in acquiring both cognitive and process skills.

One of the reasons generic study skills have not been as successful as one might expect is that processes for studying tend to be specific to tasks of the content area. Finding the balance between teaching study skills and academic content can be tricky, but adroit integration of the two has proved useful for first-generation college students (Leathwood, 2006). Therefore, it is helpful when syllabi identify specific steps in the process required of students to complete projects and assignments, as well as the content that will be covered.

Teaching *using knowledge surveys*

A strategy for fostering active learning is the knowledge survey (Nuhfer, 1993; Nuhfer & Knipp, 2003). It consists of questions that span the breadth of a course and are posed at all levels of Bloom's Taxonomy (Bloom, Englehart, Furst, Hill, & Krathwohl, 1956). Knowledge surveys can be administered at the beginning, middle, and end of a course and can be completed outside of class time using computer answer sheets or web-based courseware—or in class using electronic testing tools. In general, the students are asked to indicate "their perceived ability to answer questions about course content" rather than actually answering the questions (Wirth & Perkins, n.d.). The results provide an indication of the depth and scope of students' knowledge, serve as a self-assessment tool for students, and (when used with other strategies) prompt peer discussion of content issues that promote improved learning (Jacobs, 2008). Short knowledge surveys can be followed by quizzes on specific content so that students can compare their certainty ratings with their performance on the quiz.

Questions at the levels of Bloom's Taxonomy might look something like this:

- What are the five theories of forgetting? *(knowledge level)*
- Does the Decay Theory involve long-term or short-term memory? *(comprehension level)*
- Identify which of the five theories applies to a specific description of memory loss. *(application level)*
- Compare the Incomplete Encoding Theory with the Retrieval Failure Theory. *(analysis level)*
- Create a mental model for the type of forgetting you find most common in your field of study. *(synthesis level)*
- Identify the type of forgetting you find yourself experiencing the most and suggest a plan for eliminating this problem. *(evaluation level)*

Students respond in terms of their comfort level in answering the questions. Examples follow (Wirth & Perkins, n.d.):

- ❐ I don't understand the question. I'm not familiar with the terminology, or I'm not confident that I can answer the question well enough for grading purposes at this time.
- ❐ I understand the question and (a) I'm confident I could answer at least 50% of it correctly, or (b) I know precisely where to find the necessary information and could provide an answer for grading in less than 20 minutes.
- ❐ I'm confident that I can answer the question ... well enough for grading at this time. (p. 2)

A professor of chemistry and biochemistry at the University of Notre Dame, Dennis Jacobs (2008) uses collaborative learning and clicker-response technology with knowledge surveys in large lecture classes for general chemistry. He has found that the combined pedagogy assists at-risk students in their development of problem-solving skills and improves student attitudes and perception about the study of chemistry. In the long term he also found for at-risk students a 55% increase in completion of the first year of general chemistry, a 50% increase in those who successfully completed second-year organic chemistry, and a 50% increase for those who pursued a major in science (Jacobs, 2008). While Jacobs' strategy has many benefits for the under-resourced student, it will behoove the instructor to monitor for students who give answers they think the instructor wants to hear, rather than honestly assessing their ability to answer the question.

Teaching *question-making skills*

A great service that instructors can offer students is to help them develop their question-making skills in general and to guide them toward asking higher level questions. This includes self-questioning, which develops abstract thinking and metacognition while reading and writing. Inadequately mediated students who have difficulty dealing with data (Sharron & Coulter, 2004, p. 60) and are discouraged from asking questions by their parents often lack the ability to formulate and respond appropriately to questions. Encouraging students to develop their own higher level questions, such as the ones that might appear on a test or quiz, can be a tremendously beneficial exercise. Not surprisingly, this is not an easy task for most under-resourced students. A few "rules," such as the suggestions below for developing multiple choice questions, will help avoid pitfalls.

1. Write the question or question stem.
2. Write four possible answers.
   a. Only one answer can be the right answer.
   b. One wrong answer must be funny (hidden rule for humor/entertainment; requires higher level thinking).
   c. Students may not use "all of the above" or "none of the above." (Although this configuration appears on many tests, students could use "all of the above" or "none of the above" option as a way to avoid the task of writing thought-provoking distracters.)

After students have developed the skill of writing questions, the process can be expedited by giving them question stems, starting with content questions. Sample content question stems include:

1. What is the main idea of the passage?
2. From the passage, the reader can tell …
3. Which of these best describes the reason the author wrote this passage?
4. Which statement is the best summary of the passage?
5. What can the reader tell about _____ from information in this passage?
6. From this passage, how might _____ be described?
7. In paragraph ____, what two things is the author comparing?
8. What conclusions can be drawn from this passage?
9. Which of the following is the opinion of the passage?
10. If the author had been _____, how might the passage have been different?

Note. From *Learning Structures* (pp. 66–68), by R. K. Payne, 2005, Highlands, TX: aha! Process. Copyright 1998 by aha! Process. Adapted with permission.

Not only are analytical questions more challenging and lend themselves to deepening class discussion, analyzing questions that might be on a test or quiz can be helpful to students' understanding of the demonstration of knowledge. The instructor can distribute samples of students' questions (without student names on them) for class discussion about what makes a good question. In this process students are invited to look at the peer-generated questions and ask:

❏ What is the question asking?
❏ Is there only one right answer?
❏ Does the question stem need a qualifier in order to
   make one answer choice better than another?

Note. From *Trainer Certification Manual* (p. 167), by R. K. Payne, 2001, Highlands, TX: aha! Process. Copyright 2001 by aha! Process. Adapted with permission.

Students can be encouraged in their question formulating to play a few rounds of "Jeopardy!" as a course review (all answers must be in the form of questions). While there may not be time for this in the classroom, teaching assistants, supplemental instruction tutors, or even residence hall staff might help students form study groups and encourage this type of thinking to make learning more fun. Challenging students to "think like the teacher" or the test maker can lead them to thought processes that will enhance their mental/cognitive skills in preparation for tests.

Teaching *planning skills*

Planning constitutes a significant portion of the cognitive skills necessary for students to complete (or even begin) projects and develop autonomy—and is often lacking from their earlier skill development and family history. Instruction in how to plan can help students identify precisely what is to be achieved, as well as to keep them from wasting time and effort. They need to be directly taught how to analyze steps in the process, identify the resources needed to complete each step, work backward, and learn how and where to gather needed resources.

When assigned long-term projects, under-resourced students benefit from first writing down in their own words their understanding of the project requirements. These descriptions should be checked against the instructor's expectations so gaps can be filled in. Sometimes not understanding the nuances of vocabulary can render directions incomprehensible.

The next stage in the process is to identify the key steps that need to be taken in order to complete the project. If these steps are large and complex, they can be reduced to a number of smaller steps. *Mind Tools* ("Drill Down," 2009) refers to this process as "drilling down." Drilling-down activities can be demonstrated for an entire class or group initially, then (as the semester progresses) completed by individual students as a required project component to which points are assigned. As needed, such planning skills are worth explaining further to students on an individual basis.

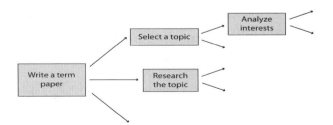

When drilling down, the students are to be instructed to write down the project goal on the left-hand side of their paper, then list the steps that make up the next level of detail on the assignment to the right of the goal. Students complete the same process for each of the points. Drilling down continues until all steps that can be generated are listed and fully expanded.

The drill-down strategy is important because it helps students break down a large and complex problem into its component parts, an input skill that many students, especially those from households where projects seldom are tackled by the entire family, have not acquired. This step helps students develop plans to identify the parts of a whole and to know how to deal with these parts.

Another beneficial tool can be a simple step sheet that lists the steps that must be followed for task or project completion. In order to make the process concrete and meaningful, step sheets might best be developed jointly as a class project early in the semester, later in smaller groups, and ultimately by individual students—possibly as part of the grade for a project.

Steps	Amount of Time Required
1.	
2.	
3.	
4.	
5.	

Note. From *Learning Structures* (p. 17), by R. K. Payne, 2005, Highlands, TX: aha! Process. Copyright 1998 by aha! Process. Adapted with permission.

For each step, students are expected to estimate the time that will be needed. Accurate time estimation is a skill essential to effective planning, without which students often fail to recognize the full complexity and difficulty of an assignment. Students must ensure that their total time estimate allows for finishing such details as editing, proofing, and printing for a paper, as well as personal emergencies, such as sickness or breakdowns in equipment. Once this step has been completed, students can be expected to prioritize actions in order of importance. Viewing a list generated as a group or by the instructor, students can then label the steps from "A" as most important to "C" as least important. Initially it is essential to set intermediate deadlines, giving students targets toward which to work.

Students then can use a calendar to plot out their steps, beginning at the end and working backward to account for the time required. Planning backward is a straightforward approach to helping students to plan for deadlines and due dates.

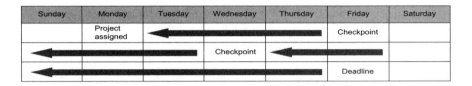

Sunday	Monday	Tuesday	Wednesday	Thursday	Friday	Saturday
	Project assigned				Checkpoint	
			Checkpoint			
					Deadline	

Students benefit from envisioning the concrete end product ("What does the final project look like?"), then working in reverse to outline the steps needed to achieve the final product, ("What would be the step you need to do just before that?"), and so on. In one situation when this planning technique was introduced, the student, an aspiring artist, responded with gratitude, "I never thought to plan how to finish my project like that. I'm going to do that for *all* my projects."

Many students who are under-resourced also have been under-affirmed. When a student's plan has been successfully executed, it is a good time to formally celebrate. For an individual, this celebration might be in the form of a personal note. For the class, it could be refreshments, an entertainment break, formal presentation, or award. The instructor's recognition of work well done can be intensely important to students.

Teaching *time management*

A variety of input skills affects one's ability to manage time. Given the present-focused time horizon usually associated with poverty, time management can be a huge issue affecting the under-resourced students' success in college. Instructors and student services support staff might remind students that they are not actually managing time—the clock ticks away no matter what they are doing—but they can manage themselves.

According to Sharron and Coulter (2004), Feuerstein points out that "[t]ime has no material existence; it is an abstract phenomenon and children who are well orientated towards time are also well orientated to some elements of abstract thought" (p. 65). They further explain that students "with poor orientation in space and time ... do not care where they start or move to next" (Sharron & Coulter, p. 65). In the college setting, an under-resourced student might take two months to select a topic for a research paper, not realizing until it is too late that this particular task should have been completed several weeks earlier.

"Feuerstein gives the interesting example of prisoners whose escape attempts increase as the time of their release from prison draws near" (Sharron & Coulter, 2004, p. 64). Students who do not have cognitive control over time also "lack the cognitive controls to analyze and gain insight into their emotions and so [cannot] adopt strategies for coping with their distortion of time" (Sharron & Coulter, p. 64). Some will drop out of school during their last semester. Therefore, guidance is needed for students to develop an understanding of the length of time required for particular tasks, as well as practice in experiencing time periods during stressful situations, such as testing or waiting for help.

Inadequate understanding of time, along with emotional factors, can lead to habitual procrastination. Many under-resourced students may not realize what procrastination is, much less its effects. Procrastinators may attribute their low score on an assignment or test to lack of ability rather than poor time management. In addition, procrastination can lead to feelings of guilt as one thinks about all the things he or she should be doing. Habitual procrastination can even negatively influence the way one is viewed by others. Students who are consistently late for class can be made aware that this behavior is considered rude and disrespectful—of the instructor and other students—giving a negative impression. It is important to recognize that procrastination is frequently about self-concept and motivation. Thus it may be equally important to show students how effective time management skills can provide structure, peace of mind, and greater control over their lives. Suggestions, such as the following, may be helpful:

- Setting their watches and cell phone clocks a few minutes ahead of the actual time so they arrive places with time to spare
- Setting two alarm clocks so that they are certain to wake up with enough time to get to class
- Practicing timed writing assignments or tests outside of class beforehand; students can be urged to frequently monitor available time, thus separating "emotional time" (what the time situation *feels* like) from "actual time" (the clock on the wall).

Many students need help with planning study time. Most students who lack intergenerational transfer of knowledge are only vaguely aware that instructors assume students will spend considerably more time studying outside of class than they spend in class, a major change from high school. Many study skills textbooks and helpful hints about academics in college will suggest that students plan to spend from *two to three* hours each week studying outside of class for every *one* hour in class—perhaps more for the under-resourced student until skills and strategies for college survival and success are in place. Finding this amount of time to study requires time management strategies, self-discipline, and practice until the behavioral changes are internalized and time management becomes an everyday habit. Suggestions for study-related planning strategies might include:

- Semester planners or at least monthly ones, which can be completed in an hour using the syllabi distributed to students in the first week of classes
- Weekly grids, which can be completed in 15-minute time increments as students decide on short-term goals needed to complete larger tasks, such as term papers and special projects (often with other students).

As students use planners, they may need guidance in evaluating their success with the self-management strategy. They can be prompted to ask themselves such questions as:

- Did I allow enough time for planning and studying?
- Did I use the allotted time as planned?
- What might I give up in order to allow more time for studying?

The following points also may be beneficial to students as they plan study time:

- Space reviews by breaking study time into manageable amounts of time to avoid boredom and loss of concentration. Sessions lasting 20–30 minutes are generally more productive than study sessions lasting several straight hours because individuals retain best what they study first and last.
- Review material several times regularly each week; such "spaced repetition" is very helpful with the mental inculcation and absorption process.
- Use spare time wisely. For example, read through notes or study a text while waiting in line at a grocery store or doctor's office.
- Include color coding when recording information in planners, designating different colors of ink for different types of activities. An examination of color-coded task components can provide a means of evaluating how effectively time has been used.

Finally, instructors might consider giving daily quizzes on required reading during the first five minutes of most class periods. This helps students view their reading assignments as manageable chunks. Further, giving the quiz during the first five minutes of class gives students extra incentive for being on time, as well as actually *doing* the reading assignment prior to class.

Teaching *sorting skills*

Some students have difficulty in college because they have not learned to sort what is important from what is less important when reading or taking (and reviewing) class notes. Compiling data for research papers becomes overwhelming without the ability to sort, especially given the availability of massive amounts of information through technology (which has made the ability to evaluate and sort information more important than ever), as illustrated in the following example:

> *Dakota was a college freshman who was struggling to manage his 15-hour course load and his 30-hours-a-week part-time job. Four weeks into the semester the history professor announced a quiz the following Monday. Dakota stopped by the professor's office after class to announce that he was dropping out of college. "There is no way I can study all of the notes I've taken in time to prepare for the quiz," he explained. The professor asked to see his notebook and discovered that Dakota had attempted to write down every word she said. Dakota didn't know how to sort what was important from what was unimportant.*

Successful students are able to distinguish relevant from irrelevant details when researching, reading texts, or listening to lectures. Less successful ones tend to lump all details together, with each carrying the same importance. Strategies that can be used within a lesson or course, as well as strategies that students might be introduced to on an individual basis, are outlined below. It is worth noting that after a certain point gathering information for a research paper can be a form of procrastination—when it seems easier (even more fun) to keep researching than to start the harder work of organizing material and writing. Students need to be reminded of this up front, particularly when a term paper is being assigned, and checkpoints need to be monitored.

Similar sorting skills are necessary when listening to lectures. One of the first things college students need to learn about taking lecture notes is that although everything an instructor says is important in some respect, everything presented and discussed in class is not equally important in terms of taking notes, studying for tests, and preparing for success in a course of study or career. Strategies can be developed to help students distinguish between more important and less important lecture information.

For instance, near the beginning of a term, an instructor or tutor might follow up on a reading assignment by asking students to recall, either individually or as a group, as many facts/details from a portion of text as they can remember. After listing them, the students might sort the facts/details as "relevant" and "irrelevant" based on their significance to assignments, tests, and projects—as well as for relevance to the overall content area. For students who may be still struggling, it could help to discuss why other class members chose certain facts/details as relevant.

Devoting the last five minutes of each class session to reviewing important points, highlighting and numbering points in notes, and deleting unimportant information is another strategy for enhancing students' sorting skills. Again, daily quizzes also assist some students in identifying important information, particularly early in the term. This strategy helps students schedule, plan, and allocate time, as well as distinguish significant from less significant information.

The use of information sorters can be modeled for the class and later assigned for students to develop independently.

Information Sorter for History

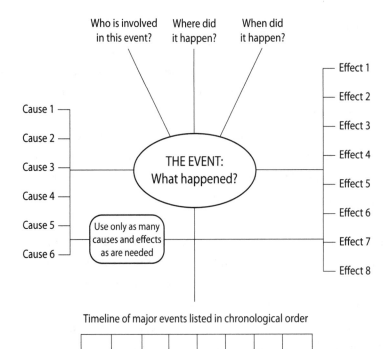

Note. Reprinted from *Success, Your Style! Right- and Left-Brain Techniques for Learning* (p. 65), by N. L. Matte and S. H. G. Henderson, 1995, Belmont, CA: Wadsworth. Copyright 1995 by Wadsworth.

Information Sorter for Literature

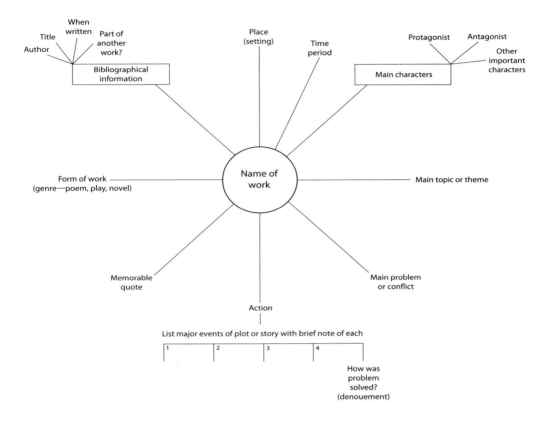

Note. Reprinted from *Success, Your Style! Right- and Left-Brain Techniques for Learning* (p. 66), by N. L. Matte and S. H. G. Henderson, 1995, Belmont, CA: Wadsworth. Copyright 1995 by Wadsworth.

Instructors and student services staff can show a class or individual what behavioral and verbal cues an instructor may use that designate given pieces of information as important during a lecture. Examples include repetition of information, information presented in more than one way (verbally and visually, for example), and such clues as tone of voice or use of key words. In addition, there are words and phrases within a textbook or lecture that signal direction of thought and level of importance, such as:

This is important ...	*You'll see this again ...*	*You'll want to take notes about this ...*
The basic concept is ...	*Listen carefully ...*	
The main idea is ...	*Please focus on ...*	*If you forget everything else, remember this ...*
The steps are ...	*In other words ...*	
In essence ...	*In conclusion ...*	*The key point is ...*
To sum up ...	*It means this ...*	

From the instructional standpoint, lecturers should be sure to include such words and phrases, thereby giving students verbal cues to help them become more aware of how an instructor enumerates both the high points and logical flow of a lecture. Some instructors choose to give students discussion test questions at the start of the semester—a strategy that effectively supports students' note-taking and study skills.

A strategy that can help students sort more important from less important information when writing research papers is to first assign students to work in groups to determine which facts from articles or texts would or would not be relevant for a given research topic. This would build on the early-term exercise of sorting facts/details. Outlining also can help students organize facts. Many graphic organizers described earlier in this chapter aid as well in the sorting and organizing of information.

Teaching *organizing skills*

Organization refers to keeping things in predictable places or arranging things in an orderly or structured manner. It is a skill developed through mediated learning during early childhood and is normally part of planning behaviors. Students from poverty often lack organizing skills because of insufficient mediated learning, coupled with inadequate space for sorting and storing items where they have lived. In order for students to experience success in the college setting and in the workplace, organizing skills must be a standard component of the process skills that are routinely taught.

Specific organizational course requirements and activities can benefit students who have seldom if ever had a system of organization imposed on their lives. Instruction, ranging from reminders and hints to course requirements, should relate to course materials, information, and files. Whenever possible, examples of well-organized projects should be shown to students in order for them to develop a mental model of what the finished product should look like.

Organizing materials for class

Instructors, particularly in introductory or orientation courses, might require students to use three-ring binders for storage of notes, syllabi, assignments, and handouts. Many students use the same notebook for all their classes, then become overwhelmed when getting ready for a test and trying to find all the appropriate and significant materials. For some students, the excuse that their books were stolen is a reality. If everything is stored in one place, then the notes and papers for all classes could be lost all at once. Three-ring binders offer a number of advantages over spiral notebooks. For instance, notes can easily be inserted and removed for reorganizing or reviewing, and supplementary course papers can be added using a hole punch, which means all course materials are in one place for easy access and study. In addition, dividers can be inserted for separating syllabi, notes by major topic, handouts, quizzes, note cards, and assignments. The inner pockets that many three-ring binders contain allow for routine storage of papers to be read at a later time or turned in. Students also could be encouraged to use color coding to distinguish one course from another so that they are sure to bring the correct notebook to the correct class. Becoming systematic helps students begin to free themselves from the tyranny of the moment—and develops input strategies related to organizing space and using data effectively.

Organizing information

Organization for college students involves not only organizing personal space in order to locate items when needed, it also means keeping information in order so it can be understood, processed, and retrieved in a timely fashion. Information that is organized is easier to recall from memory, and the process of reorganizing information following a reading assignment or lecture is an effective way for students to review and retain new material. Good organizing skills also diminish distractions and reduce procrastination.

Information obtained from lectures, textbooks, and other sources can be organized using a number of strategies, and students benefit from routinely *seeing* these strategies, perhaps deliberately demonstrated by the instructor using material covered in class. Just before quizzes, tests, or exams is a good time for instructors to stop and guide students through information organization. Students later can be required to organize information individually by using the most appropriate tools for the content, with points designated for implementation of organizing requirements.

Organizing tools are discussed in numerous study skills textbooks and at websites. The Frayer (1969) model, for instance, is a four-cell box arrangement that summarizes the essential characteristics, noncharacteristics, examples, and nonexamples of a central idea, theme, or process. The top row of the Frayer box below is for the characteristics of the central idea, while the bottom row is for examples. The right-hand column of the box is for characteristics and examples that illustrate the central idea, while the left-hand column is for characteristics and examples that do not illustrate the central idea. This strategy reminds the student that understanding a concept is also about knowing what the concept does not include.

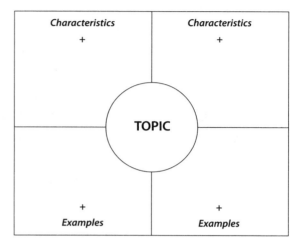

Note. Adapted from *A Schema for Testing the Level of Concept Mastery*, Working Paper No. 16 (pp. 5–6), by D. A. Frayer, W. V. Fredrick, and H. J. Klausmeier, 1969, Madison, WI: Wisconsin Research and Development Center for Cognitive Learning. Copyright 1969 by Wisconsin Research and Development Center for Cognitive Learning.

Organizing data on computers

Organizing files on a computer is a much needed skill among students and workers at all levels. A student might think of his or her computer organizationally like one's house. Dishes generally belong in the kitchen, the lawnmower is kept in the garage, etc. A student's computer is no different: "A place for everything—and everything in its place."

If a course requirement involves storing materials in e-folders, students need to be instructed how to organize their folders for that course. Each course would, of course, require its own unique system, but the following are pointers for helping students get started:

- Files must be stored in the Documents section, rather than the desktop, for easy retrieval and in order to avoid clutter.
- Students can be expected to create a folder for the course, then brainstorm (drill down) the broad topics (subfolders) within the main folder.
- Files and subfiles work best when they have readily recognizable names. How one names a file is an individual matter—but quick recognition should be the goal.

(A more detailed description of how to organize items in a computer may be found in the Appendix.) Many instructors periodically check whether students save their files in the appropriate folder—and award points or other incentives for properly organized computer files.

Computers can be used for time management and planning strategies as well. Students might create folders labeled "Daily," "Weekly," and "Monthly" on their desktops as reminders of regularly scheduled tasks. Another approach is to create a folder for each month for storing forms or task reminders that need attention at particular times of the year.

Teaching *note-taking skills*

Under-resourced students entering college without the benefit of knowledge transferred to them from parents or grandparents who attended institutions of higher education often struggle with tasks that many erroneously consider to be naturally acquired abilities. One approach to helping students acquire note-taking skills is to identify a procedure that faculty members are willing to use and teach their students. Note-taking skills build on sorting and organizing skills. Instructors might consider collecting notebooks regularly—or at least walking through the classroom on occasion to review students' efforts to find note-taking strategies that work for them.

The instructor might even assign a small percentage of the students' grades to their consistent efforts to take usable notes. To further develop note-taking skills, instructors might give hints about main topics and cue words during lectures early in the term (as noted earlier in the 15 suggested phrases), later removing this scaffold as students become more independent and skilled as note takers.

A system, such as the Cornell Note-Taking System (shown at right), offers a plan for getting started and following through with note taking.

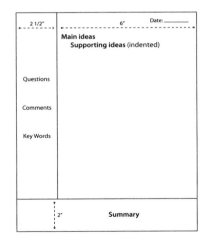

Note. Adapted from *How to Study in College*, by W. Pauk, 1974, Boston: Houghton Mifflin. Copyright 1974 by Houghton Mifflin.

Additional tips that faculty can share with students include:

- Use abbreviations, but use them consistently.
- When information is missed during the lecture, skip several lines and fill in later.
- Date notes for each class session.
- Write the general topic of the class at the top of the page.
- Leave areas of white space on the page; it is easier on the eyes when reviewing.
- Record assignments in a space separate from the lecture notes.
- Use symbols, such as asterisks, arrows, or exclamation points, for emphasis.
- Review notes on a regular basis.

Students should be encouraged to review notes and add missing information as soon as possible after the lecture. Research (Fry, 2000; Walter, Siebert, & Smith, 2000) indicates that 80% of new material can be recalled if students review notes within the first 24 hours after a presentation—and, of course, cleanly typed notes are easier to read and highlight.

Language Resources

In the absence of sophisticated writing skills, the language of poverty is primarily oral, and, in the absence of descriptive, abstract vocabulary, the oral language of poverty is highly dependent on nonverbal assists (Hart & Risley, 1995). The challenges related to the development of language skills for under-resourced students are multifaceted, ranging from the basic task of understanding and appreciating the written word to cultivating an appreciation for and a command of vocabulary. Rose describes the dichotomy:

> Writing and reading are such private acts that we forget how fundamentally social they are: we hear stories read by others, and we like to tell others about the stories we read. We learn to write for others and we write for others to read us. (1989, p. 109)

In a world of spoken language, most under-resourced students do not rely heavily on the written word. Language as written on paper is more abstract and often less interesting than communication through stories and humorous anecdotes. Therefore, written language—along with the paper on which it is written—is less likely to be taken seriously among under-resourced students. They may be less likely to complete necessary documents for the institution or even to turn in homework. It can be surprising to the middle-class observer how much difficulty many under-resourced students have when filling out applications or other forms due to this lack of familiarity with the abstract world of paper and the meaning that paper represents. This difficulty frames the challenge many institutions of higher education are facing. It further illuminates the need for support services staff members who not only explain forms and documents (and the importance they represent to new college students) but also give timelines for the completion and return of such documents, then follow through to make sure the task is completed.

It is not difficult to understand why storytelling is a major vehicle for communicating in communities of poverty, and it is also clear why these stories usually start with the most exciting event, given time constraints and the need to entertain in many households. In order to meet middle-class expectations, however, under-resourced students must learn to organize ideas chronologically in formal register. An effective—actually a fun—way to teach this skill is to have students write in casual register, then translate to formal register. For example, a character from a literary piece who returns home from war would not share his adventures with friends and family by starting at the outset of his or her story. The soldier would jump into the middle of a fierce battle or how someone saved his or her life. College students can be assigned to write such a story first in casual register, then translate the story into formal register, moving chronologically from beginning to conclusion. With the same example, students could demonstrate the body language that would likely accompany the casual telling of war stories. At that point the class could brainstorm vocabulary that could be used to relay the emotions that the nonverbals portray, then retell the story using vivid vocabulary.

Most abstract vocabulary exists in the formal and consultative registers. Therefore, language is the tool that translates the concrete to the abstract, and the lack of adequate abstract language creates communication problems. In fact, students cannot get to higher levels of thinking if they lack the requisite language. We have all experienced the "tip of the tongue" phenomenon where we know we have a word in our vocabulary, but we cannot find the right way to make it surface. Among inadequately mediated people the rigidity is particularly severe (Sharron & Coulter, 2004, p. 120) and is one of several considerations related to the effects of poverty, middle class, and wealth on language development.

The importance of the deliberate teaching of vocabulary is apparent. Feuerstein's work (as cited in Sharron & Coulter, 2004) makes it clear that, in addition to discipline-specific terms, attention must be paid to concepts that instructors might erroneously assume students fully comprehend—ideas such as "identity" or "similarity" (p. 65). When attempting to compare two objects, characters, or events, for example, some inadequately mediated students will simply describe first one object or event, then the second, etc., without ever describing similarities or differences.

Coming full circle, by focusing on helping develop under-resourced students' vocabulary, college personnel can have a positive impact on students' reading, writing, and speaking skills as well.

TEACHING VOCABULARY

Vocabulary is the tool by which the mind categorizes information (like and different), sorts the information, assigns the information to a pattern or group, and then communicates shared meaning. Vocabulary literally is the key tool for sharing understandings; hence teaching vocabulary and vocabulary building skills is essential on multiple levels.

College instructors recognize the importance of content-specific vocabulary for courses, but the lack of instructional time and the "commonly held viewpoint that vocabulary acquisition is the responsibility of the student" (Cengage Learning, n.d.) tend to preclude direct instruction.

> [T]ime spent on teaching the meaning of terms will replace time spent on explaining misunderstandings about text that are the direct result of unfamiliar vocabulary, [and] time spent on modeling strategies [for vocabulary skills acquisition] will result in empowered students. … If students learn a technique for remembering the meaning of a word, then they can "own" that word. (Cengage Learning, n.d.)

Vocabulary can be acquired incidentally through exposure to words and intentionally through explicit instruction in specific words and word-learning strategies. Based on his review of numerous research studies, Marzano (1992), along with Michael Graves and Susan Watts-Taffe (2002), identified three critical components of effective vocabulary instruction:

- Direct vocabulary instruction and word-learning strategies
- Fostering word consciousness
- Wide reading (allowing for multiple exposures to words).

Strategies that build on these components are discussed in three sections.

Direct vocabulary instruction and word-learning strategies

Robust vocabulary instruction actively engages students in thinking about and using words, as well as in creating relationships among terms. Direct instruction begins with strategies that help students analyze their understanding of the words, terms, and phrases they will encounter in their texts. Some strategies—using mental maps, pictures and symbols, and graphic organizers—particularly encourage students to elaborate on their understanding of new words.

Knowledge rating charts

Similar to knowledge surveys, knowledge rating charts can foster metacognitive awareness when implemented in the context of direct vocabulary instruction. Using a graph like this, students are to list in the first column the words to be studied. They evaluate their knowledge level of each word and check the appropriate box. If they have some idea of the meaning, they write in their guess. Following discussion or study, they write the definition in their own words. Thus students are exposed to the meaning of the term, but they learn to make their definitions meaningful to themselves.

Word	Know	Think I know	Have heard	Definition attempt	Definition
Saline				A liquid for contact lenses	A salt solution

Note. From *Under-Resourced Learners* (p. 49), by R. K. Payne, 2008, Highlands, TX: aha! Process. Copyright 2008 by aha! Process. Reprinted with permission.

Ideally, a list of essential vocabulary for courses can be attached to the course syllabus, distributed at the beginning of the semester, and monitored regularly to ensure that students have an understanding of key terms early in each unit of study.

Another similar approach is to present students with a list of words and have them arrange them in columns of words that seem *totally familiar, somewhat familiar,* and *totally unfamiliar.*

Sketching

Marzano's (1992) research summary underscores that one of the most effective ways for students of all ages to elaborate on their understanding of new words is through pictures, symbols, and mental images. Having students sketch their understanding of vocabulary terms can be both revealing (the instructor can determine if the student's presumed understanding is accurate) and solidifying (if a student can sketch the word, he or she almost certainly understands its meaning and remembers it). One particularly effective approach is for students to compile a visual dictionary for upcoming students to use to preview the course. In this activity both the process and the product have value. Visual images can be recorded in many formats; the key is that instructors require and regularly monitor the results.

Concept flash cards

Although not a new idea, concept flash cards are a good tool for reinforcing paired information, such as words and definitions or usage. Students simply write the term or concept on one side of a 3x5 index card. They also could include a visual image or symbol on the front of the card to aid in association and to trigger memory. They then write brief definitions or descriptions of the term or concept on the other side of the card. Participation in this and similar vocabulary building activities also connects with other areas of cognitive development. For example, the use of concept flash cards prior to the beginning of a unit of study can guide students in note-taking and data-collection skills.

Fostering word consciousness

Graves and Watts-Taffe (2002) suggest that word consciousness is a disposition toward words that is both cognitive and affective. Students who are word conscious are interested in words, find words intriguing, and gain satisfaction from using them well and hearing them used well. The following illustration demonstrates how word consciousness can be developed:

> *Nathan is a college sophomore doing very well in his study of aviation. One of Nathan's fondest memories is an airplane ride with his grandmother when he was nine years old. When he felt the airplane move he said, "Grandmother, we're moving." "Yes, we're taxiing," she replied. "Grandmother, we're going up!" he exclaimed. "We're beginning our ascent," she responded. Several minutes later he said, "Grandmother! Look at how high we are!" "We've reached cruising altitude," she replied. "I want to fly an airplane when I grow up," Nathan added. Grandmother smiled and said, "So you will study aviation." Later Nathan summarized the conversation and demonstrated word consciousness by stating: "Grandmother, we're going down, and I'm sure there's a word for it!"*

Graves and Watts-Taffe (2002) suggest the following approaches to fostering word consciousness: modeling, recognizing, and encouraging adept diction; promoting wordplay;

and involving students in original investigations about etymology and the use of words. According to Graves and Watts-Taffe, if students can be enticed to play with words and language, then the goal of creating the sort of word-conscious students who will make words a lifetime interest is at least partially realized.

Graphic organizers

Pairing printed text and graphic organizers also can aid in the learning process. In one study an example of this is illustrated when education majors were presented with a graphic organizer for a concept in psychology and printed text, while a separate group was exposed only to the printed text. Those who received both forms of data learned the information better and were more confident about their learning (Hirumi & Bowers, 1991). Graphic organizers can take many forms, including semantic maps, spider maps, herringbones, and flow charts (as discussed earlier in this chapter).

Semantic feature analysis

Semantic feature analysis activities require students to examine the relationships among identified information. Concept maps simply define a single concept, whereas a semantic feature analysis requires the students to first read the assignment. The instructor then gives them a matrix of key terms and concepts from the reading with the superordinate information on one axis and the subordinate information dividing the other axis. Working individually, in groups, or as a class, the students complete the chart. Presence/absence symbols, for example, may be used to indicate relationships among the informational elements. The following semantic feature analysis compares the elements of two major learning strategies—mental models and mnemonics. It shows that while both strategies accelerate learning and assist with learning the concept, only mental models also reflect patterns and structures and assist with short-term memory.

Teaching strategy	Reflect patterns, structure of discipline	Accelerate learning	Assist with short-term memory	Assist with understanding concept
Mental models	+	+	+	+
Mnemonics	–	+	+	–

Note. From "Getting Them Unstuck: Some Strategies for the Teaching of Reading in Science," by J. Walker, 1989, *School Science and Mathematics*, 80(2), p. 130. Copyright 1989 by School Science and Mathematics Association. Reprinted with permission.

As a final note on teaching vocabulary, instructors frequently find it necessary not only to teach selected terms but also to specify vocabulary that is from casual register, which should be avoided in formal settings. A college instructor who overheard a student teacher tell the children in her class to "Shut up" was horrified with this breach of professionalism. During the follow-up conference, however, it became apparent that the student was surprised to learn that "Shut up" was less acceptable than "Please be quiet" because this distinction had never been made explicit to her.

Wide reading (allowing for multiple exposures to words)

Extensive reading gives students repeated or multiple exposures to words and is also one of the means by which students see vocabulary in rich contexts. Swanborn and de Glopper (1999) conducted meta-analysis of 20 studies to determine the effects of incidental word learning (vocabulary growth that isn't intentional) and determined that during natural reading circumstances students will spontaneously learn the meaning of about 15 words of every 100 unknown words they encounter. They also report that students improve in their incidental learning ability over time. Nagy and Scott (2000) add that students need metacognitive and metalinguistic abilities to play an active role in their word learning and to assume responsibility for their own vocabulary improvement.

In order to build vocabulary through the incidental word learning approach through wide reading, instructors and program designers might include activities and assignments that encourage students to read multiple articles on the same topics so that exposure to word usage is increased. Students would therefore experience the vocabulary of the content area from different voices, perspectives, and even thinking levels.

DEVELOPING READING SKILLS

To model helpful metacognitive reading skills—in any college course—the instructor or tutor is advised to "think out loud" occasionally in order to model strategies used by good readers in that field. The following analytical questions are usually already in a good reader's repertoire, but they need to be introduced to the students who are low in this resource. Notice the progression through the *what/why/how* mediation that corresponds with comprehension, evaluation, and application of the material being read.

1. *What* can you say this passage is about?
2. *What* does the author give you reason to believe?
3. *What* are the opinions versus facts in the passage?

4. *Why* is the author writing this passage?
5. *Why* is this information important to the reader?
6. *How* does the author make his or her point clear? (e.g., examples, lists, comparisons, etc.)
7. *How* does the author expect the reader to react to the passage? (note basic information, change an opinion, move to action, etc.)

Initially, success is achieved through such highly structured exercises. As class members develop their skills, however, more originality tends to occur, and the class develops its own lexicon that "fast-forwards" class discussion of assigned reading materials.

Many of the strategies, such as note taking and creating questions and mental models as reading occurs, can be helpful suggestions for students who struggle to read. A big portion of getting students to read is their motivation; if they see a particular reading's relevance to the course and of importance to the instructor (with whom they have built mutual respect), they are more likely to complete reading assignments. And, as has been suggested earlier, if brief quizzes in the first five minutes of most class periods test what has been assigned (and read), the amount of outside reading is likely to increase.

DEVELOPING WRITING SKILLS

Craig Paulenich, an English professor at Kent State University, studied under William Coles and David Bartholomae and has been teaching developmental composition for more than 30 years. The following section offers his practical strategies for developing the writing skills of college students while simultaneously eliciting and shaping the complex stories and wisdom they bring to the classroom but have not yet found ways to talk about. He (personal communication, November 14, 2008) presents the following ideas:

Labeling

A lexicon of both questions and "labels" allows the instructor to use the students' own writing assignments (always anonymously) as class texts in what amounts to a workshop format. Though this may seem challenging as a teaching method, using actual student texts grounds the work in the real world for the students, and they are able to see their own progression as writers/thinkers. Usually in such cases, students may be either thrilled or uncomfortable to see their work discussed. Ground rules for discussion may be necessary so that feedback is constructive.

The techniques of questioning and labeling enable students to quickly assign meaning to their own and others' work. Differences in questions have powerful implications. For example, asking the class members what they would do if the instructor wrote in the margin "This paragraph needs further development" (a question about which most instructors would be glad to elaborate) should yield results that reflect the baggage the students carry. Responses might include "More ideas," "More examples," "Correct the mistakes," "Think more and work harder," or "I don't know." In contrast, the labeling and questioning techniques below create certain kinds of invitations:

1. To open up the text rather than shut it down
2. To imagine new points of entry
3. To reenvision the text
4. To hold students accountable for their language and their text through questions that indicate the instructor is taking them seriously, that language matters
5. To better enable students to discover for themselves
6. To complicate

Labeling requires identifying shared meaning for the kinds of writing found in student texts. Therefore, ask the students: "How does this text sound? Where have we heard this sort of talk before? How would you label it?"

An example (C. Paulenich, personal communication, November 14, 2008):

A student writing sample is shared with the class. It begins: "Are you a person who loves excitement? Do you like being outdoors in nature? Then you should take up cross-country skiing." The teacher asks, "How does this sound? Does it remind you of anything?"

A student might respond saying, "This sounds like one of those Ronco commercials late at night on TV." This then would be labeled by the class "the Ronco voice" for the rest of the term. When the instructor writes "Ronco," the students automatically understand exactly what is meant.

By establishing this kind of shared lexicon in class discussions, it's far more likely that students will grasp the meaning of the "Ronco" label on their paragraph rather than a lengthy, abstract explanation. Other examples of labeling marginalia might be:

Student text	Labeling marginalia
"I taught him in 15 minutes."	Magic dust
"Being a student means different things to different people."	Golly gee whiz
"Work hard and be patient."	"Be good" advice
"It was wrong, it was bad."	Bad guys/good guys
Conclusions that don't conclude but rather stop or dodge	Pinning the tail on the donkey
Introductions that don't introduce—or simply repeat from the assignment	Warming up

Questioning

Another type of marginalia commentary on writing assignments is short but powerful questions, also useful in prompting class discussion. C. Paulenich (personal communication, November 14, 2008) offers as examples the following:

1. How so?
2. In what way?
3. How, do you suppose? How do you account for such a thing?
4. Meaning what, exactly? What does one do when one ... (works hard, is patient, uses his or her mind, reads, studies)?

The four questions above can become a "routine" to the extent that students, in an effort to avoid the marginalia, begin asking the questions of themselves and their papers *prior* to submitting the assignments. Additional marginalia questions for writing assignments and student conferences include (C. Paulenich, personal communication, November 14, 2008):

1. How might it be argued that ...
   a. Your introduction fails to really introduce anything?
   b. Your conclusion fails to conclude anything?
   c. You've neglected, underestimated, skipped _____?
   d. You've failed to do justice here to what you know?
2. How might it be argued that this text could have been written by someone who has never actually (for example) visited the Grand Canyon, raised a family, been a teacher, been a student, read *Paradise Lost?*
3. Where would you go in this text if you wanted to point to things large or small that make this text somehow better than others we've seen?
4. What difference does it make if I scramble the order of the paragraphs? If it makes little or no difference, how do you account for it?
5. If you could retain only one or two places in this text, where would it be?

6. Plug in another activity (text, play, poem) in place of the one being written about. If it doesn't change the text very much, what might that indicate?
7. What does your audience know? Would they know this? What would they need to know to understand this as you understand it? What does _____ have to do with _____?
8. Given what you've written in the body of the text and all the time you've spent thinking it through, what might you now conclude regarding …?

Only three or four of these questions should be used on any one text, and it is important to keep class discussions supportive of the student. It is also useful to refrain from editing—from pointing out punctuation, spelling, grammar, and usage errors—in order to focus fully on the act of writing rather than the mechanics. Rose (1989) and Mina Shaughnessy (1977) point out the futility of concentrating on grammatical mistakes. For the under-resourced student, as with many basic writers, "error is more than a mishap; it is a barrier that keeps him not only from writing something in formal English but from having something to write" (Shaughnessy, 1977, p. 11). Rose (1989) adds:

> The assumption is that error can be eradicated by zeroing in on the particulars of language. And that assumption seems to rest on a further (erroneous) assumption that grammatical error signals some fundamental mental barrier to engaging in higher level cognitive pursuits: until error is isolated and cleared up, it will not be possible to read and write critically, study literature, or toy with style. (p. 141)

Students first must come to the realization that they have ideas to express—and that they are able to express them. *Then* grammar and syntax become relevant because the students want to share their ideas and their writings—and they realize that in order to be taken seriously, the paper also needs to be grammatically and syntactically sound.

Sequencing

The impact and effect of labeling and questioning techniques are exponentially increased in a sequenced, recursive, semester-long series of assignments on a given theme. Sequencing is an epistemic approach to teaching writing, based on the idea that language modifies the self and creates reality. "[T]he way we use language … seems not only to reflect but in part to determine what we know, what we can do, and in a sense, who we are" (Dowst, 1980, p. 72). The assignments are based on developing understanding of how writing shapes reality, the self, and the audience response. While a strong process is at work, the process is not the main focus for students. Instead, student writers build from an *experiential base* with such topics as teaching and learning, freedom and confinement, problem solving, and economic class. Assignments require students to access prior knowledge, read more about it, think more about it, and attach new ideas to what they once knew (Coles, 1992).

> [A]s a pedagogy, sequencing can be thought of as both a model and an argument for the value of sustained thinking: [Q]uestions result in responses, which in turn can become the basis for more searching questions and richer, more complicated responses. In practice, then, a sequentially constructed writing course becomes a way for [an instructor] to offer writing to students as a mode of learning, a special way of thinking and coming to know, thereby enabling them to understand the activity of writing as an activity that can have meaning, to them as students and to them as more than that. (p. 1)

It is beyond the scope of this book to do justice to this rich pedagogy. The reader is encouraged to gain further knowledge through such works as Coles' *The Plural I—and After* (1988), Bartholomae's *Ways of Reading* (2005), and Shaughnessy's *Errors and Expectations* (1977).

How instructors integrate these strategies with the passion they have for their discipline is highly personal, even intimate. Rose (1989) once again lends his eloquence to describing the development of a mind at work:

> Teaching, I was coming to understand, was a kind of romance. You didn't just work with words or a chronicle of dates or facts about the suspension of protein in milk. You wooed kids with these things, invited a relationship of sorts, the terms of connection being the narrative, the historical event, the balance of casein and water. Maybe nothing was "intrinsically interesting." Knowledge gained its meaning, at least initially, through a touch on the shoulder, through a conversation of the kind Jack McFarland and Frank Carothers and the others used to have with their students. My first enthusiasm about writing came because I wanted a teacher to like me. (p. 102)

CHAPTER 6

In Action—the *Why* and the *How* of Instructional Design

Making Explicit the Implicit

Instructors go into the classroom to help students learn and process information deemed important to the curriculum and necessary for completion of a degree or certificate. But before entering the classroom, instructors and facilitators usually take time to plan and create a syllabus or agenda to share with students. That process is the focus of this chapter, with an emphasis being on what is necessary to examine in terms of instructional design so that the student finds benefit in every class session, assignment, and project. Mano Singham (2007), however, warns:

> What ... syllabi often omit is any mention of learning. They list the assigned readings but not the reasons why the subject is worth studying or important or interesting or deep, or the learning strategies that will be used in the course. (p. 52)

It is important when designing a curriculum for any instructional setting—whether for the classroom, tutoring sessions, or a series of programs in the residence halls or at career services—that the person who delivers or implements the curriculum has a deep understanding of not only *what* the students should gain but also *why* this information is important to the overall learning process for the program, as well as *how* the student will interact to learn the information. Though the under-resourced students (as noted in Chapter 5) may be just 18 or 19 years old, many of them have had life experiences that warrant their being considered "adult learners"—by most definitions, being 24 years or older. Adult learners usually have multiple competing demands for their attention. Adult learning theorists tell us that college learners have certain desires and expectations relating to how they want to be treated and thought of as learners. Reviewing these theories can be beneficial to the instructional designer.

Adult Learning Theorist	Premise
Lindemann (1961)	Andragogy: the art and science of helping adults learn
	Values experience, discovery, and relevance
	Four assumptions serve as foundation to adult learning theory: 1) Education is life itself, not a preparation for it 2) Its focus is nonvocational 3) Learning occurs best through situations, not subjects 4) Learners' most significant resource is experience
Brookfield (1986, 1987)	Education is a transactional process, with instructor and learner continually engaged in negotiating priorities, method, and criteria of evaluation
Knowles (1990)	Adult learners want to be more independent and self-directed than our formal educational system normally allows
	Learners need to be guided toward independence and self-direction
	Expanding on Lindemann's assumptions 1) Learners have a strong need to know the rationale for what they are being taught 2) Adults have a need to be seen as self-directed; related to self-concept 3) Adults' experiences must be seen as a vital resource
Mezirow and Associates (1990)	The heart of adult learning is critical reflection—self-examination and assessment of one's assumptions and beliefs, which leads to perspective transformation
	Learning perspectives are sets of assumptions built over time, through which new experiences are filtered and understood
	Through reflection, learners' perspectives become more inclusive and integrated
	Three types of perspective "distortions": Epistemic—look critically at accepted and internalized concepts as representing right/wrong, good/bad Sociocultural—result from generalized beliefs about specific populations Psychic—assumptions that produce anxiety and block certain behaviors

Note. Adapted from *Learning Assistance and Developmental Education* (pp. 35–68), by M. E. Casazza and S. L. Silverman, 1996, San Francisco: Jossey-Bass. Copyright 1996 by Jossey-Bass.

In a sense these are the hidden rules of adult learning that neither the instructor nor the student usually discusses in an instructional setting. Getting students and instructors "on the same page" about their unspoken beliefs, procedures, expectations, and outcomes for a class might facilitate the process for both parties. Making explicit what is implicit at the instructional table enables everyone involved to more deeply engage in the learning event.

What hidden rules do *instructors* bring to the instructional setting? The following questions may test expectations and assumptions about students' needs and determine the extent to which an instructor's rules are stated or hidden (note that any instructional setting, such as a residence hall program or study skills workshop, may be substituted for "classroom"):

1. What is your driving force in the classroom?
   In your field of study?
   In your college and/or program?

2. In your classroom, who has power?
   If you say that you intend for it to be shared, how is that negotiated?

3. What skills do you assume your students have when they begin your class?
   What level of skills is expected of your students by the time they complete your class?
   How do you inform students about their areas of strength or need?
   What remediation—offered from beginning to end—is available for your students?
   How and when do students find out about student services available and relevant to them?

4. Are your logistical rules stated or unwritten (hidden)?
   Do you have hidden rules (unspoken expectations) around the issue of time? For example, tardiness, deadlines, makeup work, and attendance?
   Are these explained in your syllabus, website, course or program materials?
   Do you offer procedural guidelines and rubrics for expectations with your assignments?

5. To what extent do you expect students to think about their community, their own life, or the lives and worlds of others?
   To what extent do you assume your students have had experience outside of the communities they grew up in or live in currently?

6. What role does the syllabus play in your program and classroom?
    To what degree do you expect students to rely on it?
    How and when, and even how often, are students shown the importance of
        a syllabus or other program documentation?

7. What value do you place on the use of formal register in your classroom?
    In your field?
    Why?
    Do you teach students about registers of language?

8. In your field of study, what is the hierarchical structure of educational
        achievement (i.e., associate degree, bachelor's degree, etc.)?
    How are students in your classes or programs made aware of this and the
        meaning of it?
    Do students understand the variety of vocational options and wages
        associated with particular certificates and degrees?

9. When a student completes a degree in your program and gets a job, what
        effect (or effects) does that job have on his or her family—both positive
        and negative?
    Are these hidden rules discussed with students?
    If so, is it early enough in a program for students to make decisions and
        understand their choices? (For example, certain doctors must be "on call,"
        which may routinely interrupt and circumvent family events.)

10. What type or types of personality are best suited to the careers in your field?
        (Smart & Feldman, 1998; Smart, Feldman, & Ethington 2000)

11. What types of students do you get along with best?
    What types of student bring out the worst in you?

12. What tools do students need for success in your programs (textbooks,
        reference books, lab coats, goggles, paints, brushes, calculating
        devices, etc.)?
    Are these tools listed on your syllabus?
    What assistance is available (and visible to students) for helping secure
        these tools?

13. How are students expected to dress for success—beyond your classroom?
    At what point will students be expected to have the proper attire?
    When are they notified of this need?
    Is there assistance available for students with limited wardrobes?

14. What is the hierarchy of administration in your college or program?
    Who holds power over what?
    How and when is this explained to students?

15. What is your theory of assessment?
    How are students' grades determined?
    Do you give credit for process as well as product?
    Is reflection built into your students' assignments?
    Are students given choices and support when working on assignments,
        individually or in groups?

16. How might hidden rules of socioeconomic class apply to your students'
        work in their careers?
    How might this topic and other hidden rules be discussed in class?

As instructors examine the degree to which their learning theories and course expectations are made clear to students, the more likely they are to engage students in the course materials, resulting in deeper learning.

Where Does This Lead Us? Instructional Planning/Design

With all of this in mind, a model for teaching and learning is needed that includes an understanding of expectations and effort for mutual respect, adequate practice, and performance in contextualized settings, as well as feedback and reasonable reinforcement for learning. Closely resembling such a model is Keller's (1979) theory of motivation, performance, and instructional influence—a "macro theory that incorporates cognitive and environmental variables in relation to effort, performance, and consequences" (Keller, 1983, p. 392).

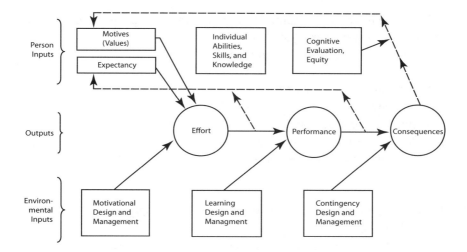

Note. From "Motivational Design of Instruction" (p. 392), by J. M. Keller, 1983, Hillsdale, NJ: Erlbaum. Copyright 1983 by Erlbaum. Reprinted with permission.

Within this model, instructors can build mental/cognitive, motivation/persistence, and integrity/trust resources by designing instructional activities to better suit and support the under-resourced student. John Keller's model asserts that attitudes gained from learners' life experiences have an impact on their motivation to succeed. These life experiences may range from fear of failure to fear of success—all of which create resistance to learning at the college level, leaving students feeling as though they do not have control of their learning. Therefore, one productive aspect of the teacher-learner relationship is mentoring in which the facilitator/teacher is modeling Aristotle's secret, "Learning is enjoyable." According to Singham (2007), a "mind-set that is endemic in our schools and college" (p. 52) is that education prepares students for something else. Further, he points to a "prevailing model of education as medicine ('Take it; it may taste bad now, but it's food for you, and you'll feel better later') that dims the focus on learning as *"worth doing for its own sake"* (Singham, 2005, pp. 13–14). These factors create a downward spiral for the under-resourced learner as described by Weiner's (1986) attributional theory:

> [O]ur explanations, or causal attributions, for why we succeed and fail directly affect our motivation because they imply that our academic performance is either controllable or uncontrollable. Thus, "lack of ability (intelligence)," or "poor instruction" are not controllable by us, and when we believe they are the cause of our failure, we feel unmotivated which, in turn, leads to poor performance. … Controllable attributions give us a sense of more personal control over our academic performance, and in turn, more motivation to achieve. (Perry, 1999, p. 17)

This zest for learning requires understanding, which according to Grant Wiggins and Jay McTighe (2005) in their book on instructional design, is "not mere knowledge of facts but inference about why and how, with specific evidence and logic—insightful connections and illustrations" (p. 86). To ensure that those connections can be made, attention to basic underlying skills must be provided, especially introductory courses and those that are part of a sequence. McKeachie (2002) agrees that "most students cannot write like a scientist unless they are taught scientific writing. Domain-specific approaches to learning are especially critical in introductory courses" (p. 276). Understanding the *why* and the *how* of learning in a particular domain or discipline makes claiming the *what* of that domain much easier. In fact, without the *why* and the *how,* the *what* tends to be merely memorized and isolated facts. Lee Shulman (1986) explains:

> The professional holds knowledge, not only of how—the capacity for skilled performance—but also of what and why. The teacher is not only master of procedure but also of content and rationale, and capable of explaining why something is done. The teacher is capable of reflection leading to self-knowledge, the metacognitive awareness that distinguishes draftsman from architect, bookkeeper from auditor. A professional is capable of not only practicing and understanding his or her craft, but of communicating the reasons for professional decisions and actions to others. (p. 13)

The information that instructors and academic support staff often take for granted is referred to as tacit knowledge. The assumption is sometimes made that students come to the instructional setting not only with the prior knowledge (the *what*) but also the thinking skills, the know-how, and the desire to delve deeply into the learning process. In fact, under-resourced learners frequently come to the college classroom displaying thinking skills and participatory behaviors that reveal their attitude that academic learning is merely memorizing and regurgitating facts. Nilson (2003) points out "exposure to uncertainties in our knowledge bases helps students realize that often there is no single superior truth, nor can there be, given the nature of rational knowledge" (p. 15). When instructors present these complexities, students will mature from "surface learners" to "deep meaning" (Caine & Caine, 1991)—or from "dualism" to "relativism" and beyond (Perry, 1981). The following chart outlines several theorists' perspectives on the progression of students from basic to the more advanced thinking skills.

Perry (1970, 1981)

| Dualism | Multiplicity | Relativism | Commitment to relativism |

| Received knowledge | Subjective knowledge | Procedural knowledge | Constructed knowledge |

Belenky, Clinchy, Goldberger, & Tarule (1986)

| Received knowledge | Subjective knowledge | Procedural knowledge | Constructed knowledge |

Mezirow (1981), Habermas (1971)

| Technical | Practical/interactional | Emancipatory |

Caine & Caine (1991)

| Surface knowledge | Felt meaning | Deep meaning |

Note. From *The Development of Learning for Nontraditional Adult Students: An Investigation of Personal Meaning-Making in a Community College Reading and Study Skills Course,* by K. A. Becker, 1993. Copyright 1993 by K. A. Becker. Reprinted with permission.

So what does this mean with regard to teaching in the classroom? If students come to class assuming that learning requires the lower levels of thinking described above and that knowledge is dispensed only from authority figures whom they are not sure they trust, then most of what transpires in the classroom is learning for the sake of the test—rather than the ideal of learning for the sake of learning. Students are more likely to advance to deeper learning when there is a relationship with the instructor. Instructors who seek deeper development of their students' thinking might assess their students' prior knowledge, incoming skills, and procedural knowledge (for accomplishing tasks related to the learning process) and share the expected outcomes of the course with the students. Beginning learners—that is, students who are learning something new for the first time, at any age—need all three components of mediation: the *what,* the *why,* and the *how.* The challenge is for the expert to relinquish his or her automaticity for understanding the subject and return to the *what,* the *why,* and the *how* of the subject matter in order to present it logically to the learners.

Parnell (1995) points to a similar focus for curriculum building, especially in high schools and community colleges where students are being prepared for four-year programs. He claims that because most instructors tend to teach as they were taught and administrators tend to continue organizing school as it always has been, the *why* of mediation is an essential element to share with students from the start.

Much of the research and teaching on instructional design at the college level supports Payne's (2001, 2002) design theories for planning curriculum, including the idea of "unpacking" the course—or differentiating the *what,* the *why,* and the *how,* which will build the abstract architecture inside the student's mind: in effect, a blueprint for learning. While instructors benefit from thinking through how a discipline translates from the sensory to the abstract representation of its content through examining the purpose, structure, and patterns, it is also essential to look at the big ideas, conceptual lenses, and the glue that holds the field together. Making explicit the implicit is recommended. Illustrating the paradoxical complexity and simplicity of this thought, Palmer (1998) writes

> Each discipline has an inner logic so profound that every critical piece of it contains the information necessary to reconstruct the whole—if it is illuminated by a laser, a highly organized beam of light. That laser is teaching. (p. 123)

What follows is a diagram for curriculum designs adapted from Payne Lesson Design (Payne, 2005c) that helps dissect the *what,* the *why,* and the *how* of a course.

Curriculum Design

Mental Model (story, analogy, drawing, movement)	**What**	**Vocabulary** **Content**	
	Why	**Connection to the discipline** (structure, purpose, pattern, process, standards)	
	How	**How for the teacher** **Instructional plan/activities** 1. 2. 3. 4. 5. 6.	**How for the student** (processes, step sheets, question making, sorting)
	*Proof	____Rubrics ____Assessments ____Task completed	

* This should be shared with students.

Note. From *Learning Structures* (p. 90), by R. K. Payne, 2005, Highlands, TX: aha! Process. Copyright 1998 by aha! Process. Adapted with permission.

Instructional or curriculum design begins with the conceptual framework of the course, breaking down the parts and rebuilding the whole, including vocabulary, applications, and implications (the *what,* the *why,* and the *how*). When instructors have completed this process, they in turn are better prepared to help students gather and process the materials necessary for the next course in the sequence, the job, or life in general. When this is accomplished, the learning outcomes become more meaningful because students can grasp all dimensions of the learning necessary to accomplish their goals.

UNCOVERING THE *WHAT*

Big ideas are a core construct in many postsecondary curriculum development techniques or models (Wiggins & McTighe, 2005; Conley, 2008). These ideas are what the instructor may tend to take for granted or tacitly assume—and may actually be difficult to put into words for the expert who is enmeshed in his or her work. The big ideas, however, tend to be neither basic nor obvious to most under-resourced students; in fact, said ideas are often abstract to novice learners. As the conceptual anchor for making facts and insights more understandable, big ideas must first be uncovered by the instructor who, as suggested above, may have been inclined to internalize the thinking processes needed to use the information on a regular basis.

The more that instructors or student services staff share the units of thought in their curriculum through visual representations, stories, analogies, and hands-on activities with under-resourced learners, the more the students will understand and make connections with the materials being explained. Giving examples or telling stories is not a last resort for instructors; rather, these methods lie at the heart of great teaching. Indeed, at the root of this process is the need for classroom teachers to be cognizant of their personal transition from expert student to novice teacher, suggesting that to access one's content knowledge might include creating an "intellectual biography—that set of understandings, conceptions, and orientations that constitute the sources of their comprehension of subjects they teach" (Shulman, 1986, p. 8). This self-examination might remind instructors of the mental models they started with and how they adapted them as their understanding became more sophisticated. Relating this change and growth, then, to students will motivate some students to see that they too must take strides to understand the materials little by little.

With the sharing of mental models, instructors can encourage students to think differently about the course or content by suggesting controllable attributions they encountered: "It took a lot of time and effort on my part to understand this concept. I can share some of my process with you in this mental model I made up—or was shown to me." Once the *what* is understood by the instructor and subsequently shared with students, the amount of time it takes to understand, remember, and transfer use of the important concepts is reduced. With increased exposure to mental models, students are likely to be autonomous in their use of them.

One suggestion for instructional designers is to see the big ideas as linchpins—the essential devices for keeping curricular wheels in place. Without grasping these ideas and using them to hold related content together, "we are left with bits and pieces of inert facts that cannot take us anywhere" (Wiggins & McTighe, 2005, p. 66), and thus the *what* of a course or curriculum is intangible to the under-resourced learner. Facilitators can address questions central to the key issues and not only promote understanding for themselves and their students but also ignite the connections referred to throughout this book as necessary for learning. Wiggins and McTighe call them "essential questions" and state that they can be generated from content standards for the field of study. In a ranking of dimensions of instruction, Feldman (1989) found that "stimulation of interest in content" was the primary correlate for improving faculty evaluations and ranked fourth (of 17 dimensions) as necessary to achievement for students. "Clarity of objectives and requirement" ranked seventh on the scale for both faculty evaluations and student achievement. Thus it is clear that making the implicit explicit is beneficial. As instructors present the *what* of content, their passion and deepest level understanding of the materials also must be freely and openly shared. For instance, in a biology course, an objective or outcome might be that "all students will apply an understanding of cells to the functioning of multi-cellular organisms, including how cells grow, develop, and reproduce" (Wiggins & McTighe, p. 119). The essential question might be: "How can we prove that cells make up living things? If we're all made of cells, why don't we look alike?" (Wiggins & McTighe, p. 119).

To move from big ideas to essential questions, Wiggins & McTighe (2005) offer their own set of questions to facilitate the process. In this model, the first two questions act as a filter for those that follow:

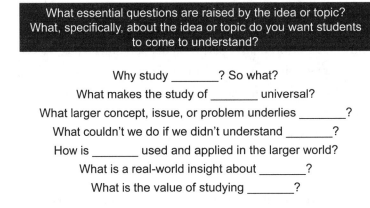

What essential questions are raised by the idea or topic?
What, specifically, about the idea or topic do you want students to come to understand?

Why study _____? So what?

What makes the study of _____ universal?

What larger concept, issue, or problem underlies _____?

What couldn't we do if we didn't understand _____?

How is _____ used and applied in the larger world?

What is a real-world insight about _____?

What is the value of studying _____?

Note. From *Understanding by Design* (p. 137), by G. Wiggins and J. McTighe, 2005, Alexandria, VA: Association for Supervision and Curriculum Development. Copyright 2005 by Association for Supervision and Curriculum Development. Adapted with permission.

As questions like these are answered, instructors will simultaneously be identifying important terminology for the course. This terminology, vocabulary, even jargon are the tools by which the mind categorizes, sorts, and organizes information into patterns or groups—and then is used to communicate shared meaning (Payne, 2008b). In the Curriculum Design (see p. 151) based on the Payne Lesson Design model (Payne, 2005c), the *what* includes the vocabulary needed for the lesson or course—and should not be limited to new terms for the content of focus but should include a preview and review of terms that may be unknown or unclear, including demonstrating how students might do this on their own.

UNCOVERING THE *WHY*

Mental models, also discussed in Chapter 5, can enhance the *what, why,* and *how* of curriculum design. More specifically, they constitute a key component in lesson plan development, as they reflect the purpose, structure, and patterns of the discipline. Mental models can be used to support the development of each class session throughout a college term, especially in helping students connect to the relevance of the course topics. Adult learning theory reminds us that when students can make this connection, motivation for learning is increased.

In-class, online, and out-of-class knowledge surveys are ideal tools for assessing students' prior knowledge and ongoing understanding, in addition to developing knowledge throughout a course. Using tools such as these reduce the natural tendency for instructors to function from their own assumptions about the material *and* the students by giving shy students an anonymous opportunity to participate in the class. This provides a much more comprehensive picture of students' learning than relying on the feedback of only the students willing to participate orally. It also sheds light on where and how to sift and sort the curriculum concepts for students so that they understand the application of the subject in relation to themselves and other concepts in the discipline.

Along with making vocabulary and terms of the content clear, Payne (2002) recommends being explicit about *why* the content information—including its purpose, structure, and patterns—is connected to the discipline at large. For example, the *purpose* of chemistry is bonding; the *structure* for bonding includes such theories as VSEPR (valence shell electron pair repulsion) or Gillespie and Nyholm (1957) based on the idea that the geometry of a molecule is determined by repulsion among pairs of electrons associated with a central atom; and the periodic table represents the *patterns* of bonding. The equations used in chemistry provide the process for calculating bonding (adapted from Payne, 2008b, pp. 65–66). As instructors unpack the big ideas, their purpose, structure, inherent patterns, and even the processes they represent in the content area are illuminated. This helps clarify presentations—whether it be through lecture, lab experiments, group work, or individual assignments.

Shulman (1986), who specialized in the cognitive psychology of instruction at Stanford University, found that a primary difference between a good instructor and an excellent one is the depth of understanding the instructor has of the content area. In fact, he suggests three categories of content knowledge that an instructor would do well to develop:

1. Subject matter content knowledge—the ways of discussing the content structures of knowledge that differ by subject matter
2. Pedagogical content knowledge—"the ways of representing and formulating the subject to make it comprehensible to others," which should include a "veritable armamentarium of alternative forms of representation" from both research and practice
3. Curricular knowledge—the full range of options for teaching the subject, including the "indications and counterindications" that the curriculum is being addressed and learned adequately. (Shulman, pp. 9–10)

He adds that the "ultimate test of understanding rests on the ability to transform one's knowledge into teaching" (Shulman, p. 14).

Without this wide lens of the big idea being made clear by the instructor, under-resourced learners in particular will likely struggle to find the information meaningful and relevant.

Identifying a discipline's structure and purpose for oneself as the instructor and then as part of instruction for the students helps both parties discover what is more important and what is less important (Payne, 2002, p. 59).

Content Area	Purpose
Biology	Identifying living systems and relationships within and among those systems
Physics	Using matter and energy through mathematical applications
Algebra	Solving for the unknown through functions
Geometry	Using logic to order and assign value to form and space

Note. From *Understanding Learning: the How, the Why, the What* (p. 58), by R. K. Payne, 2002, Highlands, TX: aha! Process. Copyright 2002 by aha! Process. Adapted with permission.

Exposing the content's purpose or big ideas is significant because it helps students better sort out what is relevant in their studies from what is less relevant. For more on big ideas or purposes for varying content areas and fields of study, see Land, Meyer, and Smith's *Threshold Concepts within the Disciplines* (2008).

UNCOVERING THE *HOW*

Abstract elaboration processes, such as those described by Payne (2005b), are the *how* that accompanies all learning. If the *what* is presented without mindfulness of students' need for the *how,* learning is less likely to occur. For instance, students were given an assignment to access several websites and critique them for reliability, relevance, and user-friendly qualities. No one handed in the assignment for review on a checkpoint day, and the instructor assumed the students felt confident enough not to ask for any feedback or suggestions. Nor did anyone hand in the assignment on the due date. When questioned, students revealed that most of them really did not know how to access websites, let alone judge them. Therefore, they had not attempted to complete the assignment. The instructor backtracked and taught the steps and procedures for critiquing written documents. In teaching the basic computer literacy skills necessary for the assignment, including processes for using the Internet, some students revealed they did not understand e-mailing procedures either.

While most instructional design models take the next step—addressing the *how* for the instructors by directing them to plan the teaching steps and activities of the lesson— Payne (2002) observes that the *how* for the students is often overlooked in the classroom. Unless the students are assessed for their understanding of the *how* and then taught the necessary processes, they may not have the tools to complete the task. These tools include the planning strategies and the thinking and organizing skills introduced in Chapter 5. Making clear to the students *how* they will be evaluated or assessed on individual assignments, as well as for the course as a whole, aids in students' understanding of expectations. These items should be included on every college syllabus and discussed at the outset of the term. The use of rubrics makes explicit the grading expectations (see Appendix for a sample rubric). Ultimately, students can benefit from participating in the design of their own learning assessment rubrics for assignments.

In Sum

Most teaching is based on the belief that students are competent with processing (the *how*) the information (the *what*) of a course—and are willing to find the motivation and relevance of the concepts discussed (the *why*). However, under-resourced students who lack mediated learning experiences and future stories also frequently lack sufficient motivation to see them through a college course that does not supply more than the what. As noted at the outset of this chapter, such issues may be addressed in the syllabus through a careful examination of the course concepts before the instructor sets foot in the classroom.

Palmer (1998) invites instructors to embrace paradox in their planning and teaching. Without a healthy appreciation for paradox, a misleading dualism can occur, separating head from heart, facts from feelings, theory from practice, and even teaching from learning. Encouraging curriculum and course designers to "view the world in which opposites are joined so that we can see the world clearly and see it whole" (p. 66) and to induce "creative tensions" (p. 74), Palmer offers this description of how he plans for teaching:

> When I design a classroom session, I am aware of six paradoxical tensions that I want to build into the teaching and learning space …
>
> 1. The space should be bounded and open.
> 2. The space should be hospitable and "charged."
> 3. The space should invite the voice of the individual and the voice of the group.

4. The space should honor the "little" stories of the students and the "big" stories of the disciplines and tradition.
5. The space should support solitude and surround it with the resources of the community.
6. The space should welcome both silence and speech. (p. 74)

Such pedagogy—both in theory and in practice—is in keeping with many of the themes relevant to designing instruction for the under-resourced learner in the college setting.

Remembering the theme of expert and novice might assist curriculum designers in focusing on the tasks of planning and teaching. Wiggins and McTighe (2005) remind us that ideas at the core of the field of study are "hard-won results of inquiry, ways of thinking and perceiving that are the province of the expert. They are *not* obvious" and, in fact are "abstract and *counterintuitive* to the novice, prone to misunderstanding" (p. 67). Therefore, the instructor's quest to more fully know the subject—in order to make the implicit explicit—is key to classroom success, especially for the under-resourced learner.

CHAPTER 7

Paradigm Shifts in Higher Education

The demographics, changing expectations of stakeholders, and needs of college students have shifted—and the pace of these changes is accelerating. Higher education is challenged to keep the best practices of the past while evolving to maintain its leadership and relevance in the future. As described in *America's Perfect Storm* (Kirsch, Braun, Yamamoto, & Sum, 2007), the socioeconomic survival of the United States is at stake. The convergence of low literacy levels, poverty, an aging population, immigration, and the globalization of business means that working with the growing and significant segment of the population that comes from generational poverty is no longer only a moral obligation. It also has become an economic imperative.

Meanwhile, across the nation, government, business, and communities are asking for changes in the very nature and premise of higher education. Stakeholders are demanding stronger linkages between education and jobs for a more productive economy. Educational institutions are being told: "In a global economy, communities will thrive or decline based on how well they do to ensure sufficient numbers of high-value jobs and an ample supply of 'knowledge workers' to fill them" (Jenkins & Spence, 2006, p. 4). And then: "The task ahead is not simply to respond to the labor market, but to help construct and defend the significance of work and employment as the generator of social wealth in this country" (Jacobs, 2007, p. 23).

In providing a skilled workforce, proponents of professional and technical education sometimes are at odds with educators who see the purpose of education as developing the critical, creative, practical, and reflective thinking skills and knowledge base to inform individual choices and foster civic engagement, sometimes referred to as the "equity agenda." Both approaches have a place. Educational missions need to address all aspects of the poverty research continuum (see Chapter 2) by supporting individual achievement, which contributes to human and social capital in the community, which in turn affects sociopolitical and economic structures.

The Equity Agenda

Education ➔
      Individual achievement
      and economic stability ➔
               Human and social capital ➔
                       Sociopolitical and economic changes

Accreditation bodies in higher education argue convincingly for major curricular changes to more realistically foster greater civic engagement. Instilling creative and reflective thinking, which is necessary for active participation in society and the workplace, must be a priority for postsecondary education. Without it, education becomes essentially skill training, and students graduate prepared perhaps to function in technical roles but probably not well prepared to analyze, craft new ideas, reflect on and evaluate experience, communicate their ideas to a range of audiences, and continue in a lifelong learning process. In addition, a nation of critical thinkers strengthens democracy when myriad messages are coming from the media, particularly in election years. The equity agenda supports the belief that education is the great equalizer and the principal pathway to prosperity, full participation, representation, and parity within the socioeconomic and political structures that shape our communities. However, if under-resourced students cannot make it through developmental education and gateway courses, much less the technical training to get good jobs, it is likely they will remain unstable economically, trapped in the tyranny of the moment. Economic instability perpetuates reactive, concrete problem solving and saps the energy necessary to participate, leaving the equity mission largely unrealized.

Although the Council on the Advancement of Standards in Higher Education (Dean, 2006) has articulated a holistic array of Learning Outcome Domains that support the development of the 11 resources discussed in Chapters 3 and 4, a few of the group's pre-suppositions reflect the kinds of misperceptions in higher education that are not useful in building programs to support under-resourced students. For example:

- Students seek higher education in responsible ways and will, when encouraged to do so, access appropriate educational resources when they are provided, made known, and relevant to students' felt educational and developmental needs.
- Institutions of higher education are purposeful and function as social and cultural resources to provide opportunities for students to learn and develop in holistic ways.
- Institutions of higher learning reflect the diversity of the society and cultures in which they exist. (Dean, 2006, p. 7)

These concepts are drawn from an earlier era when students were likely to be middle class with parents who had attended college. Today's students attend college for a variety of reasons, some of which might not be considered "responsible." Examples include:

- "I came to college because it was the next thing to do."
- "I couldn't find a job, so I took out a loan and thought I'd take some classes until I can get a job."
- "I'm not sure why I'm here; I didn't know what else to do."
- "It's keeping me off the streets" (i.e., required to attend on parole/probation).

"Relevance to the student" is sometimes lacking in postsecondary programs as has been discussed. Although a number of institutions do indeed purposely offer social and cultural resources to their student populations, this does not necessarily translate to actual access, support, and opportunity for students. Many programs are prohibitive and even invisible to the student who has a family or a job—or does not know the hidden rules of middle class and the college environment. Finally, while diversity is a focus of accreditation bodies, many institutions are isolated from the poor and working-class populations of their local communities. It is much more common for colleges to have high levels of racial and ethnic diversity than economic diversity—within both the faculty and student body.

These paradigm shifts call for changes across the board—from the classroom to student services, from accreditation standards to the institution's partnerships. This is not to say that traditional higher education is obsolete or misguided, but rather that the typical college/university perspective needs rethinking. The traditional expectation that students will mold themselves to the institution's expectations and norms is simply too big a leap for too many students, especially those in the under-resourced demographic.

While these shifts are occurring simultaneously and sometimes overwhelmingly, a synergy exists among them, which, if properly tapped into, can be transformational for students, staff, the institution, and the larger community.

REFORMULATING THE PREMISES OF HIGHER EDUCATION

Traditional Assumptions	New Paradigms
Students	
Students prepared with internal and external resources, focused on educational priority	Under-resourced students with multiple learning barriers, less-than-ideal background preparation, and competing demands brought on as a result of highly complex life conditions
Unprepared students seen as remedial, high-risk	Under-resourced students seen as problem solvers and creators
Learning Environment	
Faculty as discipline-specific experts Unsupported, autonomous, competitive learning environments	Faculty as learning facilitators using discipline-specific expertise to engage students in supported, relational, cooperative learning environments
Didactic teaching of decontextualized and theoretical knowledge	Knowledge created through service and community engagement models involving multiple individuals from diverse backgrounds, formal planning documents, and work for a given cause
Students isolated from each other and the community in the learning tasks	Contextualized and situated learning connects students to each other and to the community in the learning tasks
Institutions	
Enrollment-driven	Student retention, persistence, achievement, and completion as top priorities
Pricing and funding	Focusing on cost and value as the instructional recipe for student success
Development of human and social capital secondary to scholarship and research	Intentional structured development of human and social capital for achievement, sustainability, and prosperity
Institutional outcomes connected to self-sustainability and infrastructure	Institutional outcomes become connected to community sustainability
Accreditation based on institutional assets and fiscal resources	Accreditation based on learner outcomes
Relatively low accountability	High accountability

Note. From *Helping Under-Resourced Learners Succeed at the College and University Level: What Works, What Doesn't, and Why* (p. 3), by K. Krodel, K. Becker, H. Ingle, and S. Jakes, 2008. Copyright 2008 by aha! Process. Adapted with permission.

Postsecondary Programmatic Responses to New Paradigms and Under-Resourced Learners

There is no shortage of ideas for enhancing the effectiveness of college education. More than 90 interventions to improve outcomes for under-resourced students were recently funded under the *Achieving the Dream* community college program. These strategies are significantly influenced by a growing concern to address the deleterious effects of poverty in the classroom.

Most faculty and student services interventions appropriately target the individual student and/or seek to build support around the student. For example:

- **Developmental education and ongoing, consistent support services** for academically under-prepared students work best when delivered by full-time staff with specialized training. These are two of the most necessary interventions to get students college-ready (Bailey & Alfonso, 2005).
- **Financial incentives** have a positive impact on student persistence, full-time attendance, courses passed, and reenrollment. Incentives are a concrete representation of the value of education and achievement. The encouraging results ended, however, when the incentives ended (Brock & Richburg-Hayes, 2006).
- **Advising, counseling, and peer tutoring** are ways to provide some social capital or relationship support for students. First-semester freshman seminars, for example, are effective in teaching students how to manage their work within the academic environment through orientation and direct-teaching of planning and study skills (Bailey & Alfonso, 2005).
- **Student integration programs** that concentrate on external resources—such as supportive relationships, employment, and money—appear useful for student retention. Scheduling classes and on-campus events to accommodate the needs of working students, as well as creating meaningful interactions among students and teachers, are effective interventions (Bailey & Alfonso, 2005).
- **New media and technologies** like blogs, wikis, media-sharing applications, and social-networking sites can become vehicles for informal conversations, collaborative content generation, and knowledge sharing that give learners access to a wider range of ideas and representational skills to demonstrate their learning. Facilitating the access to, and ability to use, these technologies is as important as developing the sites and programs themselves.

- **Service learning** integrates community service experiences with academic instruction as it focuses on critical reflective thinking and civic responsibility (Robinson, 2001). Students move from mediated sources of information to experiential learning in which they practice new skills and roles.
- **Learning communities** seek to build social capital on campus through shared academic experiences. These communities enroll student cohorts in clusters of courses, often around a central theme, thus promoting deeper academic inquiry, cooperative learning opportunities, and relationships with both peers and faculty. For students with many other demands on their time, this model works well when it provides an engaging, motivating environment that does not require them to spend time in activities outside their classes. Of all the options presented here, learning communities have the most empirical evidence of success, according to Bloom and Sommo (2005).

A Common Issue: The 'Righting Reflex'

Improved outcomes are often modest at postsecondary institutions. A major flaw that can prohibit improvement in most programs is the well-intentioned though misguided "righting reflex" identified by William Miller and Stephen Rollnick (2002). The righting reflex cuts directly to the corrective action for the student, without creating a clear understanding of *what* issues are being addressed, nor explaining *why* the situation or condition occurred. In this incomplete mediated learning experience, students are told *how* to do something to "make themselves better" without an explanation of *what* and *why* these issues are being addressed for them. Being told *what* to do without understanding *why* one is doing it provokes resistance, and it fosters distrust of and alienation from the institution, resulting in (among other negative effects) high dropout rates. Many programs operate without an intentional understanding of who an under-resourced student is—and *why* this occurs—before prescribing *how* students should change. The righting reflex perpetuates perceptions of under-resourced students as being deficient and needy. This isn't to say that identifying problems is wrong or bad. In fact, identifying problems *correctly* is vital to actually changing conditions. Deficit thinking comes into play when members of the dominant culture define the problems of other cultures and blame individuals, then determine how the individuals should change. As a result, the students have little ownership in the changes they are being asked to make—and, concomitantly, little lasting success in the area or areas being addressed.

A Holistic Approach to the Challenge

The challenge of integrating what is known about adult learning theory, economic class, and effective teaching practices is considerable. There is a need to make higher education more learning-centered so that the educational experience increases in value and promotes a more genuine learner agency that teaches autonomy, engagement, and mastery. To do this, higher education must surmount the wide range of hurdles and organizational barriers that most under-resourced students experience between the real world and their academic community.

Research into the outcomes of service learning programs demonstrates the need for a broader systems approach: "Civic engagement is insufficient for active citizenship if it is not supported by experiences that provide more systematic or policy-related understanding" (Ehrlich, 2005). Without a framework, the result tends to be effort more than positive outcomes. An engagement model that uses the under-resourced students' situated approach to learning to build meaning and understanding of the symbolic hidden rules and resources of economic class—then translates that learning into new problem-solving techniques to an ever higher level of abstraction—would be a means of empowering graduates with the capacity to participate in the highly conceptual world of policy and organizations.

> When we work diligently to design learning tasks that are in simple and sound sequence and that reinforce learning, we address the disparity in political power more directly than if we preach loudly on social and economic injustice. These rather technical principles and practices—reinforcement and sequence—are tough to use. They demand attention and diligence in design. When you do that hard work, you are in fact addressing sociopolitical-economic inequities. It's all of a piece. (Vella, 2002, pp. 13–14)

In the ensuing chapters, this book explores application of economic class theories in a very specific, process-oriented course design—and also considers broader institutional implications and opportunities. The additive model is based on a new understanding of the pedagogy for working with the outcomes of poverty. This practical approach allows staff persons to apply and practice what they seemingly "already know" but had not previously given meaning to. This model is a vehicle for achieving the 16 Student Learning and Development Outcome Domains set forth by the Council for the Advancement of Standards in Higher Education (Dean, 2006). A framework is provided to:

- Build, through both academic and student services, new instructional programs
- Transform student learning

- Support student persistence and completion
- Create a vibrant participatory environment that taps students' problem-solving skills.

Formerly under-resourced students become active producers of knowledge, given the social and economic reality in which they are operating. This system works for today's students who seek greater control of their own learning in contextualized settings that relate to their everyday lives.

The model integrates teaching and learning by first meeting students "where they are," then guiding a process of self-discovery and cognitive transformation. Building on adult learning theory, along with the relational and cognitive teaching strategies already presented, the model offers the *Investigations into Economic Class in America* (DeVol & Krodel, 2010) curriculum that can stand alone or be integrated into civic-engagement strategies. It is high-impact civic engagement that amplifies the effect of experiential learning, with the promise of generating systemic change.

In the brave new postsecondary world, which is being shaped in significant ways by the emergent demography of under-resourced students, there is likely to be a continued blending of formal and informal learning. This model synthesizes the attributes of personalization, active participation, and content creation that give value to the world of the under-resourced student, resulting in educational experiences that are more productive, engaging, and community based. The framework also builds beneficial partnerships and addresses some of the more daunting accreditation issues.

The following chapters explore innovative approaches that can be integrated at multiple levels to improve student performance; to inform students, staff, and educators; and to adapt to the new paradigms in postsecondary education.

CHAPTER 8

In Action—Facilitating the *Investigations into Economic Class in America* Curriculum

Meeting the challenge of identifying content and pedagogy that (1) capitalizes on the skills and learning styles of adults, (2) bridges the language and cognitive gaps of under-resourced learners, and (3) helps institutions respond to and embrace student engagement and change is explored through application of the curriculum and process described in the following chapters.

This book is companion to *Investigations into Economic Class in America,* which is based on DeVol's work with adults from poverty in a community setting. Program evaluation reports revealed that people who used the 30-hour *Getting Ahead in a Just-Gettin'-By World* (DeVol, 2006) group process were able to achieve astounding results for themselves. For example, among three programs that used *Getting Ahead* in Indiana, Montana, and Minnesota, a total of 216 individuals increased their monthly income by an average of $1,978 (*Circles Campaign: Early Results,* n.d.). In Ohio, a group of individuals categorized as low wage and low skill saw full-time employment increases from 31% to 76% (Krodel, 2008).

Over the past few years, faculty and staff in a variety of postsecondary settings have adapted DeVol's original work. These early adopters have used it in literacy programs, as a bridge program for adults seeking to return to school, as the foundation for orientation programs, and as a credit-bearing course. Anecdotal reports from several states and Canada also indicated positive results—ranging from successfully recruiting under-resourced students into educational programs to higher levels of program completion to stories of transformational changes in participants' perspectives and goals.

As adapted for the postsecondary environment, *Investigations into Economic Class in America* provides an eminently adjustable framework, as well as offers elements of a curriculum using economic class as the analytical context. Employing the causes of poverty as framework and economic class as lens, faculty and students can create a new landscape within which to build knowledge, skills, relationships, and resources. Economic class becomes the context for situated learning, and the process provides the vehicle to develop cognitive abilities needed for success in education, work, and civic engagement. This chapter describes how the curriculum, as developed by DeVol, works.

First and foremost, the *Investigations* curriculum is intensely engaging for students because it allows them to investigate and discuss with peers a number of relevant topics—especially their lives, families, and the impact of economic class. *It prepares students for their new roles in school and society by using life itself as the context for education rather than positioning education as the preparation necessary for life.* The under-resourced students' emphasis on the immediate time horizon, relationships, and solving the problems of the day provides a springboard for research and exploration into the *what,* the *why,* and the *how* of economic class. Through their own investigation, the students learn what class is; what it means; why some people have more resources than others; and how individuals, communities, and societal systems act and react to perpetuate or reduce the impact of class structure. *Investigations* provides a bridge to what is expected for educational and work/life success—abstract and analytical thinking (Brown, Collins, & Duguid, 1989)—by beginning with a situated learning approach (Lave & Wenger, 1991) that relates to the experiences and circumstances of the under-resourced students themselves. The immediate result is a successful, college-level learning experience.

From the instructional standpoint, a facilitator guides the group's co-investigation of the four identified causes of poverty and their effects on individuals and society. Tacit knowledge bases—including how to use hidden rules of the three economic classes, how to build resources, and how to work with aspects of cultural diversity—are explored. Students translate their thinking from concrete to abstract by creating mental models or paradigms based on their life experiences. The facilitator provides resources and works collaboratively to review, explore, and direct through open-ended questioning of students' work. Learning opportunities draw on Surowiecki's "wisdom of learning from the crowds" theory (Surowiecki, 2005). The process creates learner-generated content that is not prescribed by teachers acting as dispensers of information. Rather, content is discovered and created by the students as they become actively engaged in the construction of the knowledge base they perceive to be needed in their real world.

The curriculum is designed deliberately to create spaces of cognitive dissonance where new learning can occur. Students develop the abstract models that help them understand the tension—and develop their own concrete strategies that provide a means to act and create a new future story. The dissonance or tension is resolved by creating change; by the end of the curriculum, many students are empowered to use that dissonance to fuel change. Long-term assignments involve assessing and planning to develop resources, learning about exploitation, and analyzing political and economic structures that influence economic class. Community assessment exercises encourage debate about strategies to address poverty and institutionalized classism, as opposed to blaming only oneself for the current reality. Upon completion, students have moved from the concrete learning approach developed while growing up in a low-resource environment to reasoning with causal models at ever higher levels of abstraction. Students are prepared to participate at the planning tables of such middle-class institutions as schools, businesses, and governmental bodies. This curriculum and the correlating investigative process lend themselves to service learning and community engagement strategies—and speak to many of the paradigm shifts now occurring in higher education.

Within this new landscape of economic class, students develop a lexicon and shared understanding of both hidden rules and resources. Their learning is immediately transferable and relevant to their own emergent problems and dilemmas, gifts, and strengths. A new support system is created among their peers who likely share similar characteristics—and who also desire to stay and succeed in school. Problem solving, which includes using their newfound knowledge of hidden rules and resources, allows students to share and challenge each other's strategies and assumptions.

The *Investigations* curriculum is unique in that it is an "investigation," not a "class" in the traditional sense of the word. Students are co-investigators with the instructor and affirmed for their ability to creatively solve the sorts of problems confronting them on a daily basis in low-resource environments. The instructor is the guide or facilitator—and co-investigator. Facilitators do not need to defend the course content to students but rather present it as a conjoint investigation. Instead of lecturing, instructors are facilitators of the group's process; they guide students to the necessary sources of information and allow them to draw their own conclusions. Whether the instructor/facilitator is from the middle class or was once in poverty and is now working in the middle-class world of higher education, he or she will most likely be perceived by the group as being from the dominant culture and hence will need to consciously work to build trust and mutually respectful relationships. The facilitator's role is to assist the process of self-discovery in such a way that students recognize and articulate their own motivation for change—if in fact they choose to make changes in their lives. There is a difference between achieving economic stability within one's economic class and moving from one economic class to another. Many middle-class families would like to have more income so they can have more things and more security, but they do not necessarily desire the lifestyle changes necessary to "fit in" to wealthy society. People from poverty may feel the same way; having more income and economic stability is different from wanting to enter the middle-class rat race. Although a number of politicians emphasize the desirability of middle-class values and lifestyle, it is important not to project that onto students; they will define their own desires.

As a result of this investigative process, most students come away with three things:

- They have learned to develop mental models that enable them to conceptualize large, abstract concepts, connections, relationships, and options.
- They have realized the necessity of having someone in their life who understands both the world of poverty and the world of middle class in order to help bridge the gap in hidden rules.
- They have used a defined process to explore life while simultaneously learning new information and skills. The process, the vocabulary, the relationships, and the abstract models enable people to see the difference between what is and what can be—and to develop their own future story, along with realistic plans for getting there.

Theory of Change

Investigations provides a process for change that is well grounded in adult learning theories mentioned earlier—and described as follows:

> **[First,] understand the problem:** Poverty traps people in the tyranny of the moment, making it very difficult to attend to abstract information or plan for the future—the very things needed to build adequate resources and financial assets. There are many causes of poverty, some having to do with the choices

of the poor, but most stemming from community conditions and political/economic structures. The theory of change must take all this into account.

Our theory of change: People in poverty need an accurate perception of how poverty impacts them and an understanding of economic realities as a starting point both for reasoning and for developing plans for resolution. Using mental models for comprehension and reasoning, people can move from the concrete to the abstract. Using Payne's definition of the resources necessary for a full life and her insights into the hidden rules of class, people can evaluate themselves, choose behaviors, and make plans to build resources and climb out of poverty. The community must provide services, support, and meaningful opportunities over the long term. In partnership with people from middle class and wealth, individuals in poverty can solve community and systemic problems that contribute to poverty. (DeVol, 2006, pp. 1–2)

The Sequence

The sequence of the curriculum is significant and intentional. It is designed to move from the personal to the external, from small problems to big ones, from concrete to abstract and back again. There have been occasions when well-meaning but uninformed individuals have wanted to extract portions of the curriculum to address or even "fix" a particular aspect of student behavior or learning need. This isolating approach misses the point that most under-resourced students come from extremely complex situations, and the means for developing economic stability and educational success are similarly complex. Taking the material out of context and out of sequence, as tempting as it may be, will likely not have the intended outcome—and may well be damaging. Students might feel they are being insulted, stereotyped, told "how to act," or once again being dominated by the mainstream middle class.

On the other hand, as individuals follow the process, the hidden rules and driving forces of poverty are validated as essential within that context. This, incidentally, is the essence of the additive model. The ensuing process of discovery uncovers and discloses what students already know, adds a broader perspective, and guides them toward new knowledge of familiar themes. Likewise, trying to compress the information into a shorter time frame takes away the time necessary for students to process the material in order to find personal meaning in it. This is not a class on diversity in which there is a test on Monday; it is a process of self-discovery and development—and time is essential for reflection and interpretation.

The *Investigations* sequence begins as a situated learning experience, with a discussion of the students' personal experience, because this is usually what students can best describe. The goal is to establish a comfortable, "around the kitchen table" atmosphere to encourage sharing and problem solving. A cohort group of 10 to 20 people with one or two facilitators is established, and a set of ground rules (social norms) are agreed upon so that people feel respected and safe as they share information about their lives and experience—and build relationships with each other and the facilitators. Students draw upon their own life experiences (sharing stories, situations, problems, and dilemmas) in order to develop an understanding of economic class that moves from concrete to abstract thinking. Next, the theory of change on which the course is built is explored so that students begin to think about what their thinking might result in. This introduces the process of metacognition—the ability to think about one's thought processes—a foundation for college success.

Once the group has stabilized initially, there is intensive investigation into both the causes and effects of poverty. Students find new vocabulary to express what they already know and are learning, as well as information and theories to support their arguments. History, economics, sociology, business, psychology, finance, and health issues emerge—and students are encouraged to extrapolate and explore what is most relevant or meaningful to them. The intersection of race and poverty is explored for two major reasons: first, to present information about the economic and personal effects of national policies on individuals and second, to explore the significant differences between culture and economic class. The group and individual activities encourage students to step back and consider the role of the individual in a class-oriented society, along with the role of a class-oriented society in relation to the individual.

With this new understanding of the personal, community, and societal causes and effects of poverty, students have some fun exploring the hidden rules of economic class. They are encouraged to brainstorm how the rules manifest themselves in their own families—and where they see examples in the media and entertainment. By now the students share at least a foundational lexicon and framework to use in analyzing their own life and actions, as well as what is happening around them in their family, their community, and/or on the national and international stages. The time and attention given to language and story structure help students develop additional ways to communicate through oral discourse and written assignments.

After examining the research areas regarding the causes of poverty and how knowledge of hidden rules enhances survival in any given class, the next step is the exploration of the 11 resources. The facilitator previews relevant information, and students practice scoring or rating the levels of resources possessed by people in case studies. During this phase additional information about resources necessary to create change, such as motivation and persistence, exposes students to resources on and off campus that will support their efforts.

The theory of change is revisited to again draw attention to the personal process under way and to illuminate the changes that have already occurred. This sets the stage for the objective self-assessment regarding resources and a general exploration of methods to build resources.

An assessment of the social and human capital available in the community may reveal that constraints in one's environment have had a significant impact on one's family. This again helps students step back from self-blame. The community assessment is followed by an intense period of personal planning based on self-assessment, the resources the student wants to build, and the resources available in the community to sustain that plan.

The Triangle—a Mental Model for the Design of the Curriculum

The mental model at right summarizes the six elements that students will be guided through in this curriculum. The co-investigative process is the foundation, meaning everyone in the group, along with the instructor, will investigate every element of the triangle.

Note. From *Getting Ahead in a Just-Gettin'-By World* (p. 3), by P. E. DeVol, 2004, Highlands, TX: aha! Process. Copyright 2004 by aha! Process. Reprinted with permission.

The following overview summarizes the goals related to each of the six elements of the curriculum. Activities and theories of why concepts are implemented throughout the process will be briefly outlined.

1. UNDERSTANDING POVERTY

The bottom three sections of the triangle constitute the foundation and entry point for the course, starting with the understanding of what is meant by poverty. Thus, when broaching the subject of poverty, the first class meeting is a critical test for the facilitator/instructor. The students will make judgments about the instructor's willingness to listen—whether the facilitator is there to tell them what to think or do—or to work with the group. The sense of curiosity and energy transmitted from facilitator to group sets an important tone for the co-investigation process.

The first major activity, the creation of mental models or drawings of "What it's like now," helps students tune in to the concrete realities of their lives and is a foundational piece for the entire course. The models usually include the fundamental mathematics of poverty: low wages, trying to make ends meet, cyclical debt, and other frequent realities—such as time spent at agencies, family crises, abuse of various kinds (including domestic violence, drugs, and alcohol). Further, the mental model provides the opportunity to honor and affirm the students' problem-solving skills brought to bear most often—and what the implications of that problem solving might be. (In poverty, there is little time to plan and prevent. Problems need to be solved now: The electricity needs to be turned on now, the baby is sick, and it's the last day to pay the tuition bill.) Resources for stability are scarce. The mental model becomes an abstract representation of life; it begins to put some structures and definitions behind the episodic crises. This first mental model is to be labeled, as are all subsequent group mental models, and kept available each class session for reference—and as a record of the group's investigation of poverty.

Other activities provide investigative assignments that examine personal income and expenses, linking students to the research continuum on the causes of poverty. As students crunch the numbers regarding the cost of college and the impact on their personal debt, they also calculate the likely effect of a college education on lifetime earnings, the ability to get fair credit, and the capacity to build assets. The discussion that ensues will be highly informative as students verbalize their insights into what life is like in poverty, for example:

- Full-time minimum wage won't support the family.
- Relationships are needed to survive.
- There is almost no power or influence.
- You have to "hustle to make it."

The facilitator is advised to avoid the temptation to simply hand such insights to the students—instead trusting the process and letting the students discover and own the knowledge.

In the second major activity, students are exposed to other causes of poverty. They will likely come to the realization that poverty is caused by more than individual choice. When creating their original "What it's like now" model, students may not have yet recognized exploitation and predatory lenders as features of their landscape. At this stage, students might be encouraged to rethink and revise their mental models. Within this examination of the causes of poverty, students are introduced to the concept of community sustainability, which brings the research continuum to life as they use that framework to support analysis of solutions to poverty.

The Community Sustainability Grid (CSG) is introduced as a planning tool for communities working to end poverty (see chart below). Students who complete the CSG discover that ending poverty requires strategies for all four areas of poverty research. They also may come to realize that cooperation is necessary among individuals, community organizations, leaders (including the business community), and makers of public policy. Discussion as to each person's beliefs and roles regarding poverty's causes and solutions can be liberating and exciting for all participants.

RESEARCH AREAS				
		Behaviors of Individual	Human and Social Capital	Exploitation	Political/ Economic Structures
Action Items	Individual Action				
	Organizational Action				
	Community Action				
	Policy Change				

Note. From *Bridges Out of Poverty Workbook* (p. 59), by P. E. DeVol, R. K. Payne, and T. D. Smith, 2006, Highlands, TX: aha! Process. Copyright 2006 by aha! Process. Adapted with permission.

DeVol makes the point that using the CSG to map the many efforts going on in a community may give the impression that there is both access and opportunity—and that the causes of poverty are being addressed. If it is used as a research and planning tool, however, students will see that, for example, the availability of Workforce Investment Act training money translates to only 100 people in the county being retrained each year. As students discuss the various efforts under way, it may become apparent that the majority of activity is generated by community organizations focusing first and foremost on the behaviors of the individual. Only in a secondary way is the availability of human and social capital in the community being addressed. And in most communities precious little gets done on the right-hand side of the CSG to reduce exploitation or create systemic changes in the political and economic structures that govern society.

In fact, students will likely discover that for the most part "society has given the work of ending poverty to the community organizations" (DeVol, 2006, p. 29). Yet it is quite clear that community organizations cannot do the work of the school system, the healthcare system, the employment system, and the business community—and they are not terribly effective, by and large, in public policy. Thus comes the realization that ending poverty will require action at *all* community levels: business people, politicians, clergy, and other leadership. Key questions may include:

- Which financial institutions make fair credit available?
- Which businesses value and invest in their employees—and provide decent benefits and wages?
- Which school districts or principals in buildings make it a priority to hire master teachers?
- Which agencies create access to quality healthcare?

As students consider these questions, they also will understand that effective solutions require their input. Often the people making the plans and running the programs come from middle class and have not learned about the theories of economic class, hidden rules, and resources. The viewpoint that poverty is essentially caused by individual behaviors is fairly common and precipitates narrow solutions. The CSG gives students a mental model to evaluate programs and focus their thinking.

Race as it relates to economic class, as a reservoir of hidden rules and resources, is first explored metaphorically through analysis of the bias toward "right-handedness" of modern society and what it does and does not mean to the dominant (right-handed) versus the oppressed (left-handed) cultures (Valenzuela & Addington, 2006b). Students explore how normalization affects individuals and society. A variety of media can be used to demonstrate how profoundly race impacts the individual's experience. Once again, the strategy of moving between the personal and the political, the individual and the society, provides a means to process complex theories that may have had profound personal impact. The discussion surrounding the personal, cumulative effect of race on the individual may shift the perception of the students who are white with regard to what the students of color have and will continue to experience, regardless of their income or wealth. Strategies for survival and for creating a more equitable community/society take into account both the role of individual action *and* how individuals can interact with and impact the community and policies that affect them. Part of the ensuing resource assessment encourages students to build the networks and strategies that may ameliorate the effects of racism, help them address racial inequalities in income and wealth, deepen their understanding of racism, and heighten their appreciation of diversity.

2. UNDERSTANDING ECONOMIC CLASS: PAYNE'S *FRAMEWORK*

Economic class is the primary lens through which the issues in the curriculum are studied; an important part of the picture is the "hidden rules of economic class." The *Investigations* curriculum introduces a theoretical framework filled with the sorts of rules, symbols, and well-defined problems that students will encounter in other coursework. The hidden rules are presented as a set of "laws" governing different groups in society—including people in poverty, middle class, and wealth. The driving forces, norms, and values associated with these three economic classes are powerful and foundational to the hidden rules of class that must be understood in order to move from one class to another. The driving forces of each class create a sense of identity that affects the students' perceptions and experiences as they use these normally unspoken and unwritten rules to create a different understanding of their current situations and problems.

Coming to understand the hidden rules of class is about learning *what* and *why* you do what you do—and likewise understanding the behaviors of teachers, peers, bosses, and politicians. As students realize they cannot choose the economic class they were born into any more than they can choose their race or gender, they also understand and learn the rules and how the 11 resources are prioritized and organized. Depending on one's economic background, a person can choose to behave differently and, in so doing, find access to the power structures of society. By understanding and learning *how* to use the hidden rules of economic class, students can build their own resources and reach a level of economic stability, prosperity, intellectual maturity, civic engagement, creative expression, or whatever it is they *choose*. Even more importantly, greater access to resources means a fuller life with more options and choices. In *Crossing the Tracks for Love,* Payne (2005a) refers to choice, noting that some people in poverty will opt to stay in that lifestyle even if they have a chance to move into the middle class, just as some middle-class people will choose not to enter the wealthy class and all that comes with it (pp. 19–20).

As the group explores the hidden rules from the environment and the mental models they have developed, they again revisit their first mental model of "What it's like now" and see the meaning of living to survive. This is not done to place judgment or as a way to explain status. Instead, students are likely to discover there is much strength behind the hidden rules of poverty—in that there is great resourcefulness and creativity, as well as the ability to live in the moment that many middle-class people lack. Here the facilitator must be watchful for labeling and judging people and the psychological resistance that follows. The discussion is not about success or failure; it is about defining and understanding the present reality with a new vocabulary, new information, and at a new level of abstraction. If the atmosphere in the room becomes defensive or judgmental, the facilitator might present the materials in class, then assign students to watch for and identify examples of the hidden rules around them every day—and move on. In most cases, students will recognize the hidden rules of their economic class, as well as the value judgments that were initially obscuring their perceptions.

Next in *Investigations,* the resources are defined. Objectively, it is fair to restate that having more resources makes for a fuller, more stable life. Plentiful financial resources do not buy a good life, but they do reduce many of the stressors that often accompany not having enough money. Financial stability allows for more individual choices; the ability to have and make choices is directly related to both personal and societal power.

The facilitator will introduce the resource assessment that students will use to practice evaluating the resources of people in case studies. At first, using hypothetical individuals is a way of easing into the potentially more personal, even painful process of self-examination. During the case study discussion, overgeneralized and simplistic statements are likely to emerge initially. These are precursors to deeper levels of reflection as the questions supplied become increasingly specific. Through discussion of the resources available to the case study characters, students will likely begin to recognize their own assets and liabilities—and make connections between the use of hidden rules and the acquisition of resources. This discussion will be foundational to the more detailed self-assessment of their own resources that students complete later, using a more comprehensive rubric.

3. UNDERSTANDING PRESENT CIRCUMSTANCES: ASSESSMENTS

Another goal of the *Investigations* curriculum is for students to take control of their lives by understanding change, defining their desired changes, consciously and actively moving through the change process, and monitoring their results. Students who may have been the subjects of school or agency plans, treatment plans, service plans, and care plans will become aware that some of those were the plans of (middle class) institutions attempting to identify their (the students') problems that moved directly to the "fix"—thus providing an opportunity to discuss Miller and Rollnick's (2002) "righting reflex" in action. Further, information about the process for change, based on Miller and Rollnick, is directly taught very early in the process so that students can assess their present state of change and understand their progress and setbacks. Group discussions of the barriers to change, particularly as they relate to educational goals, are useful in helping students whose past efforts in school or jobs frequently were derailed by concrete problems that demanded immediate action and took priority over school and work. Discussions such as these may be sparked as students complete an assortment of assessments throughout the curriculum.

One such assessment, the self-assessment of personal resources, is very important, and the students will have heard reference to it as a step to complete. Some of the students may be feeling apprehensive about this upcoming exercise. As the students prepare to do the self-assessment, it is important to draw their attention to the processes they have been using, particularly their analytical thinking. Facilitators will need to occasionally encourage the students to press on by using this thinking. It can be helpful to remind them that there might be a tendency to get discouraged by limited personal assets—that those resources arise not only from individual action but also from families and communities. At this juncture, the facilitator also can point out and talk about the resources in which the individual students are strong. In the subsequent planning process, students will be challenged to build resources they need to succeed. The facilitator's role is to guide the investigation toward the idea of using students' strengths and assets to build additional resources. At the end of the assignment, students will have another personal mental model, a bar chart, showing their resources—but ultimately a clearer understanding of how things in their lives "got that way."

Leading up to the self-assessment on resources is additional information about motivation, financial, emotional, and social capital resources. The latter is particularly significant and serves as the foundation for a "mental model of support for change." As students consider the differences between bonding and bridging social capital, they will evaluate the health of their bonding social capital in relation to their desire to change their lives. Like other self-assessments in the curriculum, this can be painful as individuals who have been crucial for survival in the past may now be seen as barriers or even opponents to the students' personal growth and academic/vocational success. This can be disconcerting, even dangerous, for some of the students. Careful listening that brings attention to students' strengths, as well as providing information about the campus and community counseling center and domestic violence shelters, may be needed.

The last area of assessment is the community assessment, which will reinforce the two recurring themes central to the curriculum: "poverty and me" and "poverty and the community." The community assessment supports ideas about building personal resources, as well as the information about the causes of poverty. The sequence is intentional. Intense personal work is followed by investigation of the community for two reasons: to provide emotional relief from the intensity of the self-assessment and to continually broaden each student's perspective and knowledge about the interrelationship between the individual and society. The group will create a Community Assessment Mental Model and relate it back to the concept of community sustainability.

Here the students will more clearly see themselves as potential problem solvers in the community. For instance, the interaction with the facilitator can serve as an introduction to people from middle class with whom students may want to build partnerships to solve *community* problems. Once again, two themes might emerge: "the community where I (or my family) live" and the "campus as a community." Introducing the students to one or more community leaders to interview about community strengths and weaknesses provides an opportunity to:

- Apply their knowledge about mental models
- Use hidden rules
- Gather information and build resources.

Students will use the hidden rules to understand the mindset of the person they are talking to—and will probably shape and direct interview questions accordingly. They are likely to compare their mental models of poverty in the community with those of other community leaders, then analyze the differences. Many organizing, sorting, reading, and writing skills can be brought to bear in these assignments.

4. GAINING POWER

Helping students see the "big picture" and take responsibility for their role in it without taking on all the responsibility for society's problems is another goal embedded in the *Investigations* curriculum. The concept of "power" is introduced early through the theory of change, and change is a recurrent theme throughout the curriculum. First, students identify the community agencies that work on issues identified in the group's mental model of "What it's like now." The students then evaluate whether the agencies expect people to change—and whether the agencies prescribe what the change should be (righting reflex) and the exact consequences for not changing (coercion, even intimidation). At that point students can identify how using hidden rules and understanding the driving forces of the (middle class) agencies can enable them to develop a different relationship with the agencies—a relationship that allows them to access resources without being diminished or put down by agency policy.

As the course unfolds, the personal work of developing power continues with discussion about building personal resources. Students will be exploring the space on the mental model of change between "What it's like now" and where they want to be. As students identify people, community agencies, and institutions that can help them further their plans, they may encounter the very same agencies whose righting reflexes caused the students to reject their help in the past. Students may thus learn that, by understanding and using the hidden rules of middle class, they can change their relationships with these agencies and find sources of bridging social capital and other resources to help them get what they need.

5. TAKING RESPONSIBILITY

As this work progresses, students begin to think about *what* and *why* they want to change. Another goal of the curriculum is for students to "own" these choices and take responsibility for their actions, the *how.* To help students assume even greater responsibility for their lives, they will be asked toward the end of the course to develop an individual plan for developing their own resources. It is the student who is exercising leadership and control over his or her own life, not a teacher or outside authority. This exercise demonstrates the students' move from reactive problem solving to proactive planning. Facilitators must be ready for the fact that many students really don't know how to plan. A constructive strategy is to keep this activity in class and encourage students to talk to one another and challenge/support each other in developing the plans. Even though the goal is to build individual resources, this drives home the point that social support is a key resource for change. This way the facilitator is available to talk about student plans individually and provide feedback or advice—but *only* if asked. This avoids the righting reflex trap on the part of the facilitator. Although the development of this plan is a key intended outcome of the course, overemphasizing it can backfire, so as DeVol suggests in *Facilitator Notes for Getting Ahead in a Just-Gettin'-By World,* it is best to treat it as a low-key celebration (DeVol, 2004, p. 43).

After generating their personal plans, students develop a plan to create prosperity in their community. Before moving to the community plan, two things need to have occurred. First, it is important that students have realized poverty is about more than the choices of the poor. And with that realization, second, they need to recognize that the solution to poverty does not rest solely on the community. The students are invited to see *themselves* at this point as proactive rather than reactive problem solvers—and as leaders. Their personal understanding of poverty's hidden rules, coupled with their newfound knowledge of middle-class hidden rules, puts them in a unique position to share insights and develop workable solutions with a variety of partners—from family members to neighbors to community agencies. And yes, even with others on campus.

6. TAKING ACTION: IMPLEMENTING FUTURE STORY

The process wraps up by creating a new mental model of success and a new future story by translating the students' concrete plans written on worksheets into an abstract mental model of what life will be like. The point of the curriculum at this juncture is to connect the fact that solving problems proactively and controlling their own lives introduces students to the sort of power the middle class takes for granted. By learning about driving forces, hidden rules, and resources, students become more comfortable interacting with people from all economic classes. In their final mental models, the students would be expected to identify which hidden rules come into play in their plans and how to forge partnerships with people in other classes in order to build resources, power, and personal responsibility. By the time they are done, they will have written a new—and perhaps their first—future story. Students will have learned new skills that allow them to go to the abstract despite the very real pressures they will continue to face in the "concrete" present.

In helping develop this final mental model, the instructor might interrupt the work periodically and ask the students to challenge each other's thinking and put greater detail into their models. Their final mental model is to:

- Include all important elements
- Identify timelines showing past, present, and future
- Distinguish between individual and community responsibility
- Show the relative importance of the different parts of their mental model
- Show relationships between and among people
- Identify the key players
- Show options and possible consequences.

Note. From Facilitator Notes for Getting Ahead in a Just-Gettin'-By World (p. 34), by P. E. DeVol, 2006, Highlands, TX: aha! Process. Copyright 2006 by aha! Process. Adapted with permission.

The culmination of the *Investigations* curriculum is meant to bring students to the point of action—perhaps in a new direction or at least in a more focused direction than they had when they first came to college. Concluding the course with a celebration that allows students to talk about the process of the group and their personal journey, as well as clarify their future story, is in order. Before the last class session, allow time for the students to plan the final meeting.

The future stories that students have created will require developing partnerships with people from middle class and a different level of social capital than most had at the start. The students and/or campus community may want to continue to meet to support plans and future stories. The facilitator needs to clarify with the participants regarding the level of post-class commitment that might be expected of the students, as well as the facilitator, who is likely to be seen as the students' primary bridging social capital during the course. Students are to be encouraged to acquire additional bridging capital over the near to long term by reinforcing other sources and strategies for building support.

It is also important to support students if they want to contribute to community problem solving. That support includes preparing the larger community and the college itself to accept them at the planning table. There are many opportunities to build support and champions for change on the college campus and beyond.

Educational Theories Support the Process

The tables that follow demonstrate the relationship between learning theories and the *Investigations* curriculum and process.

Relationship Between Structured Cognition and *Investigations* Process

	Beginning stages of *Investigations* Just plain folks	Intermediate and end phase of *Investigations* Student	Ending phase and post-*Investigations* Practitioner
Reasons with	**Casual stories** Students examine personal stories as the context for the course	**Laws** Students apply hidden rules of economic class to understand past and present realities	**Casual models** Students use the poverty research continuum and theory of change as analytical frameworks to support arguments
Acting on	**Situations** Students act on current situations, build bonding relationships	**Symbols** Students investigate personal and community resources, build bridging relationships	**Conceptual situations** Students investigate social, political, and economic structures; take political action to address community resources
Resolving	**Emergent problems and dilemmas** Students apply new learning and accept support from new relationships	**Well-defined problems** Students proactively plan to build resources identified in personal resource assessment	**Ill-defined problems** Students engage and seek relationships to solve problems identified in community resource assessment
Producing	**Negotiable meaning and socially constructed understanding** Students build community and shared language to understand poverty	**Fixed meaning and immutable concepts** Students establish a lexicon and framework of ideas that can be applied to individual plans	**Negotiable meaning and socially constructed understanding** Students engage and use new language to reflect on issues and assign meaning

Note. From "Situated Cognition and the Culture of Learning," by J. S. Brown, A. Collins, and P. Duguid, 1989, *Educational Researcher, 18*(1), p. 35. Copyright 1989 by American Educational Research Association. Adapted with permission.

Many other theories of Lindemann (1961), Brookfield (1986, 1987), Knowles (1990), and Mezirow and Associates (1990), discussed in Chapters 4 and 5, are put into practice through the *Investigations* process as shown below.

Adult Learning Theory Related to *Investigations* Process

Adult Learning Theory	Application in *Investigations into Economic Class in America*
The learner's most significant resource is his or her experience.	*Investigations* places value and meaning on the under-resourced students' experience with the effects of economic class on their personal lives.
Learning occurs best through contextualized situations.	The contrast between life and the new situation on the college campus is used to illustrate concepts.
Learners value experience and discovery.	Students use their life experience to create questions for investigation—about how economic class affects a person and community. The richness of the subject allows for tangential exploration and extrapolation.
Relevance is important. Learners need to know the rationale for what they are being taught.	Examining one's life situation and experience is highly engaging, and doing so in the context of creating a successful stable life and/or succeeding in college is highly relevant.
Education is a transactional process, with teacher and learner continually engaged in negotiating priorities, methods, and criteria of evaluation. Adult learners want to be more independent and self-directed, yet learners need to be guided toward independence and self-direction.	The *Investigations* process of co-investigation is a transactional process, and students work independently and in groups to investigate issues of personal interest and relevance. The facilitator acts as co-investigator, resource, and guide.
The heart of adult learning is critical reflection—self-examination and assessment of one's assumptions and beliefs, which leads to perspective transformation. Perspectives are sets of assumptions built over time, through which new experiences are filtered and understood.	*Investigations* provides a process for self-assessment of resources and analysis of one's driving forces and use of hidden rules, leading to transformation of the students' assumptions and perspectives about economic class, their role as students, and their choices.
Through reflection, learner's perspectives become more inclusive and integrated. Perception distortions are (1) epistemic—internalized concepts as representing right/wrong, good/bad; (2) sociocultural—generalized beliefs about specific populations; and (3) psychic—assumptions that produce anxiety and block certain behaviors.	Students look critically at perspective distortions, such as racism, classism, their own generalizations and stereotypes compared with others', and how their personal perspectives affect their behaviors.
The process of learning and becoming educated is fundamentally different from vocational skill training.	*Investigations* is not vocational training, but it does develop the language and behaviors expected by both the workplace and the school setting.

This curriculum also is highly responsive to the new paradigms affecting postsecondary education described in Chapter 7.

Adapting Concepts from *Investigations* to the New Practices and Assumptions in Higher Education

New Paradigms	Approaches Operationalized via the *Investigations* Process
Contextualized and situated learning connects students to each other and the community in the learning tasks	*Investigations* uses economic class as the context for a cooperative investigation that is personally relevant and evidenced in the community
Students seen as problem solvers and knowledge creators	*Investigations* moves students from reactive problem solving to proactive planning, knowledge creation, and "future story"
Supported, relational, co-operative learning environments	*Investigations'* group process provides the vehicle and relationships with a network of peers, faculty, and staff
Student retention, persistence, achievement, and completion as top priorities	▪ Resource assessment provides affirmation and leads to clear personal plans to build resources for academic achievement ▪ Creates "future story" ▪ Relational learning increases social capital ▪ Social network provides support and linkage to services

Note. From *Helping Under-Resourced Learners Succeed at the College and University Level: What Works, What Doesn't, and Why* (p. 8), by K. Krodel, K. Becker, H. Ingle, and S. Jakes, 2008. Copyright 2008 by aha! Process. Adapted with permission.

This unique analytical framework, along with practical strategies that help educators teach more effectively, can now help under-resourced college students take charge of their learning processes and develop future stories for a fuller and more stable life. There are many variations and opportunities to explore for delivering this curriculum. For instance, *Investigations* may be an optional path in a first-year experience or as an orientation alternative. The course also could be employed in a learning community that uses reading and writing exercises to remediate academic gaps, either for credit or as a non-credit "bridge" program. Facilitating change from poverty to stability is a work in progress with no easy answers, so instructors and staffs are encouraged to join the dialogue and contribute their own experiences as well, from which others can benefit. As students learn these concepts and apply them, they also start to see institutions—including their place of postsecondary study—through different lenses. The last section of the book introduces the role of the college in community sustainability, along with ideas to weave this material into the larger tapestry of the college or university environment.

CHAPTER 9

Building Synergy Among Stakeholders

The Model: Access *with* Support

The model described in this section explores application of the *Investigations into Economic Class in America* curriculum and strategies to shift the culture of higher education institutions in such a way that colleges are better positioned to understand and respond effectively to under-resourced learners. While the *Investigations* curriculum alone can effect significant personal change and improve student retention and achievement, additional synergy is created by coupling this introductory course with a process that supports student engagement within the actual structure of the institution. Beyond creating their personal plans and building their own resources, students are likely to connect to the institution within the campus environment and practice the planning and negotiation skills as part of service learning, work study, or other vehicles. Indeed, campus culture may shift as a result of their participation.

This entire model, then, supports the vision articulated in the "Platform for Economic Justice" (aha! Process, 2007) by offering a holistic, systemic approach that addresses all four causes of poverty—the behaviors and choices of the individual, the absence of human and social capital in the community, exploitation, and political/economic structures. Here the platform's concepts (originally applied in the context of the broad definition of individual and society and shown on subsequent pages in bold-faced statements) are focused on the microcosm of the college environment and are applicable on both commuter and residential campuses. Admissions, financial aid, advisers, developmental education instructors, faculty, administrators, et al. ... all can create access to higher education for the under-resourced learner. Access without support, however, is not opportunity, as Tinto (2004) points out in a paper of the same name.

All involved in the process outlined and described will find their work transformed. Instead of the middle class dispensing solutions to students from poverty, every class is drawn to the table together as problem solvers—working toward sustainable communities—whether that is the classroom, campus, adjacent community, or greater communities in which the students and institutions are involved.

The model addresses the personal experience of poverty.
It is the students' experience that underscores and fuels the motivation for change. When the under-resourced students' experience, knowledge, and problem-solving skills are brought to the discussion about transforming a campus or community, a wealth of knowledge and wisdom that otherwise would go unrecognized fuels the process and production of the work at hand. The *Investigations* model is based on the premise that by becoming multicultural through intentionally learning the hidden rules and patterns of poverty—and developing language to articulate the experience—the impact of poverty can be much better understood. This information is acquired from people in poverty and is used to inform the design and delivery of programs and services on campus.

Colleges and universities have both a moral obligation and an economic imperative to work to end poverty and build sustainable communities.
Higher education has a long history of leading transformational change and generating new knowledge and applications. College personnel may choose to use the *Investigations* curriculum's concepts within their own unique setting and circumstances—in order to forge change for all. Thus, when faculty, staff, and students intentionally engage in (1) an investigation of the personal experience of poverty, (2) the social and human capital the college contributes to the community, (3) a candid assessment of the legacy of exploitation, and (4) discussion of how power structures influence society, they will be able to justify and support the need for change.

By looking at poverty through the lens of economic class, colleges will be able to work to build resources for individuals and the larger community.

Economic class provides a perspective that is less emotionally charged than race, gender, and/or ethnicity. While colleges should continue in their leadership role regarding diversity and tolerance of individuals and cultures, they also can assume leadership in endeavors as small as teaching/learning the hidden rules of all classes and as large as promoting economic justice. Based on understanding the causes and effects of poverty, along with patterns (not stereotypes) of economic classes, postsecondary institutions can foster the intentional creation of resources, economic stability, and mutually respectful relationships, all of which are tools for working toward ending poverty. In so doing, retention and graduation figures will improve. A cycle of change can develop that continues to build toward greater good, both locally and beyond, as graduates are inspired and empowered to take their knowledge into their community and career settings.

The process of investigating all four causes of poverty, not just one or two as is often the case, provides a comprehensive and holistic approach to ending poverty.

The process mitigates the polarizing, blaming debates that tend to narrowly target either individuals or societal structures to the exclusion of other causes of poverty. During the investigation a lexicon develops—language to define and help explain poverty, middle class, and wealth. As students learn and use the language to articulate the causes of poverty, learn how these factors affect their resources, and learn how to strengthen their own lives with choice and future stories, other tools become necessary for creating change. As a planning tool, the Community Sustainability Grid enables students and colleges to evaluate their work, determine areas that are not being adequately addressed, and locate areas of overconcentration that may reflect outmoded thinking about poverty. Rather than blaming individuals and institutions, this process invites all stakeholders to come to the table to contribute their perspectives and resources.

Students from poverty are an integral part of ending poverty, as well as designing college programs that stabilize students' economic conditions and build resources.

Under-resourced students are experts regarding the concrete realities of their lives and how to solve problems. Students get prepared to participate in committees by learning about poverty and economic class—and by developing analytical thinking skills, proactive problem-solving techniques, and vocabulary through the *Investigations* curriculum. The problem-solving skills developed in low-resource environments are first identified and honored, then further developed in the classroom, and ultimately put to use in service learning and community engagement courses and projects. Colleges can work *with* students rather than simply design programs *for* them. These newly resourced students will likely then move out into their community or on to other communities to bring change and to carry on what they have learned.

Including people from all groups (economic, racial, religious, gender, etc.) on committees and planning teams will move the college community toward accountability and reduce exploitation.

Using the lens of economic class encourages further examination of the numerous ways different groups intentionally or unintentionally gain advantage over others. Relationships built on mutual trust and respect become the foundation for identifying both blatant and hidden exploitation—and ending it. This new level of understanding and the ability to build relationships, along with the language for discussion, heightens students' awareness of and desire for accountability.

An integrated effort linking curriculum to student services and learning assignments creates experiential educational opportunities for students.

In the systemic approach employed by *Investigations,* all parties are educated and speak a common language about a complex and personally relevant subject that affects everyone on campus, as well as the larger community. The co-investigative process sparks new ideas that can help faculty design curriculum that motivates students and accelerates learning. Integrating the cognitive development of students with the examination of economic class and cultural issues creates dynamic educational opportunities. Projects—for specific classes or in general for a course of study that includes service learning—offer the opportunity for students to gain meaningful experience for their résumés and future occupations.

Businesses play an important role in education by creating demand for an educated workforce, jobs with sustainable wages, and internships and apprenticeships for students.

Businesses will engage with colleges when they see how this model improves retention and produces better employees. The evidence will come first as people from poverty complete the semester-long *Investigations* curriculum with a new outlook, along with a new set of tools and resources that support their ability to work. (In the language of workforce development, this is "soft-skill training." In fact, it is much more.) Next, some businesses will engage in community strategies and open more internship positions for students. Later, as the model evolves, businesses will see students from poverty graduating with technical and professional degrees, thereby enabling them to compete for high-skill, high-wage jobs. The presence of a skilled workforce is a major factor in locating business in the profit sector and so more jobs—and better jobs—will become available, thus improving the prosperity of the community. The networking between the institution and the business community will gain both momentum and reciprocal benefits in many ways.

High-impact civic engagement intentionally works on the causes of poverty.
Colleges can begin to improve relationships with under-resourced students by using the *Investigations* process and relational teaching methods. Prepared with new knowledge, skills, and a future story of their own, students can be included at the planning tables and committees that work on changing and designing programs at the college level. Such committees begin by examining the student life cycle—the concrete experiences of students as they enter and progress through the institution—then look at examples of best practices and develop strategies to improve recruitment, retention, and graduation unique to the campus and student body.

As other faculty and student services providers begin to use the constructs, more courses, services, and events will address economic justice, the causes of poverty, and the building of sustainable communities. No single intervention—or even set of coordinated interventions within a single institution—will be effective in ending poverty. But by building partnerships both on and off campus, institutions can engage the wider community in their vision and activities.

Looking Back, Looking Forward

We have examined the *what* and the *why* of under-resourced students. We then looked at teaching strategies and instructional design, as well as introducing a curriculum that focuses on the investigative process (the *how*) to build critical-thinking skills and a knowledge base in relation to highly personal, relevant, and complex issues. A single instructor can apply these methods and use the curriculum to engender positive effects. In turn, these tools can be expanded upon to build an institutional culture that can be tapped to develop much broader solutions.

BEYOND THE CLASSROOM, WHAT DOES THIS MODEL ACCOMPLISH?

1. Brings all economic classes to the table
2. Applies strategies that cover all causes of poverty

3. Extends mutual accountability to all partners and the community
4. Provides ownership of the work to everyone at the table
5. Works to expand the partnership to build sustainable communities. (aha! Process, 2007, p. 12)

Practically speaking, how is this done?

1. Develop a dynamic landscape for learning

- By integrating the *Investigations* curriculum into orientation, general education requirements, or learning communities (Chapters 10 and 11)
- By building competencies of faculty and staff (Chapter 10).

This results in a shared language (or lexicon) and knowledge of specific constructs (hidden rules, resources, causes of poverty), analytical methods (co-investigation and relational learning), and tools (personal, institutional and community assessment, and planning processes).

2. Create a participatory environment

- By involving students in planning committees (Chapters 10, 12, and 13)
- By mapping the student life cycle and making adjustments (Chapter 11)
- By "strategic doing" (Chapter 13).

This results in all classes being at the planning table to determine root causes and real solutions to students' potential barriers to access and success.

3. Reach out to the broader society

- By building community partnerships (Chapter 13).

This results in more opportunities for student engagement, access to social capital in the community, genuine civic engagement through Circles™ Campaigns and *Bridges* steering committees, improved business climate, and a better economy for the community.

Now we will explore specifically *how* colleges might use these tools to integrate the building of resources and sustainable communities into a systemic and holistic approach that enhances personal resources, adds to the human and social capital in the community, and prepares leaders to function successfully in their communities, as well as the larger political and economic structures of society.

CHAPTER 10

Resources and the College Campus

Colleges and universities continually strive to develop strategies to better meet the needs of their under-resourced students. Specific strategies typically have included connecting students to the campus through freshman orientation and first-year experience programming, then linking them to jobs via career pathways. Both approaches and many others can be made more real and relevant by incorporating the *Investigations into Economic Class in America* curriculum.

Reimagining Student Orientation: Using College Campus as Context for Investigating Community Resources

First-year experience programs and freshman orientation programs are intended to create a more engaging and inclusive college experience, with the longer term objective of improving retention and graduation rates. Such programs also are created for students who delayed college by a year or more after graduating from high school. Many student orientation programs divide students into subgroups based on similar characteristics, such as age, major, or interest area in which they learn more about registration and their plan of study in the context of their group. During these first-year programs, the advising of students regarding their prospective plans of study may be enhanced and more targeted based on students' needs, and students may have a "college success" course in their schedule. These experiences build a sense of belonging and social support essential to student success. Incorporating these types of experiences into required courses emphasizes their importance and keeps them from being marginalized as extracurricular. The "college readiness" agenda, however, must be supported with content and methods more relevant to under-resourced students; otherwise it might be perceived as just so much "middle-class noise" to be tuned out.

Directly teaching the hidden rules of college, for example, helps students realize that, unlike high school, *you must achieve a passing grade in a course in order to advance.* Going beyond teaching planning skills to actually modeling the semester-long planning process helps students apply this abstract concept while they also experience significant relationships. This will enable them to have the essential tools—including knowledge of hidden rules, bridging relationships, language proficiency, responsibility, and abstract thinking and analytical skills—that those in higher education often assume are operative across all social classes of society.

The *Investigations* process includes two major activities relevant to the goals of college orientation and first-year experience courses. The activities—the Personal Plan to Build Resources, along with the Community Assessment—relate directly to the goal of orienting students to the campus environment, culture, and resources. Both activities target the development of the students' internal and external resources by helping them responsibly take control of their learning, as well as access resources available on campus or off. It is important to realize that these exercises take place in the broader context of the co-investigation of economic class. Without that context, the exercises are like many others—and become far less relevant to the situated learning approach for the under-resourced student.

After completing a self-assessment of their own resources, the students begin to develop a plan for improving the resources that they determine are priorities. Later in the curriculum, the students do an investigation of community resources. This exercise can be modified to enhance orientation and first-year experience objectives by asking students to investigate campus services that contribute to building personal resources—in other words, to explicitly treat the campus itself as a community. Relating this investigation of campus services to their personal plan not only exposes students to the resources available through the school, it directly addresses the lack of intergenerational transfer of knowledge about college life with which many first-generation students must cope. At institutions where a large percentage of students are first-generation college students, the need to bridge the gap caused by the lack of knowledge transferred from family members and friends who have previously gone to college is vital to student success.

Because of their ongoing daily pressures and problems, or because they feel that the campus activities are part of a world that is "not for them," under-resourced students often do not notice student support services and related student life activities. Through the assessments in the *Investigations* curriculum, however, students examine directly how the financial aid office, student counseling services, writing and math centers, and student recreation and health centers can help them acquire the skills, resources, and support necessary to both thrive during their college years and finish school—at relatively little cost to them.

The self-assessments and community assessments in *Investigations* provide context that supports the situated learning approach upon entry to postsecondary education—and thus concretely links orientation and first-year experience to a personal plan. The curriculum helps students become more intentional in their educational efforts by helping them learn to plan and consider their own responsibility for the achievement of their goals.

In addition to building personal resources through campus services, students will be analyzing the institution and holding it accountable for protecting all its members (DeVol, 2004). This creates the conditions necessary for developing social capital and community engagement strategies described in the next two chapters.

'Career Pathways' Intentionally Addresses Needs of Under-Resourced Students

"Career pathways," which emerged in the late 1990s, is a trend in organizing education and services for low-wage and low-skill students, particularly adults. Career pathways projects are usually closely tied to labor market conditions—seeking to train the unemployed and retrain dislocated workers for jobs in high-growth or high-demand industries. Such programs respond to students who want to enter for short-term noncredit training, as well as those who may reenter multiple times for more education while also working. In order to meet the needs of this type of student, pathways programs include more intensive student services—such as case management, transportation and childcare assistance, mental health services, addiction counseling, and support for students with disabilities.

Common curricular features of career pathways programs include stackable, modularized curricula aligned with the occupational ladder to put technical/career coursework ahead of the general education requirements of degree programs. This allows students to achieve more rapid labor market payoff for their efforts—that is, finding a job in their field of choice (in some cases even before completing a two- or four-year degree).

Within these pathways programs, developmental or remedial curriculum might be contextualized around occupational training to increase relevance to the student (i.e., nursing students learning metric conversion in the context of calculating drug dosages). The problem with this approach is twofold, however. First, it presents problems of scale for smaller schools that do not have or cannot schedule full classes of developmental health and human service majors, education majors, engineering majors, etc. Second, it asks developmental education faculty to possess some level of expertise in all these areas of vocational study as well. In contrast, economic class as discussed in the *Investigations* curriculum creates a context for remedial education relevant to students in any major, as well as the instructors.

Hence, by incorporating the *Investigations* curriculum as the context for remedial education, the institution does not have to develop a multitude of occupation-specific developmental education assignments. Instead, the co-investigative process allows students to learn about the hidden rules of work and college, thereby helping them take control of their learning and become employable. By this point students understand how internal and external resources affect their success and are thus better able to self-organize and complete programs. This curriculum also provides a touchstone for students as they enter, leave, and reenter education programs because many of their peers and instructors are sharing the *Investigations* experience.

Career pathways programs tend to be prescriptive in nature and heavily invested in the righting reflex (Miller & Rollnick, 2002), the impulse to "fix" low-skilled students and produce, as rapidly as possible, employees to serve the needs of business and industry. The value of the career pathways programs may lie in the sometimes accelerated timeline for completing certificates and degrees that lead to jobs with sustainable wages. After all, it is difficult to achieve economic stability without money. The righting reflex, however, largely fails to deal with down-to-earth realities and usually interferes with the goal of developing self-regulating citizens responsible for their own learning and achievement. Some students will learn to "act" the way employers want them to act—but by not developing the knowledge bases about hidden rules and resources the student/employee will be more prone to simply *react* to stress. This reaction pattern tends to follow the familiar hidden rules of poverty, which often are not congruent with employers' expectations. As a result, another "failure" occurs.

In Sum

These college-readiness or work-readiness programs intend to connect students with local resources—on or off campus—thereby enhancing the likelihood of success. The *Investigations* curriculum offers a context for situated learning that deepens the postsecondary experience and broadens students' resolve both to be educated and to find meaningful, long-term employment—even "a career" rather than "just a job."

CHAPTER 11

Developing Human and Social Capital on the Campus and in the Community

In the middle class a driving force is achievement; this is the foundation for most higher education systems. These systems, combined with faculty and staff with limited training in working with under-resourced students, set up situations that erode or even break the relationships that students need in order to progress. Building the social capital of the campus with knowledge and skills that will support these relationships is key to sustaining the success that institutions seek for all their students. Not only will students benefit from this curriculum, so will the faculty and professional staff who commit themselves to the process. The students and the representatives of the postsecondary institutions who so engage will have the opportunity to analyze the student life cycle, which in turn leads to developing social capital for individuals, as well as the campus and even the local community. At any point in the student life cycle, if students experience a break in relationships (one of the primary driving forces for people in poverty) due to feeling disrespected, devalued, stereotyped, and/or poorly served, they will find a reason (justified or not) for leaving the system. This pattern is similar to what happens in the work setting for many people from poverty who quit their job when they get angry with someone at work (Payne, 2005b, p. 58).

The present chapter explores what a college or university might do to enhance the postsecondary work/teaching/advising experience for the faculty and staff, as well as improve the process of building social capital from the students' perspective. Benefits for faculty and staff will be found through professional development, facilitating and/or co-facilitating the curriculum, and the opportunity for continued mentoring and support for students who engage in the learning process described in this book. The second part of this chapter describes how the student life cycle can form a foundation for both students and staff to analyze and inform change. The final section describes how the *Investigations* curriculum enhances student engagement through learning communities and service learning.

Professional Development

There is growing interest and demand on many college campuses for improving the connection between teaching and learning—with research through professional development and the alignment of faculty incentives and rewards. Such initiatives for many institutions are frequently set in place for accreditation purposes, and they serve to define the need for new modes, media, and methods of contemporary instruction. Since the 1960s there has been growing interest in addressing the effects of society on the learning process. The "development culture" of higher education furthers the personal and professional growth of all members, values planning, and assumes an inherent desire for personal maturation and helping others succeed (Bergquist & Pawlak, 2008). Professional development—inclusive of faculty development to improve teaching and scholarship, instructional development to improve curricula and pedagogy, and organizational development to improve the institution's ability to support faculty and students—will enhance application of the concepts and strategies presented here.

It is very important to develop a knowledge base among faculty, staff, and administration about the framework of poverty, the constructs of economic class, the reasons class differences exist, and how resources impact students' ability to achieve academic and work goals. Faculty and staff will better understand and serve the under-resourced learners at their institution when they use the lens of economic class to design and evaluate curricula and programs. At the heart of this is building language and relationships for bridging social capital. Developing techniques for fostering mutually respectful relationships is just as applicable for program coordinators, administrators, and board members as for faculty and the institution's support staff. People who do not understand the concepts are more likely to say and do things that break relationships of mutual trust—and thus have the effect of turning some students away.

In addition to participating in workshops and seminars, individuals are encouraged to talk to students from poverty as an excellent way of building knowledge about economic class. DeVol (2004) explains how acquiring bridging social capital—relationships with people from the dominant culture—is necessary for people in poverty to further their plans for a more stable life. Likewise, members of the dominant culture, in this case postsecondary education staff, are encouraged to seek out and build mutually respectful relationships with people from poverty. This provides an authentic and ongoing source of knowledge that enables one to validate or correct perceptions and interpretations of behaviors and situations. It also allows one to witness firsthand a more free-spirited, even existential, lifestyle than many in middle class have. This is a point Payne makes in *Crossing the Tracks for Love* (2005a, pp. 127–128); there are trade-offs, regardless of one's level of wealth and station in life.

An institutional challenge in meeting these professional development goals is the prevalence of part-time faculty. Nearly two thirds of both community college students and faculty are part time (Community College Survey of Student Engagement [CCSSE], 2007). A full-time teaching load of four or five courses per semester is equivalent to 12 to 15 hours of class time per week, so a full-time instructor also is being paid for other duties, such as preparation time, committee work, student conferences, professional development, and perhaps scholarship. Part-time faculty members are paid to teach only, not for time spent conferencing with students or for preparation. They often have little or no office space, few if any expectations of participation in planning, no voice in the governance of the institution, and little or no access to professional development to improve their content mastery or teaching ability. Since part-timers tend to teach in the evening, they also may be teaching more part-time students—a type of double jeopardy of unconnected instructors attempting to assist unconnected students. Therefore, it is important for colleges to direct resources so that part-time faculty also can be engaged with their students and the campus community.

Professional development will:

- Shift emphasis from teaching to learning and outcomes, as well as support development of learning-focused classrooms (Bergquist & Pawlak, 2008).
- Reinforce some actions already under way in any given institution and catalyze new cooperative development of curricula and scholarship.
- Provide a quality assurance mechanism to address the requirements of accreditation bodies (Farrugia, 1996).

- Inspire students to acquire new knowledge about social and cultural change by observing that faculty do the same (Patterson & Longsworth, 1966).
- Create shared meaning and vocabulary that improve communication among diverse populations.

Throughout this book, the implication is that most of the faculty and staff of the institutions are middle class. Regardless of the actual background of the professors and staff, under-resourced students will tend to see them as middle class. It should be noted that a percentage of college faculty (at some schools, a very large percentage) is from generational poverty—or grew up in a low-resource environment. Equipped with the framework presented here, these instructors can be invaluable resources to the rest of the institution from the standpoint of professional and program development.

INVESTIGATIONS FACILITATORS

Facilitators for the *Investigations into Economic Class in America* co-investigation can be instructors or faculty members who are able to intentionally establish a cooperative, relational learning environment and relationships of mutual trust and respect. The role is twofold—facilitating someone else's self-discovery (not prescribing solutions to problems) and continually learning from students about the realities of their lives. Facilitators should know the theories of economic class and the causes and effects of poverty. This would include ongoing investigation of the ethnic, racial, and religious characteristics of the participating students, as well as the pertinent political and economic circumstances affecting the surrounding community. The ability to translate between the formal and casual registers is helpful, but facilitators are urged to use their own authentic voice and be cautious about using the casual register if it is not natural. Facilitators need to model the adult voice. A curious and nonjudgmental attitude also is very important (DeVol, 2004).

Further, the *Investigations* process could be co-facilitated by a previous student participant who has attended some training in facilitation skills. Training past student participants as co-facilitators and paying them for their role assigns greater value to the process and provides evidence of the school's belief that students can be change leaders. The joint effort of a faculty member with a student as co-facilitator has many benefits—both real and symbolic—to all involved. Student co-facilitators:

- Make the material more relevant
- Bridge initial distrust by students
- Build institutional capacity through creation of experts within the student body

- Build bridging social capital
- Inform the facilitator's performance
- Earn experience and respect
- Model healthy behavior and investigation skills
- Assist translation from formal to casual and casual to formal
- Follow up with students who miss classes.

Note. From *Facilitator Notes for Getting Ahead in a Just-Gettin'-By World* (p. 12), by P. E. DeVol, 2006, Highlands, TX: aha! Process. Copyright 2006 by aha! Process. Adapted with permission.

MENTORS

The last step in *Investigations'* theory of change is building partnerships with the middle class and others to create vital social support/capital. After students have gone through the *Investigations* material, they need continued support. Ideally, professional development helps establish a campus culture where almost everyone in contact with students comes from a similar frame of reference and is willing to advocate, guide, and act on behalf of students. Realistically, though, it takes time to build that level of institutional and even programmatic commitment and consistency. In the early stages, it is critical to address directly this gap in social capital by preparing staff and student mentors who are charged with helping students coordinate and act on their plans.

CIRCLES™ CAMPAIGN

One extension of the *Investigations* theories involves some communities launching Circles™ Campaigns as a major initiative for increasing social capital. A campus could join as a partner in such an effort—or even develop it within the campus community itself. Circles™ Campaigns were initiated by Move the Mountain in partnership with aha! Process to

> provide transformational leaders a structure to engage the community in ending poverty. A Circle [consists] of a family [student] working to get out of poverty and two to four community [campus] allies, people who are willing to befriend the family [students] and support their way out of poverty. The mission of the Circles™ Campaign is to transform communities by building relationships that inspire and equip people to end poverty. The vision of the Circles Campaign is: Everyone in America has reasons, relationships and resources to thrive. (*Circles Campaign,* n.d.)

In the Circles™ model, an *Investigations* graduate becomes a Circle leader and chooses a few people from middle class with whom he or she has, or wants to have, a bridging relationship. The leader calls the Circle together to meet and advises them about making progress on his or her plans to build resources. The Circle allies do not solve the problems or directly provide the resources, but they do form the bridge. Circles™ has done much work to create a program that continues the benefits of *Investigations*. There is potential for similar support and development on the campuses of many postsecondary institutions. Professional development is available through Move the Mountain.

Using the Student Life Cycle to Inform Committee Decisions

James Champy's "Customer Life Cycle" (1995) outlines the intentionally designed process or steps that customers go through in an organization to get what they want, along with their views of the experience. The idea is highly relevant to institutions seeking to better serve diverse student populations. Postsecondary institutions have complex student life cycles, ranging from the macro-level admission through graduation cycle down to the very granular level in a particular office or classroom. If one considers how the hidden rules and driving forces of economic class influence perspectives of student life cycles, the need for some changes becomes clear.

Institutions can improve students' experiences without lowering standards or expectations by changing how elements of the student life cycle are approached. To do so requires careful examination of the assumptions and needs upon which the process was created, as well as a rethinking based on an understanding of economic patterns.

❏ To analyze the student life cycle at a particular institution, begin by defining it and understanding the experience *from the student's perspective.*

Why is the student here?	*Perhaps because he or she needs skills to get a job*
What does the student want to change?	*Gain economic security, create a more stable life, do something meaningful*
How do programs make that possible?	*Programs teach skills, allow practice; services help with money*

❑ Next, map the specific student life cycle. It may be in the classroom or in a larger academic division—or perhaps a student services office, such as admissions, financial aid, or advising. Identify and map all the elements. This should include at least six elements: initial contact, intake, data collection, planning, intervention, and evaluation.

When examining each element in the student life cycle, consider the following issues:

- Who is the step designed for?
- What decisions are made at each step?
- Who, besides the student, is accountable for the internal process behind the step?
- What behaviors allow the student to progress to the next stage?
- Is this step of the life cycle difficult or easy for students? Why?
- What could make the steps more achievable?
- What expectations can be abandoned?
- What expectations must be maintained?
- Where are relationships broken?

❑ Finally, identify the policy, environmental, or programming *adjustments* that will improve the experience without lowering expectations.

An example of student life cycle elements and issues follows. It describes the overall experience of going to college—from recruitment through degree completion. The chart also gives examples of adjustments that might make the experience more positive and successful for more students.

Life Cycle in a College Course

	Course Selection Initial Contact	Enrollment/ Registration Intake
Staff roles **Time and place**		
Who is it designed for? What decisions are made at each step? Who is accountable for each internal process?	Designed for advisers Decides schedule, possibly determines major Course catalogue Academic advisers	Designed for advisers and enrollment management staff Decide whether student is academically and financially qualified to take course Accountability varies Student is held accountable if registration is incorrect
Procedures and expectations		
What behaviors allow student to progress to next stage?	Student decides to enroll, accepts schedule, pays fees	Must be in good standing academically and financially Must pay fees
Environmental, economic, cultural issues		
Is this part of life cycle difficult for students? Where are relationships broken?	Problem areas include uninformed advisers, course catalogues that are difficult to access and use Student may have no knowledge of school's processes Potential key relationship with adviser	Paperwork or computerized processes may be difficult to understand Rudeness from staff can be deterrent
Policy, environment, and programming adjustments		
What could make them more achievable? What behaviors can be abandoned as expectations? What expectations must be maintained?	Peer advising, mentors, buddy systems Video and online video demonstrations of how to choose course schedules Need to maintain quality control for advising staff	Staff development to build understanding of socioeconomic class and how to build mutually respectful relationships Consider ways to work around issues Actual registration of student is necessary for tracking progress

First Class: In-Class Assessment Data Collection	Explanation of Syllabus Planning	Delivery of Course Content Intervention	Testing and Grading Intervention/ Evaluation
Staff roles			
Time and place			
Designed to help instructor assess student's and class's ability May influence assignments, teaching style, and timeline for course delivery Instructor is accountable	Syllabus designed to hold student and instructor accountable Instructor is accountable for providing; student is accountable for understanding	Courses should be designed for students Student is accountable for mastering material Instructor often is not held accountable Decisions to persist or drop course or withdraw along the way	Tests designed for students; grading systems designed for institutions Determines student's ability to advance Faculty responsible for administration of tests and grading
Procedures and expectations			
Student only has to take test Student may be unsure of purpose and impact of test	NA	Pass exams, complete assignments Meet with instructor, seek tutoring or support services	Students must pass tests and other assessment measures
Environmental, economic, cultural issues			
Difficulty depends on student's academic mastery Instructor's attitude toward student performance is critical to relational learning environment	Middle-class "noise" and importance and significance of syllabus If instructor is not willing to explain, relationship is broken	Student-teacher relationships of respect and trust are paramount	Many under-resourced students have experienced failure in K–12 systems Without support, insistence, and high expectations from instructor, students may repeat old patterns
Policy, environment, and programming adjustments			
Clarify purpose of test (assessment) and its impact (not part of grade)	Orally review syllabus in class, post on website As course progresses, cross off objectives that have been achieved	Professional development to teach relational learning models and build understanding of causes and effects of poverty Reward instructors for student success Maintain academic rigor and quality-assurance measures	Holistic portfolio assessments Grade also for process Teach input, elaboration, and output skills

EXAMPLES OF STUDENT LIFE CYCLE ADJUSTMENTS THAT CORRESPOND TO ISSUES OF ECONOMIC CLASS

The following suggestions are intended to improve retention, engagement, and graduation by addressing corresponding economic class issues and effects. They require new skill sets for faculty, staff, and administrators, as well as rethinking who should be involved in program design. As the CCSSE (2007) found, engagement does not happen by accident.

Recruitment

Under-resourced students are accustomed to receiving a plethora of forms, brochures, and other printed materials from agencies. Generally speaking, all that thoughtfully produced material is not necessary for actually accessing the agency services, hence it is often ignored. Access is usually obtained through the individual service provider, such as an actual recruitment officer, or by learning how it is done from another person—in other words, relationships.

Similarly, in college recruitment, many handouts or mailings, no matter how carefully written, can be replaced with videos of or phone calls from real students from generational poverty telling their stories of how they decided to go to school, how they built resources, how they completed a credential, and how they achieved an occupational and social payoff. Further, at events at high schools and employment centers live testimonials from actual students give potential applicants a chance to ask questions of someone more like themselves. Remembering the importance of people and relationships to the under-resourced students, these face-to-face interactions with current students or even graduates bring validation and credibility to the recruitment process that otherwise would be largely irrelevant to them.

Financial aid

Institutions are recognizing that financial aid favors the full-time student, making it more difficult for working adults to finance their education. In fact, 18 states in the United States offer no grants to part-time students (Jaschik, 2008). Lack of funding for critical developmental education courses is another barrier. In addition, students are vulnerable to aggressive credit card companies and predatory student loans. Almost all students, regardless of background, lack the financial literacy to create (on their own) good financial plans and practices to support their education. The financial barriers to postsecondary education are large for many students, and making errors in this area has long-term implications.

Examining the student life cycle within the context of the financial aid office will reveal numerous opportunities to help students build financial resources. Staff development in hidden rules of money and power, language, and relationship building is critical in any institution of higher education in order to build and maintain relationships that lead to graduation. They are more likely to be retained when they avoid pitfalls, including the impulse to simply give up when things seem frustrating. For example, colleges can engage students in the investigation of how to finance their college goals in the context of how to avoid predatory lenders. A proactive financial aid office can become a champion for building financial literacy programs for students.

Admissions

Students from generational poverty have likely had negative experiences with middle-class institutions and may tend to distrust them. In order to obtain such benefits as food stamps, emergency cash assistance, childcare help, and financial aid, people are required to reveal intimate details of their lives and their crises over and over again, putting them in a submissive position in relation to the dominant culture. While it might not be possible in all cases to eliminate a college department's need to collect information and determine the students' needs and eligibility, an important improvement can be made by using technology to create a common data collection process so that students don't have to give the same information repeatedly to each department in the institution. This is not a new idea; the technology is readily available. Nevertheless, the barriers may include staff persons who are more comfortable doing things "the way we always have"—plus there is the cost of the technology and human resources to initially set up and expedite the new system. Whether or not the technology changes, it is imperative that, at the institutional level, staff development about economic class includes student services personnel from all departments so that the importance of the change is known and made a priority.

Placement testing

Within the student life cycle at each institution, it is wise to investigate how many agencies (both on and off campus) under-resourced students are dealing with that require testing. For instance, local employment agencies, literacy programs, and welfare offices may require students to take the same or similar tests that the college requires for placement in order to determine eligibility for training dollars. In many cases this process is a barrier because students who may have struggled with standardized testing then are given the message that they are deficient.

One improvement that might result from this investigation would be to develop agreements with agencies to use the same tests, align the tests, or create a crosswalk between the results to reduce the amount of testing a student must undergo. In addition to easing the way for the student, such partnerships can save the institution(s) money. Until that is possible, those dealing with students who are "overtested" should at least acknowledge the inconvenience and stress created by these "hidden rules of college" and provide testing times and places convenient to all students.

Advising

There is as much variation in advising as there are institutions; therefore, this process would benefit from life cycle mapping. Advising provides another major opportunity to build critical social capital resources and to connect students to other services. Of course, the converse is possible: Breaking critical relationships has the effect of driving students away. Therefore, it is essential to apply relational and cognitive learning methods to the advising process. The communication skills and knowledge of the advisers should be regularly developed to ensure that all advisers utilize their training with under-resourced students and are aware of the resources on the campus that can best serve the students. Training faculty and staff who help students navigate the institution and troubleshoot crises is a proven practice.

Some campuses are adopting a case management approach and using success coaches for the higher risk students. Others use advisement coordinators who follow the first-time and developmental student until the student achieves a benchmark (Brock et al., 2007). Also, early warning systems may be put in place to help advisers monitor progress and intervene before negative consequences accrue. A "one stop" center that combines advising with counseling and tutoring increases accessibility. Frequency, timing, and location of advising sessions impact access for students and, hence, effectiveness.

Transfer policies

Under-resourced students tend to be drawn to two-year, for-profit schools because of condensed coursework and relatively short "time to degree." Students who have attended for-profit institutions, however, often have difficulty getting their credits accepted by accredited institutions. Many students, especially first-generation college students, do not understand the implications of transfer policies and frequently have to repeat coursework because of it. Even public two- and four-year institutions within the same state are not required, as a rule, to accept each other's credits.

Institutions that want to increase students' success and build their resources as they progress to graduation will support efforts to standardize and publicize transfer agreements and improve student advising. Gateway institutions in states without central control have an obligation to proactively advise and guide students' course choices, as well as provide ongoing monitoring of their educational goals to account for changes. Complicated and difficult credit transfer is an example of the sorts of public policy issues that perpetuate poverty by making educational achievement more difficult for students lacking the transgenerational knowledge about the hidden rules of college.

Scheduling

All student services should be made available to part-time and working students due to students' financial resources, work schedules, and family responsibilities. Evening and weekend hours are not just for coursework anymore. Students benefit from financial aid, admissions, and advising services during "after work" hours, remembering that some students are employed during variable shifts throughout the month—not just the 9 to 5 workday (CCSSE, 2007). Similarly, extended library and computer lab access, especially during academic breaks and on commuter campuses, is helpful (McSwain & Davis, 2007). Much as public libraries are open evenings and weekends, so campus offices that specialize in student services might be kept open more hours in order to accommodate a broader cross-section of both full- and part-time students.

Creating Engaging Environments

Under-resourced students with multiple commitments in addition to school usually have little time or energy to engage in the campus community—be it co-curricular activities, informal networking, or studying with other students or staff. Yet CCSSE (2007) found that engagement matters more for under-resourced students than for others. The data showed that high-risk students actually were more engaged (by their measures) than lower risk students. CCSSE suggests this occurs because academically unprepared and otherwise under-resourced students *must* get engaged in order to make the same progress as lower risk students. Therefore, CCSSE recommends that colleges maximize engagement efforts for at-risk students. Institutions must be intentional and aggressive in designing programs so that being engaged has relevance and meaning to all students and "is not what students do, but what students are" (CCSSE, 2007).

One impression gleaned from the literature review is that sometimes it is a special instructor who creates that engaging chemistry, infuses the students with his or her own passion for learning, creates the excitement and joy of discovery, and produces "off the chart" results. But such personality-based approaches cannot work on a broader scale. The *Investigations* curriculum provides a catalyst for the so-called "fire in the belly" that accelerates student engagement and learning at multiple levels. The curriculum generates such a high level of motivation and excitement because it is so relevant to the students. They succeed, and they make major strides in their attitude toward higher education. Using *Investigations* as the contextual cornerstone for learning communities and service learning creates the conditions for authentic civic engagement that does not necessarily require students to plan activities outside the class schedule. The importance and interactive nature of these two learning milieus are addressed in the remainder of this chapter.

Learning communities are a method of creating social support among cohort groups of students who take the same set of courses together during their first semester (for example, composition, psychology, and an orientation course) and perhaps beyond. Using *Investigations* as the context for coursework in (developmental or freshman level) reading, study skills/college success, and composition courses builds a common language and usually reveals some common life experiences and goals for the students. (However, given the intentional design of the sequence within the curriculum, instructors are asked to consider how to integrate their course objectives within *Investigations* rather than attempting to integrate it into an existing course. The distinction here is significant.)

In such a learning community, participants not only learn reading and study skills by reading books, essays, and articles about economic justice, they also acquire and use deeper theoretical knowledge and vocabulary to support group discussions. A composition course then teaches students to support their ideas with research and "translate" the casual register of language used during class discussion to the formal register required for school and careers. Such a process moves students from the concrete, present-focused thinking that results from growing up and living in lower resourced situations to the abstract critical thinking and analysis of college-level students and educated citizens. This concentrated examination of relevant topics across several courses for an entire semester (or longer) allows students to develop deeper and broader skills in analytical thinking, problem solving, and written and oral communication. Thinking, talking, and writing repeatedly about the same personally relevant subject matter effectively moves students out of sensory and emotionally based processes into metacognition. In the *Investigations* experience students are taught how to think about their thinking. They create mental models and return to them to check for accuracy and changes. By the end of a term, most students will have achieved some level of epistemic cognition whereby they can use theories of economic class to analyze unfamiliar situations and material. These skills are prerequisites for civic engagement.

Through learning communities, the strategies of team teaching and project-based assignments may further integrate curricula and increase faculty-to-faculty interaction, as well as faculty-to-student interaction. Some learning community programs try to keep students together for at least two courses for a second term; this, however, presents scheduling challenges. In a follow-up term, a service learning component would offer the opportunity to put theory into practice.

Service learning pairs academic content with engagement in related civic activities, often through nonprofit agencies. Students are frequently asked to do reflective writing assignments to connect their thoughts and feelings about the engagement experience as a part of a service learning course for college credit. Service learning serves to promote leadership development, along with more active civic engagement.

Service learning courses and assignments can be used to build and sustain the campus conversation about economic class, providing students with opportunities to test theories and to practice leadership skills first developed during the semester spent immersed in the *Investigations* curriculum. In essence, the framework of economic class provides a relevant construct within which to analyze and act, while the *Investigations* process offers the vehicle that moves students from situated problem solving to abstract analysis and planning.

Adjustments such as these create a campus climate in tune with the resources of all students. Staff that has been educated about economic class will relate to students more effectively and foster the bridging social capital that students need in order to be successful. Further opportunities for students to develop social capital and feel connected to the campus will have positive effects—on them personally and the community at large.

CHAPTER 12

Beyond the Classroom—Fostering Student Engagement with Sociopolitical and Economic Structures

As discussed in Chapter 7, higher education prepares students to become responsible citizens in the community, including the political and economic structures that make up society. Postsecondary programs, however, are not known for confronting this issue directly. Because, historically, higher education was developed to educate the children from the dominant culture(s), it has not been necessary until relatively recently for institutions to deal with this larger picture. Most students from the dominant cultures already know the hidden rules of the middle class that govern education and business. Further, these students generally have access to the political and economic structures due to their membership in the dominant culture and so could apply their college or university education and go on to practice good citizenship. Institutions can take a more intentional approach to directly building the knowledge and skills necessary to help under-resourced students engage with the community and the political and economic structures that govern society.

College personnel might envision a progression of activities, beginning with the engagement of students within the campus community and moving toward assignments in the external community to prepare students for involvement in policy issues. The preceding chapter looked at the student life cycle from the perspective of the *institution* making changes in order to better serve students—building social capital on campus. In this chapter, the *student* becomes the change agent within the student life cycle (and campus policies) in the context of service learning or a community engagement model. This intermediate step prior to service learning and community engagement programs with *external* partners gives students the opportunity to practice skills in an environment where a greater proportion of individuals is informed about both economic class and the intentionally designed program(s) being implemented.

Students as Problem Solvers and Program Designers

Encouraging students to investigate the degree to which the college meets its obligations to students by using the campus as the context—or even laboratory—for the investigation of community (i.e., campus) resources could have a salutary secondary impact on the institution's student services. Students who have completed the *Investigations* coursework might investigate aspects of the student life cycle and assess the school's capacity to serve under-resourced students, thereby contributing solutions for the redesign of programs. In such an educational construct, students experientially practice and develop skills that prepare them to participate in planning—skills necessary for responsible civic engagement, a possible further result of the work with the *Investigations* curriculum.

Including under-resourced students in the decision-making process benefits both the students and the college. Though colleges frequently form committees to design programs to serve students, it is only the occasional committee that actually calls for student representation. Often this is not implemented, or the chosen students come from the dominant class, members of which already are in possession of the hidden rules and resources for success. Under-resourced students can become a program's or an institution's most valuable asset in the design/redesign of policies, environment, processes, and programs. Problems must be accurately identified to keep solutions focused and relevant, as well as to avoid "deficit thinking" and practice. The under-resourced students who did not know the rules when they came to college are uniquely able to identify the root causes of pitfalls and traps that undermine the ability of programs to meet their needs, along with the needs of students with similar demographics. The *Investigations* graduates bring practical solutions and insights that can help schools address the effects of poverty on the under-resourced student. As the institution benefits from student input, students gain relationships and experiences that create bridging social capital and access to one of the political and economic structures that influence stability: the postsecondary institution itself.

Including students on committees and work teams is an excellent way to provide an experiential learning environment in which they can observe the language and behaviors of others—and practice leadership, teamwork, planning, relationship, and communication skills. Students should be informed as to the purpose of the committee and who the members are. There also should be at least one designated committee member who will help the students process what is happening on the committee. One way to cultivate this experience is for a class to engage in committee work as a service learning assignment. Perhaps the service learning committee is charged with analyzing the student life cycle within the admissions office and making recommendations for change where problems are identified. One student or the student co-facilitator could then present the findings of the service learning committee to the larger college committee. For the student to have had experience with committee work through a service learning course assignment, prior to working on an actual campus or community committee, builds the student's confidence and competence.

Another way to cultivate this experience would be to pay students for committee work outside class time, just as faculty and staff are compensated for their time around the planning table. Such an increase in meaningful campus work experience advances the engagement agenda addressed in the next chapter and offers students real-life experiences and résumé-building opportunities—thereby supporting the future stories of the students involved.

The campus itself becomes the socioeconomic case study or laboratory when students are viewed as problem *solvers* engaged in solution seeking. Students practice skills and engage in planning within an actual institution. All this can happen in class or as assignments in a course with content-appropriate research topics. Meanwhile, the institution taps into the wealth of knowledge and ideas of the students themselves that otherwise would go unrecognized and unused. Such an approach would be considered a *high-impact strategy* by Move the Mountain Leadership (MTM) Center. MTM defines high-impact strategies as affecting:

- The way people think and what they believe
- The goals of a system
- The rules of the system
- The ability of people to organize themselves

When the faculty and staff have been trained in theories of economic class and cognitive and relational teaching models—and students investigate economic class in a learning community that includes community engagement assignments within the campus setting—then the institution has created an environment that provides under-resourced students authentic access to the power structures that govern institutions. It also has created the conditions for constructive and positive change.

Developing the Institution's Role in Achieving Community Sustainability

By this time it should be clear that no service learning program or learning community alone, no matter how well crafted, will bring about significant levels of *systemic* change or have real impact on the underlying issues related to poverty. Instructors and student services personnel can be agents of change and work with under-resourced students to improve their *personal* economic status through education and work. The results of this synergy can indeed create beneficial *institutional* changes.

But what about the institution's *macro* obligation to the local community and larger society? Whether it is called "the equity agenda" or "economic justice," postsecondary institutions can in fact make major contributions to ending poverty. This book describes a framework that institutions can use to become fully engaged in the process of ending poverty. All the steps along the way—from educating faculty and staff about economic class to relational learning methods to designing the use of *Investigations* to developing assignments that require students to practice using new resources—can become part of an intentional, planned, institutional approach to community sustainability. For that subset of faculty and staff interested in this level of institutional engagement, the ensuing discussion is offered.

Naturally, engagement efforts would be well served by an active steering committee. In recent years many communities with a critical mass of people who have been educated in *Framework* or *Bridges Out of Poverty* concepts have organized *Bridges* steering committees to provide the necessary organizational structure for coordinated efforts. These steering committees lend themselves to action plans in four areas.

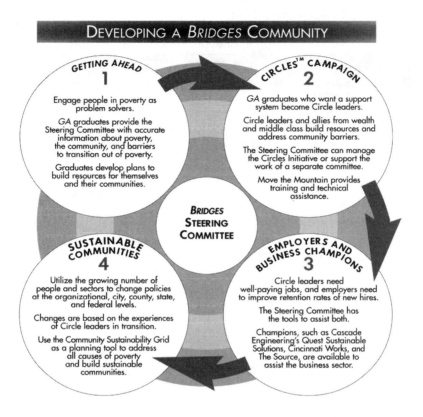

Note. From "Building Bridges Communities" (p. 10), by P. E. DeVol, 2008. Copyright 2008 by aha! Process. Adapted with permission.

Bridges steering committees are built around the core *Bridges* (DeVol, 2004) theories and are intentionally inclusive of people from all sectors, economic classes, and political persuasions. Faculty and administrators from colleges are valuable members of the committees, and *Getting Ahead in a Just-Gettin'-By World* graduates are included. The energy and experience that *Getting Ahead* grads bring to the table can serve as both guiding light and litmus test when setting priorities and establishing strategies.

There is no single prescription for how steering committees form or are organized, but generally speaking, communities that have them also have:

- Educated a critical number of people in *Bridges* constructs
- Conducted *Getting Ahead* in one form or another such that people from poverty have learned *Bridges* theories and are able to use the hidden rules of class to navigate society
- Identified one or more champions—individuals at agencies, schools, courts, hospitals, and businesses who apply *Bridges* constructs in connection with their work.

College Community Sustainability Grid:
How colleges can directly address the recurring predictable patterns—within
the four causes of poverty—through education, services, and policy

	Individual Behavior: Resources for Individual	Human and Social Capital in Community
INDIVIDUAL ACTION: INSTRUCTION		
Entering student	Placement testing Transfer credit Developmental education First-year experience	Advising First-year experience Learning communities

Investigations:
can be integrated
with all of above
	Interesting, engaging, affirming
	  entry to college
	Build personal resources
	Become Circle leader
		Help identify external resources and support to
		  build internal resources

All students	Coursework emphasizes
	  language and communication
	  skills
	Career pathways
		Coursework emphasizes language and
		  communication skills
		Team projects
		Service learning

Faculty	Cognitive teaching strategies	Relational teaching methods Circle allies
ORGANIZATIONAL ACTION: STUDENT SERVICES		

	Recruitment, admissions, and
	  financial aid all seek to open
	  doors
		Advising
		First responders
		Health services
		Circle allies

COMMUNITY ACTION: PARTNERSHIPS		

	Service learning experience,
	  internships
		Bring essential services to campus—Workforce
		  Investment Act (WIA)
		Temporary Assistance to Needy Families
		  (TANF), childcare, transportation
		Circle allies

BUSINESS ACTION		

	Work experience, internships	Community engagement models
		Service learning
		Assign to students business ambassadors who
		  are placed at worksite
		Encourage local businesses to adopt strategies
		  that use *Bridges* constructs
		Circle allies

POLICY		

	Classroom policies, due dates
	Grading options
	Use of rubrics for grading, choice
	Consistent transfer policies
	Provide credit for prior learning
	Provide more work/study
	Increase scholarship awards
		Scheduling of services and courses on
		  evenings and weekends
		Promote and provide support for
		  Circles™

Exploitation	Political and Economic Structures
INDIVIDUAL ACTION: INSTRUCTION	
Assistance with student loans to avoid exploitation	Volunteer in "Get out the vote" campaigns Vote
Expose role of predators and exploitation	Prepare students for active civic engagement as change agents
Coursework on economic justice, diversity, racism, sexism, and under-represented groups	Coursework examines political, social, and economic structures
Advocate for professional development opportunities for all instructors	Partner with other practitioners of economic justice Join *Bridges* steering committee
ORGANIZATIONAL ACTION: STUDENT SERVICES	
Financial literacy workshops offered frequently	Partner with other practitioners of economic justice Join *Bridges* steering committee
COMMUNITY ACTION: PARTNERSHIPS	
Provide financial literacy, alternative credit opportunities, Individual Development Accounts (IDAs), revolving loans	Invest resources in the campus as economic driver Join *Bridges* steering committee
BUSINESS ACTION	
Influence banks to provide fair loans	Create partnerships with education Partner with other practitioners of economic justice Invest resources in campus community as economic driver Join *Bridges* steering committee
POLICY	
Remove charges for developmental education Monitor for predatory business practices on campus	Students, staff, and faculty representing economic diversity on committees Board of trustees Include more conditional admission students if not open-enrollment school

Returning to the concept that a college campus is, in and of itself, a community within a community, some might see potential for a steering committee within the campus community. In this model, the micro committee can work intensively within the college environment to improve services, increase the success of students from poverty through *Investigations* and Circles™, and address policies and their effects on students from poverty. If this were done, it would be even more important for the college to be intentional about maintaining and building contacts with the "outside" community, as the micro committee strategy would likely feed any institutional tendencies toward insularity.

Regardless of the level of the committee, the Community Sustainability Grid (aha! Process, 2007) is a helpful tool. This is a planning tool to take inventory about what is being done in a community (or on a campus or within an agency) to address poverty. The College CSG depicts the individual actions by faculty and staff, the organizational actions through student services, and the community partnerships and policy work that are generated by this model within the microcosmic college community. All four causes of poverty are addressed, and the actions taken relate directly to the circumstances and needs of under-resourced students on campus. Communities and, more recently, colleges have been working to apply Payne's and DeVol's concepts of sharing knowledge regarding how to develop this model, given the unique culture in higher education.

The College CSG points out areas of both strengths and challenges. It helps all the stakeholders on a campus (for example, the students themselves, instructors, senior faculty, managers and administrators, academics, and student services personnel) see their current role and create new paradigms for themselves and the institution. Using the grid may mitigate the concern some staff might have at the idea of allowing students to participate in planning and oversight. Likewise, the grid can reduce anxiety students also may have. The grid shows how applying each student's problem-solving skills to the student life cycle helps the institution—and also how education helps that same student evolve to abstract analyzing and proactive planning, thus becoming a change agent rather than a subject or object. Finally, the grid shows the many integrated parts of society that work together to foster economic justice.

In Sum

So far we have looked closely at students and helped them look closely at themselves and the community. This develops the student *as* a student—and helps both students and college staff understand and relate better to one another.

Next, this understanding was applied, via the institution, to improving the student life cycle so that students have a better experience and achieve what they intended to achieve.

Then we asked the student to examine the institution as a microcosm of the larger society—to assess, analyze, and create plans to improve the institution's ability to create a sustainable community that supports all of its constituents.

Subsequently, we asked the institution to examine its role in the larger society—and measure its contribution to staff development and community sustainability.

In the final chapter we will examine ways to develop the partnerships necessary to support students and coursework, as well as to engage the institution more meaningfully with the wider community.

CHAPTER 13

Developing Community Partnerships

Payne's *Framework* (2005b) offers economic class as a prism for viewing complex issues and reshaping education, particularly within the context of the K–12 classroom. DeVol applied this knowledge to agencies and conceived of the research continuum as a way to explore the role of the individual, community, and society at large in the creation of economic stability and wealth. Throughout this book, the reader has learned new skills to teach and work with under-resourced postsecondary students, including ways to analyze and redesign programs and curricula that build students' capacities to predict and define problems and conceptualize solutions. All this has been done with the intention of improving the experience of all postsecondary students by building the institution's retention, persistence, and graduation rates, as well as understanding and honoring differences among students and faculty alike.

This last chapter of the book closes the loop for faculty, program staff, and/or administrators who see the potential to integrate the work of *Framework, Bridges Out of Poverty, Getting Ahead in a Just-Gettin'-By World,* and *Investigations into Economic Class in America* into activities that engage under-resourced learners with the larger community around the causes—and solutions—regarding poverty. For staff members who want to support the student both during *and* after the educational experience, making additional efforts to collaborate with community partners will strengthen this balanced, holistic approach to community sustainability. A deeper level of success and a more profound impact on both the individual and the community can be realized through effective collaboration. Colleges and their partners can extend the concept of the student life cycle to include postgraduation employment, lifelong learning, and civic engagement activity. While identifying partner agencies that relate to these goals is relatively straightforward, building the collaboration necessary to make a service learning or community engagement experience educational and productive is more complex.

Partnering to Provide Service Learning or Improve Student Life Cycles

The initial factor to consider in choosing a partnership is the purpose of the partnership. If the intent is to establish a service learning assignment or course, the partnership needs to connect the service learning experience to course content—and also needs to have students critically reflect and respond to the experience. In an institution that has adopted the *Investigations* curriculum, connecting service learning experiences to economic issues allows students to continue to build their causal models in a community of students with shared language and relationships established through the earlier study of economic class. For example, the service learning project in a health education course might put students into a federally funded clinic where, in addition to practicing health education skills, they analyze disparities in access to healthcare pertaining to economic class. A service learning assignment for education majors offers rich possibilities for students to see firsthand the systemic issues affecting the K–12 system related to public school funding, such as inadequate facilities; under-prepared teachers; pay inequities; and a lack of resources for nutrition, sports, art, and music programs, etc.

From the student services perspective, community partnerships might provide support and resources while the student is in school. Examples would be working with job retraining programs to increase financial resources for school and providing childcare, transportation, and tutoring services—or providing social services application processes and even entire programs on campus.

Whether the goal is to provide relevant service learning assignments or to improve elements of the student life cycle, the four steps necessary for effective partnerships are largely the same. These steps are shown below, followed by a description of each element.

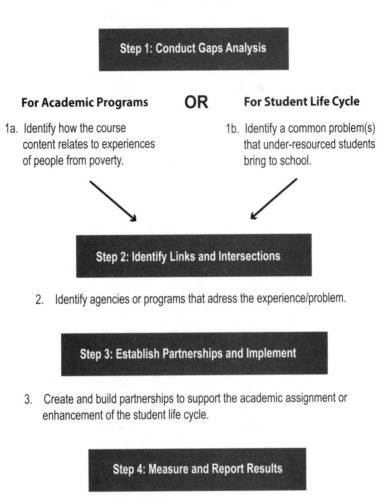

Steps to Establishing Community Partnerships for
Academic Programming or the Student Life Cycle

STEP 1A. CONDUCT A GAPS ANALYSIS FOR ACADEMIC PROGRAMMING

Almost every academic course can address one or more topics related to economic class. To incorporate aspects of economic class into an academic course, begin by identifying how the course content relates to the experiences of people in poverty. The following table gives examples of the kinds of experiences that could be explored in discipline-specific coursework.

Academic Subject	Experiences of People in Poverty
Education	Literacy, achievement gaps, remediation, school violence, low-quality schools and/or teachers, busing, charter schools, cost of college/university, poorly funded schools in poor neighborhoods
Healthcare professions	Infant mortality, prenatal care, teen/unplanned pregnancy, diabetes, hypertension, depression, substance abuse, access to healthcare, cost of healthcare
Social services professions	Income stabilization, hunger, domestic violence, child/elder abuse, job skills, homelessness, childcare, prevention programs of all types, transportation, inadequate housing, non-profit leadership
English	Language experience, literacy
Geography	Immigration, neighborhood resources/problems
Psychology	Mental health, gambling, relationships
Sociology	Family structure, immigration, racism and discrimination, sex trade, gender issues
Economics	Social services/minimum wage trap, arithmetic of poverty
Business	Subprime lending and predatory lending, downsizing/outsourcing, wage structures, dead-end jobs, temporary jobs, corporate investment in communities, redlining, migrant workers, Internet scams, organizational management, abstract paper world
Political science	Voting rights, representation, affirmative action, racism, sexism, discrimination, poorly funded schools, exploitation of natural resources
Criminal justice	Crime, gangs, courts, sentencing guidelines, minimum sentences, penal system, diversion programs
Computer science	Digital divide

These topics also can become issues of discussion within campus student services, as well as via student government organizations seeking to implement change on campus.

STEP 1B. CONDUCT GAPS ANALYSIS FOR STUDENT LIFE CYCLE IMPROVEMENT

To build partnerships that will improve the student life cycle, begin by identifying common problem(s) that many under-resourced students bring to campus. The experiences of people in poverty in the right-hand column of the preceding chart also might emerge during the mapping of student life cycles as problems facing students during school or after graduation. It is important to gather both quantitative and qualitative data to determine what issues have the greatest negative impact on student success, including their root cause(s). Perceptions are often different from the reality of the situation. For example, officials in Chicago Public Schools discovered that the single most significant predictor of their students entering a four-year college or university was whether they had completed the Free Application for Federal Student Aid (Roderick et al., 2008). Another example from CCSSE found that students didn't want to take developmental courses at a college, not because of cost or time, but because students perceived the quality of instruction to be poor in the developmental courses (CCSSE, 2007). Identifying root causes allows for strategies that speak to the problem. Regardless of whether the partnership is intended to deal with academic or support issues, the next step is finding potential partners.

STEP 2. IDENTIFY AGENCIES OR PROGRAMS THAT ADDRESS THE DESIRED EXPERIENCE (LINKS AND INTERSECTIONS)

The types of agencies or businesses chosen for partnering will be determined by:

1. The discipline
2. The purpose of the class or assignments or
3. The gap in the student life cycle at the institution, discovered in Step 1.

The following Community Sustainability Grid (CSG) gives examples of the kinds of agencies and programs typically engaged in addressing issues related to the four areas on the poverty research continuum. These are some of the partners and programs that can provide service learning and community engagement experiences for an academic course—or supplement student services to improve the student life cycle.

Sample Agencies/Activities Addressing Poverty Along the Research Continuum

	Behavior of the Individual	Human and Social Capital in Community
INDIVIDUAL ACTION		
	S.C.O.R.E., volunteer services	Circles™ Campaign
ORGANIZATIONAL ACTION		
Social and public welfare agencies	Welfare, Work First, gang prevention, credit counseling, housing projects, Section 8, abstinence/marriage incentives, parenting programs, domestic violence prevention, child support	Department of Job & Family Services, Work First, homeless shelters, childcare
Education	Schools, dropout prevention, early reading, basic literacy	Head Start, after-school programs, busing, career pathways, community colleges, parent/teacher associations/organizations, YWCA, Boys & Girls Clubs
Employment and workforce development	Vocational training, on-the-job training, retention programs	Workforce training, one-stop centers
Mental health and substance abuse	Addiction programs, drug courts	Mental health boards, prevention programs
Health	WIC (Women, Infants, & Children) programs, Planned Parenthood, food banks, crisis hotlines	Health department, Second Harvest, wellness programs, community gardens
Religion	Salvation Army	Faith-based organizations, churches, mosques, synagogues, etc.
COMMUNITY ACTION		
Economic and community development	Diversity programs	Neighborhood associations, Crime Stoppers, planning departments, community action agencies, Circles™ Campaign, transportation, small-business development
Business and industry	Employment, tuition reimbursement programs, internships and apprenticeships	Chamber of Commerce
POLICY		
Local, state, and national policy	Earned-income tax credit	Workforce Investment (WIA); local control

Exploitation	Political and Economic Structures
INDIVIDUAL ACTION	
	Bridges steering committee
ORGANIZATIONAL ACTION	
Consumer credit offices	Immigration reform
Free college guarantee, government grants and loans	Political and social science centers at universities
	WIA
Drug trafficking prevention	Courts, sentencing
	National health insurance
COMMUNITY ACTION	
Recycling, environmental programs, community development programs	Social Health Index (SHI)
Benefit programs for less than full time, fair-credit programs	Lobbyists, PACs (political action committees), labor unions, industry associations
POLICY	
Affirmative action, Medicaid/Medicare, redistricting	Political parties, tax policy, living-wage movement, right to vote, immigration

Locating community partners

While relationships may already exist between the college and community partners, some institutions are so large it is difficult to keep track of the many relationships. Further, in some cases, the existing relationship may have nothing to do with needs revealed in the gaps analysis. For faculty and staff less familiar with community agencies and programs, the following suggestions are offered to help locate community partnerships:

- ❑ Through local one-stop employment office (formerly known as the "unemployment office," this agency goes by different names in different states/areas, but generally the workers there are knowledgeable about the social services referral network, as well as active businesses in the area)
- ❑ City or regional planning departments
- ❑ Crisis line or 411 information line
- ❑ Faculty in social services, human services, or health-related fields
- ❑ Contacts in the K–12 system or teacher education faculty
- ❑ Yellow Pages listings by:
  - Agency type (i.e., substance abuse, mental health, literacy, etc.)
  - City planning department
  - Chamber of Commerce
  - Labor unions
  - State departments, such as:
    - Development
    - Job and family services
    - Education
    - Board of regents
    - Secretary of state

Other examples of service learning partnerships addressing economic class issues

The Community College National Center on Student Engagement's (CCNCSE) Accent on Student Success: Engaged Together in Service (ASSETS) is sponsoring 10 service learning projects that provide examples of connecting academic studies to service learning around issues of economic class ("Accent on Student Success," n.d.).

For example, the Borough of Manhattan Community College (BMCC) partnered with the Office of the Superintendent of Manhattan High Schools to address the growing trend of excessive credit card debt and student loan balances among college students. The BMCC Office of Student Affairs, accounting faculty, Center for Continuing Education and Workforce Development, and the Financial Planning Association of New York planned a financial literacy workshop for college students. Twenty workshop participants will subsequently be chosen and trained as financial literacy ambassadors (FLAs), will be mentored by a member of the business community, and will participate in service learning by teaching New York City high school students what they have learned. This includes visits to financial institutions where high school students open accounts and see loan application processes ("Accent on Student Success," n.d.). In this project more experienced college students are able to share their newfound knowledge with younger students who may be facing similar financial troubles as they enroll in colleges and universities. The college students, the high school students, and the community benefit from this educational process as students learn to stay out of financial debt.

In another example, Gateway Community College in Phoenix developed plans to use classes in Geographic Information Systems to identify and map high-need areas surrounding the college. College students' aptitudes, abilities, and values will be assessed at the Workforce Transition Center. Students will then be assigned to schools or agencies based on the assessment results. Social work classes will concentrate on organizational management, social policy, and/or economic development; the bilingual nursing program will provide healthcare education to residents; and students with talent in math and science will tutor elementary school students ("Accent on Student Success," n.d.).

STEP 3. CREATE AND BUILD PARTNERSHIPS TO SUPPORT ACADEMIC ASSIGNMENT OR ENHANCEMENT OF STUDENT LIFE CYCLE

Once the gap has been defined and a potential partner identified, the partnership must be developed. This is a multistage process, with each stage evolving in its own way and requiring ongoing stewardship.

Defining the nature of the partnership

Any partner relationship works better if all partners share a common understanding of each other's roles, responsibilities, and expectations. A frequent problem when building partnerships is the lack of common understanding of the relationship, usually caused by assumptions that understandings already exist. Because the roles, responsibilities, and expectations may naturally change and evolve—or may need to be purposely changed over time—a useful routine in a partnership is to regularly revisit these as committees and subcommittees meet and interact.

In considering the type of partner relationship to create, be it part of an academic course or part of the student life cycle, it is helpful to reflect on the level of involvement necessary from each partner to create successful teamwork. Paul Mattessich, Marta Murray-Close, Barbara Monsey, and the Wilder Research Center (2004) categorize three important distinctions in levels of partnerships: coordination, cooperation, and collaboration.

Committee members from both teams in the partnership may use the chart below as a planning and communication tool to assess whether everyone is on the same page regarding expectations and assumptions. For the sake of discussion and creating a transparent atmosphere, all members are encouraged to "locate" their perception of the evolving partnership in the following chart. Discussion regarding differences and similarities in members' perceptions helps the partners come to consensus about where the partnership is and how to further develop it for success and sustainability. At that point the committee might decide if the essential elements are appropriately developed for the project and, if not, what needs to be done to move the project forward.

Coordination, Cooperation, and Collaboration: A Table Describing the Elements of Each

ESSENTIAL ELEMENTS	COORDINATION	COOPERATION	COLLABORATION
VISION AND GOALS	Basis for coordination is usually between individuals. Organizational missions and goals are not taken into account. Interaction is on as-needed basis.	Individual relationships are supported by organizations they represent. Missions and goals of individual organizations are reviewed for compatibility. Interaction is usually around one specific project or task of definable length.	Commitment of organzations and their leaders is fully behind their representatives. Common new mission statement and goals are created. One or more projects are undertaken for longer-term results.

continued on next page

Coordination, Cooperation, and Collaboration:
A Table Describing the Elements of Each (continued)

ESSENTIAL ELEMENTS	COORDINATION	COOPERATION	COLLABORATION
STRUCTURE, RESPONSIBILITIES, AND COMMUNICATION	Relationships are informal; each organization functions separately. No planning is required. Information is conveyed at occasional intervals.	Organizations involved take on needed roles, but they function relatively independently of each other. Some project-specific planning is required. Communication roles are established and definitive channels are created for interaction.	New organizational structures and/or clearly defined and interrelated roles that constitute formal division of labor are created. More comprehensive planning is required that includes developing joint strategies and measuring success in terms of impact on needs of those served. Beyond communication roles and channels for interaction, many "levels" of communication are created—as clear information is keystone of success.
AUTHORITY AND ACCOUNTABILITY	Authority rests with individual organizations. Leadership is unilateral, and control is central. All authority and account ability rest with individual organization, which acts independently.	Authority rests with individual organizations, but there is cooperation among participants. There is some sharing of leadership and control. There is some shared risk, but most of authority and accountability falls to individual organization.	Authority is determined by the collaboration to balance ownership by the individual organizations with expediency to accomplish purpose. Leadership is dispersed, and control is shared and mutual. Risk is shared equally by all organizations in the collaboration.
RESOURCES AND REWARDS	Resources (staff time, dollars, and capabilities) are separate, serving individual organization's needs. Rewards are specific to each organization.	Resources are acknowledged and can be made available to others for specific project. Rewards are mutually acknowledged.	Resources are pooled or jointly secured for longer term effort that is managed by collaborative structure. Organizations share in the products; more is accomplished jointly than could have been individually.

Note. From *Collaboration: What Makes It Work* (p. 61), by P. Mattessich, M. Murray-Close, B. R. Monsey, and Wilder Research Center, 2004, St. Paul, MN: Fieldstone Alliance. Copyright 2004 by Fieldstone Alliance. Adapted with permission.

Of particular interest here are the collaborative relationships (Mattessich et al., 2004), which include a commitment to:

1. A shared vision and mutual goals
2. A jointly developed structure, shared responsibility, and agreed-upon methods of communication
3. Mutual authority and accountability for success
4. Sharing of resources and rewards.

Many public and private funders are asking for increased collaboration. True collaboration, however, requires a great deal of intentional activity and is not easily accomplished. Mattessich et al. (2004) also define 20 factors that influence the success of collaboration—and the implications these factors have for programming. Again, this is a helpful discussion tool for members to use to clarify expectations and needs. In examining this information, consider what already has been presented about hidden rules, driving forces, and resources—and how these same factors relate to relationships between/among colleges and partner agencies.

Twenty Factors Influencing the Success of Collaboration

FACTOR/DESCRIPTION	EVALUATIVE STATEMENTS	IMPLICATIONS
ENVIRONMENT		
1. **History of collaboration in community.** History of collaboration or cooperation exists that offers potential partners understanding of roles and expectations, enabling them to trust process.	▪ Agencies in our community have a history of working together. ▪ Trying to solve problems through collaboration has been common in this community. It has been done a lot before.	a. Goals should correspond to level at which collaboration is developed. b. If there is little history of collaboration, address "environmental" issues before starting work (example: advocacy for legislation or funding that promotes collaboration, requiring education of potential collaborators). c. Collaborators will have to address inhospitable environment, such as history of competition.

continued on next page

236

Twenty Factors Influencing the Success of Collaboration (continued)

FACTOR/DESCRIPTION	EVALUATIVE STATEMENTS	IMPLICATIONS
2. **Collaborative group seen as leader in community.** Collaborative group is seen as leader, at least related to goals and activities it intends to accomplish.	▪ Leaders in this community who are not part of our collaborative group seem hopeful about what we can accomplish. ▪ Others (in this community) who are generally not part of this collaboration would generally agree that the organizations involved in this collaborative project are the "right" organizations to make this work.	a. Must be perceived as legitimate leader by community it intends to influence. b. Include assessment of group's leadership image—and correct it if necessary. c. Communitywide projects will require broad legitimacy; smaller scale projects will require legitimacy of narrower group.
3. **Political/social climate favorable.** Political leaders, opinion makers, those who control resources, public support, no obvious opposition to mission of group.	▪ The political and social climate seems to be "right" for starting a collaborative project like this one. ▪ The time is right for this collaborative project.	a. Group must "sell" collaborative structure to key leaders. b. If right climate doesn't exist, partners should plan strategies to change public commitment. c. Set goals realistically to meet political and social requirements. d. Goals and process should be seen as cost-effective and not in conflict with or drain on current endeavors.
MEMBERSHIP		
4. **Mutual respect, understanding, and trust.** Members share understanding of each other and their respective organizations (i.e., how they operate, cultural norms, values, limitations, and expectations).	▪ People involved in our collaboration always trust one another. ▪ I have a lot of respect for the other people involved in this collaboration.	a. In early stage of their work, partners should lay aside purpose of collaboration and devote energy to getting acquainted with each other. b. Partners must present their intentions and agendas honestly and openly to facilitate building of trust. c. Building strong relationships takes time. d. Conflicts may develop. e. Existing connections between partners may help with communication, trust, and sharing.

continued on next page

Twenty Factors Influencing the Success of Collaboration (continued)

FACTOR/DESCRIPTION	EVALUATIVE STATEMENTS	IMPLICATIONS
5. **Appropriate cross-section of members.** Collaborative group includes representatives from each segment of community that will be affected by its activities.	• The people involved in our collaboration represent a cross-section of those who have a stake in what we are trying to accomplish. • All the organizations that we need to be members of this collaborative group have become members of the group.	a. Carefully review membership needs; who has explicit and tacit control over relevant issues? Invite them to participate. b. Monitor whether new groups or individuals should be brought in; develop formal integration/education plan. c. Membership that is too broad will become unmanageable.
6. **Members see collaboration as being in their self-interest.** Partners feel that collaboration, with its resulting loss of autonomy and "turf," will have benefits for them that exceed costs.	• My organization will benefit from being involved in this collaboration.	a. Make it clear that organizations will gain from collaboration; build those expectations into goals so they remain visible throughout life of group. b. Build in incentives for organizations to get and stay involved; monitor whether those incentives continue to motivate members.
7. **Ability to compromise.** Partners are able to compromise, since all decisions cannot possibly be molded to conform perfectly to preferences of each member.	• People involved in our collaboration are willing to compromise on important aspects of our project.	a. Representatives must have latitude in working out agreements; rigid rules and expectations will render collaboration unworkable. b. Take time and be patient. c. Members must know when to seek compromise or common ground and when to work through major decision points.

continued on next page

Twenty Factors Influencing the Success of Collaboration (continued)

FACTOR/DESCRIPTION	EVALUATIVE STATEMENTS	IMPLICATIONS
8. **Members share stake in both process and outcome.** Group members feel "ownership" both in how group works and results of its work.	▪ The organizations that belong to our collaborative group invest the right amount of time in our collaborative efforts. ▪ Everyone who is a member of our collaborative group wants this project to succeed. ▪ The level of commitment among the collaboration participants is high.	a. Devote time and resources to developing "ownership." b. Operating principles and procedures must promote feeling of ownership. c. Continuously monitor ownership and make changes in process/structure as required. d. Developing interagency work groups, participating in regular planning, and monitoring effort can solidify ownership and ongoing commitment.
9. **Multiple layers of decision making.** Every level (upper management, middle management, operations) within each organization that is part of collaborative structure needs to participate in decision making.	▪ When the collaborative group makes major decisions, there is always enough time for members to take information back to their organizations to confer with colleagues about what the decision should be. ▪ Each of the people who participate in decisions of this collaborative group can speak for the entire organization they represent, not just a part.	a. Create mechanisms to involve all layers. b. At outset of collaboration, systems should be developed to include necessary staff from each organization. c. Leadership may be insufficient to sustain major collaboration.
10. **Flexibility.** Group remains open to varied ways of organizing itself and accomplishing its work.	▪ There is a lot of flexibility when decisions are made; people are open to discussing different opinions. ▪ People in this collaborative group are open to different approaches to how we can do our work. They are willing to consider different ways of working.	a. Flexibility needed in structure and methods. b. Need and expectation for flexibility should be communicated at outset. c. Monitoring group to ensure that it remains flexible is important, since groups often solidify their norms over time, thereby limiting their thinking and behavior.

continued on next page

Twenty Factors Influencing the Success of Collaboration (continued)

FACTOR/DESCRIPTION	EVALUATIVE STATEMENTS	IMPLICATIONS
PROCESS/STRUCTURE		
11. **Development of clear roles and policy guidelines.** Group clearly understands roles, rights, responsibilities—and how to carry out those responsibilities.	• People in this collaborative group have a clear sense of their roles and responsibilities. • There is a clear process for making decisions among the partners of this collaboration.	a. Members need to reach agreement on roles, rights, responsibilities—and communicate them to all relevant parties. b. Partners may need to adjust policies and procedures to reduce conflicts and competing demands on staff who work on collaborative issues. c. People will gravitate toward their own interests; this tendency should be considered when making assignments.
12. **Adaptability.** Group has ability to sustain itself in midst of major changes, even if it needs to change some major goals, members, etc., in order to deal with changing conditions.	• This collaboration is able to adapt to changing conditions, such as fewer funds than expected, changing political climate, or change in leadership. • This group has the ability to survive even if it has to make major changes in its plans or add some new members in order to reach its goals.	a. Group should stay aware of trends, environment, and directions of community and members. b. Review vision and goals of group regularly and revise if necessary. c. As member goals and outcomes change, it is important that collaborative goals and outcomes keep pace by group continually incorporating changes as necessary.
13. **Appropriate pace of development.** Group has chosen a reasonable number of projects of a manageable size for the resources available.	• The collaborative group has tried to take on the right amount of work at the right pace. • We are currently able to keep up with the work necessary to coordinate all the people, organizations, and activities related to the collaborative project.	a. Groups should guard against taking on projects that are too large and complex for the collaborative group structure. b. Groups should agree on expected timelines for projects, monitor progress regularly, and adjust expectations as needed. c. Members must take active roles in determining appropriate pace of development.

continued on next page

Twenty Factors Influencing the Success of Collaboration (continued)

FACTOR/DESCRIPTION	EVALUATIVE STATEMENTS	IMPLICATIONS
COMMUNICATION		
14. **Communication.** Group members interact often, update one another, discuss issues openly, and convey all necessary information to one another and to people outside group.	▪ People in this collaboration communicate openly with one another. ▪ I am informed as often as I should be about what goes on in the collaboration. ▪ The people who lead this collaborative group communicate well with the members.	a. Set up system of communications and identify responsibilities of each member. b. Staff function for communication may be necessary. c. Provide incentives within and between organizations to reward or highlight effective communication.
15. **Establish informal and formal communication links.** Channels of communication exist on paper, so that information flow occurs; members also establish personal connections that will produce better informed, more cohesive group working on common project.	▪ Communication among the people in this collaborative group happens both at formal meetings and in informal ways. ▪ I personally have informal conversations about the project with others who are involved in this collaborative group.	a. Stable representation from each organization is needed to develop strong personal connections. b. Meetings, trainings, and interagency work groups promote understanding, cooperation, and transfer of information. c. Social time might be helpful for members of group. d. Review systems regularly to upgrade and expand communications.
PURPOSE		
16. **Concrete, attainable goals and objectives.** Goals and objectives of group appear clear to partners and can realistically be attained.	▪ I have a clear understanding of what our collaboration is trying to accomplish. ▪ People in our collaborative group know and understand our goals. ▪ People in our collaborative group have established reasonable goals.	a. Clear, attainable goals will heighten enthusiasm. b. Groups must experience some success in achieving objectives in order to be sustained. c. Formulate clear goals and periodically report on progress. d. Develop short- and long-term goals.

continued on next page

Twenty Factors Influencing the Success of Collaboration (continued)

FACTOR/DESCRIPTION	EVALUATIVE STATEMENTS	IMPLICATIONS
17. Shared vision. Partners share same vision with clearly agreed-upon mission, objectives, and strategy.	▪ The people in this collaborative group are dedicated to the idea that we can make this project work. ▪ My ideas about what we want to accomplish with this collaboration seem to be the same as the ideas of others.	a. Group must develop shared vision, either when it is first planned or soon after it begins to function. b. Engage in vision-building efforts and develop language and actions out of shared vision. c. Technical assistance (outside consultation) may be useful to help establish common vision.
18. Unique purpose. Mission and goals or approach of collaborative structure differ, at least in part, from mission and goals or approach of member organizations.	▪ What we are trying to accomplish with our collaborative project would be difficult for any single organization to accomplish by itself. ▪ No other organization in the community is trying to do exactly what we are trying to do.	a. Mission and goals of group create "sphere of activity" that overlaps significantly but not completely with "spheres" of each member organization. b. Mission and goals of each member of collaborative structure need to be known by all involved. c. Development of collaboration among competing organizations around goals of each member may lead to failure; less demanding attempts to coordinate or cooperate might fare better.
RESOURCES		
19. Sufficient funds. Group requires adequate, consistent financial base to support its operations.	▪ Our collaborative group has adequate funds to do what it wants to accomplish. ▪ Our collaborative group has adequate "people power" to do what it wants to accomplish.	a. Obtaining financial means for existence must be priority in forming group. b. Collaborative work may be expensive in start-up phase; money should be available at outset. c. Group needs to consider resources of its members, as well as approach outside sources, if necessary.

continued on next page

Twenty Factors Influencing the Success of Collaboration (continued)

FACTOR/ DESCRIPTION	EVALUATIVE STATEMENTS	IMPLICATIONS
20. Skilled convener. Individual who convenes group has organizing skills, interpersonal skills, reputation for fairness, and perceived legitimacy in convener role.	• The people in leadership positions for this collaboration have good skills for working with other people and organizations.	a. Care must be taken to choose convener with necessary skills. b. Leaders of collaborative groups must give serious attention and care to convener role. c. Grooming of new leaders and planning for transitions in leadership should be well thought out to avoid costly power struggles and loss of forward momentum.

Note. From *Collaboration: What Makes It Work,* by P. Mattessich and B. R. Monsey, 1992, St. Paul, MN: Amherst H. Wilder Foundation, and from *Collaboration: What Makes It Work,* 2nd Ed. (pp. 38–40), by P. Mattessich, M. Murray-Close, B. R. Monsey, and Wilder Research Center, 2004, St. Paul, MN: Fieldstone Alliance. Copyright 2004 by Fieldstone Alliance. Adapted with permission.

Building relationships of mutual trust and respect

Just as postsecondary students come to campus with experiences that shape their expectations of school (good and bad), agencies will respond to the institution's request to partner based on their preconceived notions. The same relational skills and understanding of bonding and bridging capital can be applied to improve partner interactions. Communication is enhanced when partners realize that different disciplines have different driving forces and hidden rules motivating and shaping their behavior—but with a common language so that all can be heard and participate fully in the partnership.

Establishing leadership, communication, and institutional buy-in

Analysis by the National Research Center on Career & Technical Education showed that successful collaborative programs had institutional leadership skilled in leveraging existing resources through partnerships with external partners (Bragg et al., 2007). "By building on local strengths, the leaders exhibited [a deep knowledge and] sophistication in developing policy and program components identified by key stakeholder groups as instrumental to program delivery" (Bragg et. al., 2007, p. iii). Transformational leadership from the head of the institution will accelerate progress. The reality is that usually these changes start at the "front lines"—in the classrooms and offices seeking to better serve students. Such informal leadership can be effective in creating institutional change; it just takes longer and requires political sensitivity to be effective within the institutional culture.

Internal communication is vital: up the chain of command, preferably to the college president, and also through faculty senate, student government, student affairs, curriculum committees, and other committees particular to the institution (i.e., unions, outreach, public service, urban studies, etc.). It is essential to publicize the program to the board in on-campus presentations, news articles, blogs, and other Internet venues. The college is part of the partnership and must be cultivated and tended to in the same manner, if not more, as the external partner. Without ongoing attention to disseminating information, misconceptions arise that create resistance and efforts to block programming. Nonetheless, expect debate and encourage it as a means of engaging the campus community. Some will criticize the program, and elements of the critique may well be valid. Listening to vocal opponents informs the leadership about what others are thinking (and might not be verbalizing). Program leaders would do well to become knowledgeable about the varying theories of economic class, in addition to what opinion leaders in the field are saying and writing.

Developing funding and other resources

Program funding is a major issue that also must be considered at the outset. One of the biggest challenges is the extra work and bureaucracy involved in weaving together small amounts of funding that support components of integrated strategies. Bragg et al. (2007) found other common barriers to be

> entrenched organizational policies and operations, including space and scheduling concerns, rigid curricular and assessment rules (particularly in the area of college placement testing and developmental education), faculty contractual agreements (including concerns with differential pay scales for full- and part-time instructors), and inflexible local and state-level curriculum approval processes. (p. x)

Often resources are available, however, and simply realigning them provides the funding, staffing, or services necessary. Staff can frequently be redirected to give time to the project based at least partly on the premise that this is work that should have been done in the first place—or that now is recognized as worthwhile or more effective than past practice. Portions of course fees might be used to fund service learning projects.

Some projects, however, will require additional outside funding. Given the current attention to low achievement rates at postsecondary institutions, several national foundations and government offices support grant programs to increase recruitment, persistence, and graduation of students from low-income backgrounds or under-represented demographics. The National Foundation Center Library is an excellent source of information on grants and sponsored programs.

STEP 4. MEASURE AND REPORT RESULTS; ESTABLISH FEEDBACK LOOP TO SUSTAIN COLLABORATION

Increasing emphasis on data-driven decision making from every conceivable quarter, including accreditation bodies, improves the quality of data and analysis produced by postsecondary education programs. The mediated learning experience and righting reflex are often reflected in the evaluation and research process as well. The data tend to show *what* is happening but not *why*. Many colleges are just beginning to establish a "culture of evidence," and some staff will feel resistant or even threatened by the exposure that results from data analysis. Dramatic stories that stereotype student experiences often are accepted as fact—when careful examination of the data proves otherwise. For example:

- Do under-resourced students avoid developmental courses because of stigma, because they do not have the money to pay for them, or because most of the instructors do not teach effectively?
- Do they avoid science and math courses because the liberal arts curriculum is engaging—or in order to maintain a grade point average that in turn maintains a scholarship?
- Do they fail a gateway course because the instruction is poor or because the class starts at 8 a.m.?

Investigations groups are an excellent resource for qualitative information about why students do what they do. Colleges can foster a more collaborative supportive environment by regularly reviewing data and using the information to guide decisions and monitor progress: "Transparency builds credibility, ownership, and support for change" (CCSSE, 2007, p. 7). One of the things this book adds is to include the students themselves in the discussion.

The first step in program evaluation is establishing clear baseline data. Understanding the source of the data intended to support evaluation is critical. Planning for data collection and management must occur prior to program implementation, not as an afterthought or at the end of the project when documentation of results is needed. But remember, the complexity of data collection is increased at least in proportion to the number of partners, if not more so. Each partner may have different data needs and ways of measuring and, when working with government-funded programs, may have very specific reporting requirements. If partners do not clarify, agree upon, and coordinate their efforts at the beginning of the project, they may find themselves unable to correlate their results in order to draw meaningful conclusions.

Erroneous assumptions about the accessibility, availability, or integration of data limit program evaluation and the subsequent use of information to guide program design. While many institutions have organizational research departments, lack of human resources can limit the value of such departments to new program initiatives. The rule is "never assume" that the available data are congruent with the way the partner collects data—or that internal departments necessarily have the capacity to serve the particular program needs.

Consider the following general steps of an outcomes-based evaluation:

1. Identify the major outcomes the program intends to achieve.
2. Choose the outcomes each partner wants to examine—and attach metrics or targets. There are four levels of change to consider:
   - Changes in feelings
   - Changes in learning
   - Changes in skills
   - Changes in effectiveness or performance
3. Specify a target number or percentage of change related to each outcome.
4. Identify what information is needed to demonstrate the change.
5. Decide how and when to gather the data.
6. Collect the data.
7. Analyze and report the findings to all partners after the implementation staff has had the opportunity to review the reports.

Providing executive summaries is essential for busy people to grasp the concepts and results of the program. It is recommended that these be shared with all partners, including students and former students who are part of the planning team. Sharing information establishes an atmosphere of transparency, as well as continuous improvement and collaboration.

It is beyond the scope of this book to discuss all the aspects of program planning and how they relate to goal setting and subsequent outcome evaluation. Given the increasing emphasis on data and outcomes, program planners may want to access evaluation experts. Such professionals can be found, for example, in their own institution's research department, in the public service or urban studies department, or at a local university. They may be private consultants. Major foundations and higher education professional associations also are sources of information, such as Campus Compact, Achieving the Dream, MDRC (formerly Manpower Demonstration Research Corporation), and The Community College Survey of Student Engagement.

Partnerships offer opportunities to broaden program impact and engage the institution more fully with the community, but they require maintenance and monitoring. The importance to the process of effective communication cannot be overstated. Institutions that have or develop numerous partnerships and engage with the community in multiple ways might need strategies to better manage these efforts and avoid becoming bogged down in hierarchies and bureaucracies. In addition, as the waves of "baby boomers" retire and are replaced with new generations of staff, colleges can carefully plan and create the spaces needed for open discussion—and adopt processes that both allow and encourage the participation of younger faculty and staff.

'Strategic Doing' as a Framework for Action

"Strategic Doing" is an appealing process developed by Ed Morrison (2006) of I-Open, a national leader in economic development strategies that emphasize the importance of education as the central means of developing human capital and building wealth. I-Open has consulted on numerous large regional and interstate collaborations among education, government, and the private sector that are highly complex, yet move quickly and achieve measurable results using the Strategic Doing process.

The mental model for Strategic Doing depicts four areas in which networks can foster economic development. Perhaps such groups as *Bridges* steering committees and other campus/community partnerships do not consider themselves to be economic developers, but indeed they constitute a vital civic network that does contribute directly and indirectly to any regional economic development strategy. It is helpful for members to see their role in this bigger picture. Morrison focuses on four strategic areas.

First, the focus area of brainpower described above relates to concepts about individuals building resources and systems that support their education and achievement. An educated populace is essential. Second, connecting networks for innovation is how regions build wealth through business and industry. The third element is building quality, connected places that people want to live in—where others are supportive of individual achievement and relationships. Finally, getting the word out about the transformative changes happening for individuals and the community keeps energy high and attracts other like-minded people to the networks.

Mental Model A—Strategic Doing Content

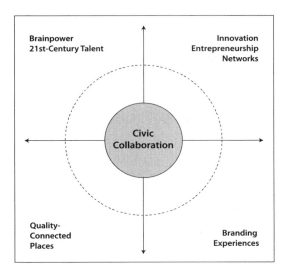

Note. From "New Models of Economic Development: White Paper Version 0.5," by E. Morrison, 2006, p. 11. Copyright 2006 by Ed Morrison. Reprinted with permission.

The underlying premise of Strategic Doing is that significant changes can be implemented through the power of networks concentrating on these four areas, as well as using open civic forums in which to work and share what has been learned. The steering committee can use this model, along with the Community Sustainability Grid, to support planning.

Strategic Doing works well in an environment of partners willing to act practically—but who perhaps are somewhat jaded by past experiences with seemingly endless planning meetings that did not seem to achieve the intended results for one reason or another. A factor in the effectiveness of Strategic Doing is the fast-forward, one-hour monthly planning/monitoring meetings that maintain focus, momentum, and accountability. Another reason for its appeal is the tenet that *all those at the table are the right people.* Plans do not have to be delayed or stalled while "the right people" are cajoled into attending. (The implication is that the group invites everyone—but works with those who come. Call it "the quorum of the present.") The people who are there act responsibly within their authority, but they act and move ahead. This energizes those who have become fatigued by working within systems built by their grandfather's generation who are now on the downward slope of effectiveness (the vertical business model), and it captivates the younger generation, individuals already on the second-curve, "new economy" businesses and practices and heavily invested in networks and relationship management.

CIVIC NETWORKS PROVIDE VEHICLE

Applying the Strategic Doing process to a hypothetical *Bridges* steering committee would begin by acknowledging the steering committee as a civic network. As such, members consider how the network might be strengthened. Just as in the *Investigations* process, members assess who is in their network (social capital, relationships) and with whom they would wish to forge stronger ties. The objective is to focus collaboration to make innovation effective. Most *Bridges* steering committees begin as an "interested community"; the members have a common interest in ending poverty but do not necessarily work together or share information. With intentionality, this group becomes a learning community in which members share information in a limited way and may help each other on projects, but they do not articulate common objectives. When the group achieves the characteristics of a network in which members commit to helping each other on specific projects and share a common objective of integration and transformation, it is then that the members have achieved the high level of trust and commitment needed to innovate.

One of the most critical attributes of effective networks is civility. Morrison describes the attributes of effective civic leadership as honesty, fairness, consistency, compassion, and integrity. Civil deliberation occurs best in an atmosphere that welcomes diversity, is open to learning, and supports innovators. Networks with these characteristics will be more effective than those dominated by personal agendas, secrecy, control, and power struggles or inertia. Each group will find different ways of building civility—perhaps using ground rules or implementing the "parking lot" strategy. The parking lot is where the "meeting after the meeting" takes place in groups having trouble with civility. Members congregate in the parking lot to say what they really think to people who probably agree with them—rather than bringing divergent views to the table for open discussion. The committee can provide members with 3x5 cards labeled "parking lot" and encourage everyone to write down anything they feel is important but are uncomfortable saying in front of the group for whatever reason. The core team of the committee can then process the information and decide how to share it with the group.

'STRATEGIC DOING' PROCESS PROVIDES RESULTS

Strategic Doing provides a theory of change and a process model to guide the network.

Mental Model B—Strategic Doing Process

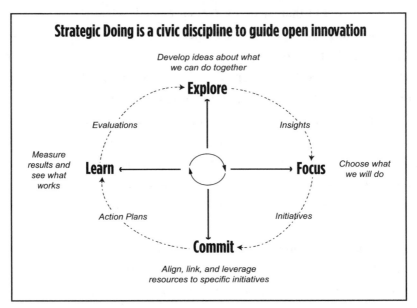

Note. From "New Models of Economic Development: White Paper Version 0.5," by E. Morrison, 2006, p. 8. Copyright 2006 by Ed Morrison. Reprinted with permission.

The deceptively simple *process* (Mental Model B) of Strategic Doing asks the members to answer just four questions during each hour-long meeting:

- Explore: What can we do together?
- Focus: What should we do together?
- Commit: What will we do together?
- Learn: What are we learning together?

What can we do together? (20 minutes)

Using the Strategic Doing mental model for *content* (Mental Model A) above, the committee begins asset mapping and documents the assets available in the community that might already be doing things in that focus area. The point here is to link first-curve assets (colleges, businesses, and specific aspects of institutions and infrastructure from the post-World War II era in particular) with emerging second-curve opportunities (new-economy businesses, innovation networks, etc.).

250

Next, committee members jot down their ideas about what these assets could be doing together, as well as how members can use the assets to do new things together. If these ideas are written on sticky notes, they can be put in the appropriate quadrant of the Strategic Doing mental model for content (Mental Model A)—either as a handout or on a flip chart or some other visual representation. Finally, the group can use the process to come to consensus about which focus area to address first.

What should we do together? (20 minutes)

The group members take time to discuss and reach consensus about what one thing they want to work on—and what the outcome should be. What might be a quick "win"? Where is there synergy? What are the most pressing/critical issues? Using questions to prompt them, the group describes what the outcome will look like.

- What will be different when it is achieved?
- What difference will the change make?

It is important to take time to paint the mental picture of where the group is going and why it is better than where the group currently is. This is fundamental to determining the strategic outcomes and understanding what needs to be tracked and measured to determine success.

Within this step, the network develops SMART goals: specific, measurable, attainable, realistic, and time-specific. Once again, a strategy advocated in *Investigations* is practiced by community leaders to strengthen and build resources for the community.

What will we do together? (15 minutes)

This step creates the action plan by working out the following details:

- What, specifically, will each person do in the next 30 days?
- How will the members link and leverage their resources to make it happen?
- What can each of the partners contribute, and what do they need?
- Who will be responsible for each step?

What are we learning together? (5 minutes)

When the group convenes for all subsequent meetings, time is spent discussing what the outcomes have been, what has and has not happened as planned, and what needs to be adjusted to improve the effort. Questions during this process might include:

- What's new?
- What didn't we know?

As the group becomes involved in more action plans, the two important questions to answer at the start of each meeting are:

- What was the outcome?
- What changes need to be made?
- What's the next step?

The ongoing challenge to the group is to build productive, focused networks around strategic issues. This type of open collaboration leads to the sort of innovation necessary for communities intending to end poverty. The general aims of *Bridges* steering committees fit well within the open source, economic development, Strategic Doing model:

1. Developing a *Bridges* community by increasing the numbers of graduates from *Investigations* is a brainpower project.
2. Involving businesses that offer well-paying jobs and/or opportunities supports innovation networks.
3. Implementing the Circles™ campaign to provide ongoing bridging relationships for families contributes to building quality, connected places.
4. Using the power of the network to change policies would, in addition to the other stories, create a powerful branding story for communities.

In this era of social networks and collaboration, a harsh reality is that nobody can tell anyone what to do. We must find ways of working together and capitalizing on the strength of our connections. Leaders are needed who are willing to listen and lead, and engaged citizens are needed to contribute ideas and participate in the solutions. All economic classes and all sectors must be at the table. When both leadership and participation levels are high, then the network, community, or region is being governed by rules of civility, innovation is supported, and prosperity grows.

An Invitation to Continue the Dialogue

The readers of this book are invited to join the online community at www.ahaprocess.com/r/college/. Here people from higher education (including students and *Investigations* graduates) and other concerned individuals working toward similar goals are invited to gather to think, to ask questions, and to find solutions. We would like to invite you to submit ideas and your stories as we expand this resource for transformative change in the postsecondary world.

An Invitation to Computer Programming

Appendixes

Appendix A
Giving Empowering Feedback
Receiving Empowering Feedback

Appendix B
Sample Rubric for Assessment of Computer Programming Project

Appendix C
Organizing Laptops
Organizing E-Mail

Appendix D
Mental Models for Poverty, Middle Class, and Wealth
Mental Model for Persuasive Reasoning and Writing
Mental Model for European Reformation
Mental Model for Developing Characters
Mental Model for Compare and Summarize
Mental Model for *Investigations* Theory of Change

Giving Empowering Feedback

Feedback is a way of providing people with information about their behavior and how those behaviors affect others. As in a guided missile system, feedback helps individuals keep their behavior "on target," and thus they are better able to achieve their goals. To be effective in working with others, we need to become skilled at giving, soliciting, and accepting feedback.

–John Luckner and Reldan Nadler

HELPFUL ATTITUDES: Your feedback is most helpful to others when you are …

1. Humble—Remember, even if you are right, you are the "better than." Monitor your attachment to seeing yourself "above" the other person intellectually, morally, emotionally, socially, physically, or spiritually.
2. Confident—Remember that you have every right to offer your honest feedback; in fact, to withhold your feedback may be selfish and detrimental to the welfare of the other person. Monitor your attachment to not upsetting the other person with honest feedback.
3. Neutral—Remember, your feedback may or may not be accurate; it is simply your best interpretation of your perception of "reality." Monitor your attachment to being "right" and your need for others to see the situation your way. Let go of pretending to know "the truth," and present your unique perspective.

HELPFUL BEHAVIORS: Feedback is most helpful to others when it is …

1. Solicited—Rather than imposed (e.g., "I have some thoughts that I could share with you about … Are you open to them?").
2. Well-timed—Earlier rather than later.
3. Clear—Able to be stated simply.
4. Specific rather than general—Avoid such sweeping comments as those that include all, never, and always; clarify what you mean by using such vague pronouns as *it, that,* etc.
5. Balanced—Offering positives, as well as negatives.
6. Focused on behavior or problem rather than the person.
7. Identifying behavior(s) that can be changed.
8. Descriptive—Rather than judgmental (e.g., "You didn't complete the work" rather than "You're lazy").
9. Presented with ownership language—"I" statements (e.g., "When you _____, I'm offended. I wish you would contribute more to the efforts of this team. In my experience … In my perception … It seems to me … As I see it … From my point of view … ").
10. Long on encouragement, short on advice.
11. Checked to ensure reception.
12. Cross-checked with others for accuracy.

Note. From *On Course Workshop II: Innovative Strategies for Promoting Student Success Across the Curriculum,* by S. Downing, 2002. Copyright 2002 by On Course Workshop. Adapted with permission.

Receiving Empowering Feedback

> *Honest criticism is hard to take, particularly from a relative, a friend, an acquaintance, or a stranger.*
>
> —Franklin P. Jones

HELPFUL BELIEFS: Others' feedback is most helpful to you when you see it as …

1. Possibly holding the key to your greater success.
2. Merely information revealing someone else's perspective (rather than an attack).
3. Separate from your worth (rather than confirmation of your flaws).

HELPFUL BEHAVIORS: Others' feedback is most helpful to you when you …

1. Ask for feedback often.
2. Check your understanding to make sure you have accurately received the information.
3. Thank the other person for his or her feedback. It is not necessary to agree or disagree. Remember, feedback is only information, and you need not take it personally.
4. Let your Inner Guide assess the accuracy of the information.
5. Respond appropriately.

If On Course feedback seems accurate, keep doing what you are doing.

If Off Course feedback seems accurate, make a plan to get back on course.

If, after careful consideration by your Inner Guide, the feedback seems inaccurate, ignore it.

Note. From *On Course Workshop II: Innovative Strategies for Promoting Student Success Across the Curriculum,* by S. Downing, 2002. Copyright 2002 by On Course Workshop. Adapted with permission.

Sample Rubric for Assessment of Computer Programming Project

Criteria	Unsatisfactory	Satisfactory	Good	Excellent
Completion of Assignment	Less than 50% of the assignment has been completed	Between 50 and 65% of the assignment has been completed	Between 65 and 80% of the assignment has been completed	Between 80 and 100% of the assignment has been completed
Presentation and Organization	No name, date, or assignment title included Poor use of white space (indentation, blank lines) Disorganized and messy	Name, date, and assignment title included Use of white space makes program easy to read Organized work	Name, date, and assignment title included Good use of white space Organized work	Name, date, and assignment title included Excellent use of white space Effective use of bold and italics Creatively organized work
Correctness	Program does not execute due to errors No error-checking code included No testing has been completed	Program executes without errors Program handles some special cases Some testing has been completed	Program executes without errors Program handles most special cases Thorough testing has been completed	Program executes without errors Program handles all special cases Program contains error-checking code Thorough and organized testing has been completed, and output from test cases is included
Efficiency	Program uses a difficult and inefficient solution Programmer has not considered alternate solutions	Program uses a logical solution that is easy to follow, but it is not the most efficient Programmer has considered alternate solutions	Program uses an efficient and easy-to-follow solution (i.e., no confusing tricks) Programmer has considered alternate solution and has chosen the most efficient	Program uses solution that is easy to understand and maintain Programmer has analyzed many alternate solutions and has chosen the most efficient Programmer has included the reasons for the solution chosen

continued on next page

continued from previous page

Criteria	Unsatisfactory	Satisfactory	Good	Excellent
Documentation	No documentation included	Basic documentation has been completed, including descriptions of all variables	Program has been clearly documented, including descriptions of all variables For each subprogram the purpose is noted, as well as the input requirements and output results	Program has been clearly and effectively documented, including descriptions of all variables For each subprogram the specific purpose is noted, as well as the input requirements and output results

Note. From *Rubric for the Assessment of Computer Programming,* by S. Bauman, n.d. Copyright 2009 by S. Bauman. Adapted with permission.

Organizing Laptops

Many colleges provide laptops for their students, in which case it is advisable to lend rather than to give the computer to the students. This lessens the possibility that the item will be sold by family members. A logical requirement would be that the computer be used by the student only.

Following are some pointers for organizing computers, many of which are from "Learning Strategies Database" (n.d.):

- All files must be stored in the Documents section rather than the desktop, in order to avoid clutter and for easy retrieval.
- Instruct your students to create a folder for your course. Brainstorm with your students the broad topics (folders) within this folder.
- Students should name folders and files with readily recognizable names. (If the student cannot immediately know what is in each file, it needs a new name.)
- Periodically check to make sure students save their files in the appropriate folder. Award points for a properly organized folder.

In the event some students are not familiar with the procedures for creating folders, following are general steps for this process:

Step 1:
Set up broad-category folders within My Documents.

Step 2:
Set up subfolders within each category. For example, create a subfolder for term-paper notes within the broad English 202 folder.

Step 3:
Use the computer's sorting function. Put "AAA" in front of the names of the most-used folders and "ZZZ" in front of the least-used ones so the former position themselves at the top of an alphabetical list and the latter at the bottom. Such numbering systems as 01, 02, 03, and so on can also be used.

Step 4:
Sort files to suit your needs. Sort by date, for example, to find the file you worked on most recently, or by kind or type to group all spreadsheets.

Step 5:
Use meaningful filenames for your documents. Remember not to use slashes, colons, asterisks, or any punctuation other than a single period preceding the file extension.

Step 6:
Keep refining your filing system so that it works better and better. Rename or rearrange folders, and archive or trash inactive ones. Avoid duplicating folders, particularly those containing photos or other large files, to avoid filling up your drive and creating confusion.

Step 7:
Reserve your desktop for items that need immediate attention. When you've completed them, file them in the proper folder.

Step 8:

Remember, if several people on a team take turns working on any one file, put an asterisk at the end of the file name before you copy it off the server to denote that it is in use. Then add your initials before the period and the file extension. You have now prevented two people from working on the same file, created a backup, and left people a trail to follow should there be any questions.

Students also can add folders labeled Daily, Weekly, and Monthly on their desktops to remind them of regularly scheduled tasks. Another approach is to create a folder for each month of the year for storing forms or task reminders that need attention at a particular time of the year.

Organizing E-Mail

If students are assigned to work groups, it can be assumed that e-mail exchanges will take place. Students must learn that well-written e-mail messages are a reflection of one's professionalism. Most colleges have established e-mail etiquette statements. Such statements should be listed or referenced on syllabi. Etiquette statements might address such pointers or requirements as:

1. Avoid using all caps. WRITING IN ALL CAPS LOOKS LIKE SHOUTING.
2. Use appropriate punctuation.
3. Avoid using shorthand.
4. Use the spell checker. Reread messages before sending.
5. Cut and paste rather than forwarding whenever possible.
6. Avoid large attachments.
7. When responding to a message, include only the portion to which you are responding.
8. Avoid using stationery, which takes longer to download and might require recipients to reformat in order for it to be legible.
9. Remember, using BCC (blind carbon copy) avoids forwarding other people's addresses.

Students can use color to be able to look at their inboxes and recognize e-mail from peers, contacts, friends, or family. With Outlook Express they need to follow the usual procedure for message rules: Go to Tools > Message Rules > Mail, then click New.

Students can be required to include a signature on e-mail messages that are sent as part of the course requirement. To set up a default signature in Windows Mail or Outlook Express:

- Select Tools > Options from the menu.
- Go to the Signatures tab.
- Make sure Add signatures to all outgoing messages is selected.
- You probably also want to deselect Don't add signatures to replies and forwards.
- Now select the signature you want to become the one automatically inserted.
- Click Set as default.
- Click OK.

To set up a special signature for replies and forwards in Outlook:

- Select Tools > Options from the menu.
- Go to the Mail format tab.
- Click on the Signature for replies and forwards drop menu.
- Select the desired signature.
- Click OK.

Students can sort e-mails more efficiently with the Rules command. In Outlook, the general directions are:

1. In the Tools menu, select Rules and alerts.
2. Click the New rule button.
3. Click the circle in front of Start creating a rule from a template, then click Move a message sent to a distribution list to a folder.
4. Click on the underlined text for People or distribution list.
5. In the new box that opens, enter the e-mail address you are creating the rule for next to the To button. If you are creating this rule for the class, enter the e-mail address of the class, rather than your own e-mail address. When you click OK, this box will close. Select Next.
6. Place a check mark by Move it to the specified folder.
7. Click on the underlined text Specified. This will cause a new box to open.
8. Scroll to the folder you created earlier for this e-mail address or group. Select the appropriate folder by clicking on it, and click the OK button. This box will then close. In the remaining window, click the Finish button.

Repeat this process for each e-mail account or individual folder you have created.

Note. From *Learning Strategies Database* (n.d.). Copyright 2009 by Muskingum College. Adapted with permission.

Mental Models for Poverty, Middle Class, and Wealth

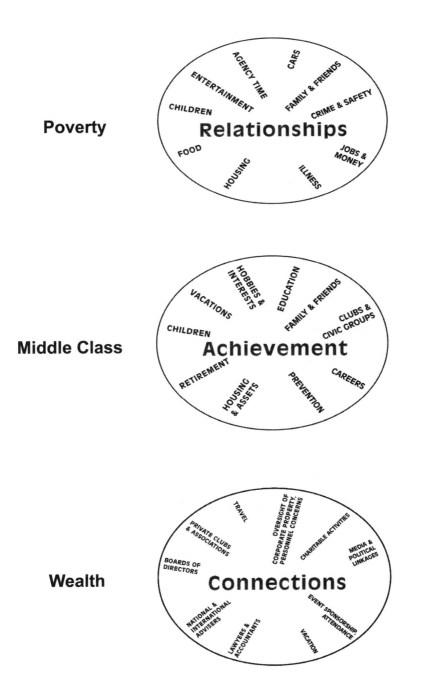

Poverty

Relationships

CARS
AGENCY TIME
FAMILY & FRIENDS
ENTERTAINMENT
CRIME & SAFETY
CHILDREN
FOOD
JOBS & MONEY
HOUSING
ILLNESS

Middle Class

Achievement

HOBBIES & INTERESTS
VACATIONS
EDUCATION
FAMILY & FRIENDS
CLUBS & CIVIC GROUPS
CHILDREN
RETIREMENT
HOUSING & ASSETS
PREVENTION
CAREERS

Wealth

Connections

TRAVEL
OVERSIGHT OF CORPORATE PROPERTY, PERSONNEL CONCERNS
PRIVATE CLUBS & ASSOCIATIONS
CHARITABLE ACTIVITIES
MEDIA & POLITICAL LINKAGES
BOARDS OF DIRECTORS
NATIONAL & INTERNATIONAL ADVISERS
LAWYERS & ACCOUNTANTS
VACATION
EVENT SPONSORSHIP ATTENDANCE

Mental Model for Persuasive Reasoning/Writing

The hamburger mental model can remind students at any level to state their thesis, provide supporting details, and to restate their thesis in the summary/conclusion.

Note. From *Learning Structures* (p. 62), by R. K. Payne, 2005, Highlands, TX: aha! Process. Copyright 1998 by aha! Process, Inc. Adapted with permission.

Mental Model for European Reformation

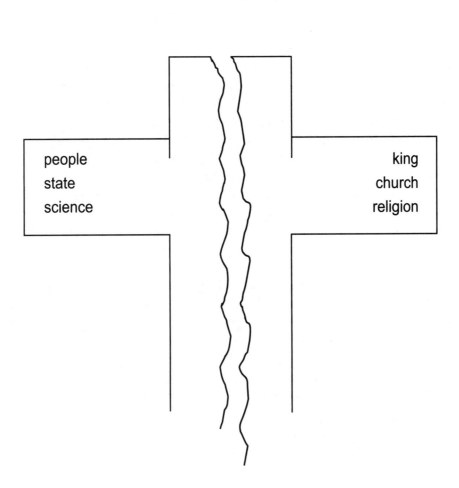

people
state
science

king
church
religion

Note. From *Mental Models for Social Studies/History: Grades 6–12* (p. 125), 2008, Highlands, TX: aha! Process. Adapted with permission.

Mental Model for Developing Characters

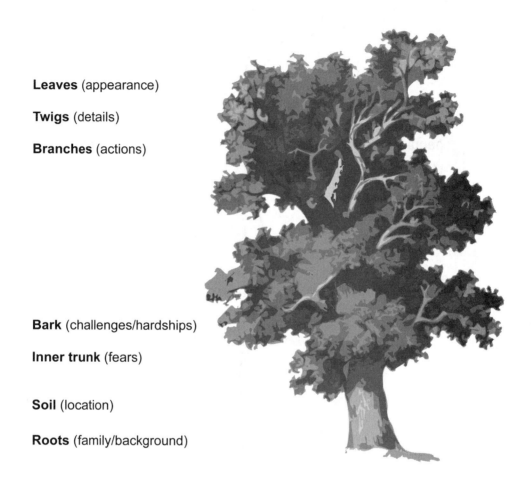

Leaves (appearance)

Twigs (details)

Branches (actions)

Bark (challenges/hardships)

Inner trunk (fears)

Soil (location)

Roots (family/background)

Note. From *Mental Models for English/Language Arts: Grades 6–12* (p. 9), 2007, Highlands, TX: aha! Process. Adapted with permission.

Mental Model for Compare and Summarize

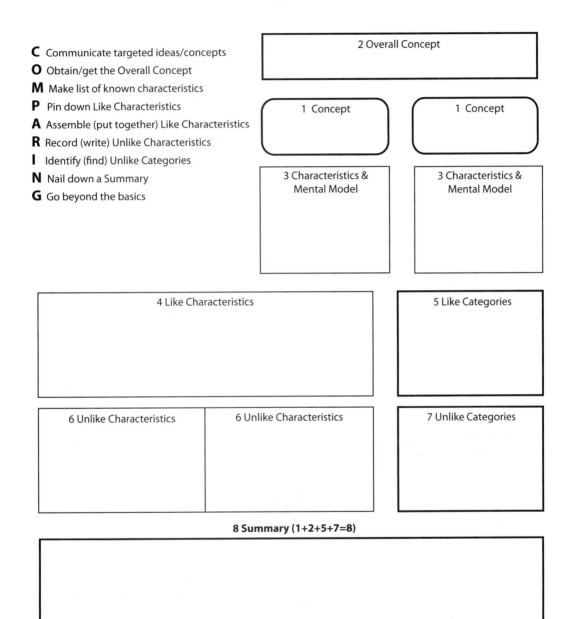

C Communicate targeted ideas/concepts
O Obtain/get the Overall Concept
M Make list of known characteristics
P Pin down Like Characteristics
A Assemble (put together) Like Characteristics
R Record (write) Unlike Characteristics
I Identify (find) Unlike Categories
N Nail down a Summary
G Go beyond the basics

2 Overall Concept

1 Concept

1 Concept

3 Characteristics & Mental Model

3 Characteristics & Mental Model

4 Like Characteristics

5 Like Categories

6 Unlike Characteristics

6 Unlike Characteristics

7 Unlike Categories

8 Summary (1+2+5+7=8)

Note. Mental model created by Marye Jane Brockinton.

Mental Model for *Investigations* Theory of Change

Theory of Change

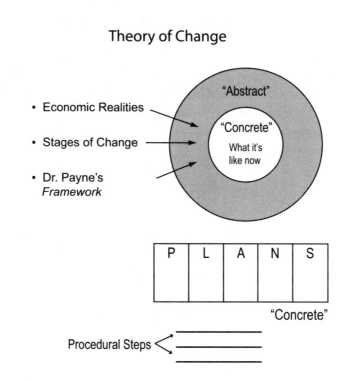

- Economic Realities
- Stages of Change
- Dr. Payne's *Framework*

"Abstract"

"Concrete"
What it's like now

P	L	A	N	S

"Concrete"

Procedural Steps

NOTE: This mental model works best when the instructor draws it as he or she explains the parts and the process.

1. Draw the inner circle and label it "What it's like now." This represents the mental model each person made of his or her own situation. Label this "Concrete" because it requires people to solve immediate problems all day long and doesn't give them the opportunity to take on abstract issues. This is where people often get stuck.

2. Draw the outer circle and label it "Abstract." Explain that these are ideas to be discovered in the course. Abstract also means becoming detached—so individuals can view problems from the outside. It's easier to work in the abstract space when lives are stable and they don't have to worry about immediate problems all the time. They have time and energy for new things. To get out of the tyranny of the moment and change their lives, they have to be able to get to the abstract.

3. Draw a set of rectangles (representing plans) and three lines (representing procedural steps) to make the point that people in poverty need concrete solutions. Label this "Concrete" also. For instance, explain that when the electricity is cut off, people aren't interested in budgeting information as much as they are in getting the heat and lights back on. The point here is that the necessary and immediate concrete solutions are not often effective long-range solutions. People have to get into the abstract to really solve their problems.

4. Now add what goes into the abstract from this curriculum: Economic Realities (the mental model of poverty and the research into the causes of poverty), the Stages of Change (so individuals can track their own success), and Payne's information (hidden rules and resources). This is the same information as in the triangle but presented in the abstract.

5. Write the word "PLANS" (in all capital letters) in the set of rectangles and "Procedural Steps" for the three lines below. This is where people begin to emphasize the importance of planning and procedural lists.

6. Now talk about how people move from the inner circle to the outer circle. How, when they're stuck in crisis, do they find ways to get to the abstract? The curriculum identifies three ways: (a) using mental models—to help them see the big picture, connections, relationships, and options without using a lot of words; (b) having someone (like the facilitator and the other students) make the information relevant because they know what poverty is like, as well as the hidden rules of class; and (c) using a process, as in the curriculum, to help folks explore their lives while learning new information—where they see the difference between what is and what can be, thereby developing their own future story.

Note. From *Facilitator Notes for Getting Ahead in a Just-Gettin'-By World* (pp. 22–24), by P. E. DeVol, 2006, Highlands, TX: aha! Process. Copyright 2006 by aha! Process. Adapted with permission.

References

Abramson, L. Y., Seligman, M., & Teasdale, J. (1978). Learned helplessness in humans: Critique and reformulation. *Journal of Abnormal Psychology, 87*(1), 49–74.

Accent on student success: Engaged together in service. (n.d.). Retrieved April 3, 2009, from http://www.mc.maricopa.edu/other/engagement/ ASSETSProjectDescription.pdf

aha! Process. (2007). *A platform for economic justice.* Retrieved March 4, 2009, from http://ahaprocess.com/files/PlatformForEconomicJustice.pdf

Andrews, A. B., Guadalupe, J. L., & Bolden, E. (2003). Faith, hope, and mutual support: Paths to empowerment as perceived by women in poverty. *Journal of Social Work Research and Evaluation: An International Journal, 4*(1), 5–14.

Ausubel, D. P. (1960). The use of advance organizers in the learning and retention of meaningful verbal material. *Journal of Educational Psychology, 51*(5), 267–272.

Bailey, T. R., & Alfonso, M. (2005). Paths to persistence: An analysis of research on program effectiveness at community colleges. *New Agenda Series* (Vol. 6, No. 1). Indianapolis, IN: Lumina Foundation for Education.

Bandura, A. (2001). Social cognitive theory: An agentic perspective. *Annual Review of Psychology, 52,* 1–26.

Bartholomae, D., & Petrosky, A. (Eds.). (2005). *Ways of reading: An anthology for writers.* Boston/New York: Bedford/St. Martins.

Bauman, S. (n.d.). *Rubric for the assessment of computer programming.* Retrieved March 23, 2009, from http://educ.queensu.ca/~compsci/assessment/Bauman.html

Becker, K. A. (1993). *The development of learning for nontraditional adult students: An investigation of personal meaning-making in a community college reading and study skills course.* Unpublished doctoral dissertation, Ohio State University, Columbus.

Belenky, M. F., Clinchy, B. M., Goldberger, N. R., & Tarule, J. M. (1986). *Women's ways of knowing: The development of self, voice, and mind.* New York: Basic Books.

Bergquist, W. H., & Pawlak, K. (2008). *Engaging the six cultures of the academy: Revised and expanded edition of the four cultures of the academy.* San Francisco: Jossey-Bass.

Berkner, L., He, S., & Cataldi, E. F. (2002). *Descriptive summary of 1995–1996 beginning post-secondary students: Six years later.* Washington, DC: U.S. Department of Education, National Center for Education Statistics.

Berkner, L., He, S., Mason, M., & Wheeless, S. (2007). *Persistence and attainment of 2003–04 beginning postsecondary students: After three years* (NCES 2007-169). Retrieved March 13, 2009, from http://nces.ed.gov/pubs2007/2007169.pdf

Berne, E. (1996). *Games people play: The basic handbook of transactional analysis.* New York: Ballantine Books.

Bess, J. L. (Ed.). (2000). *Teaching alone, teaching together: Transforming the structure of teams for teaching.* San Francisco: Jossey-Bass.

Biggs, J. B. (1986). Enhancing learning skills: The role of metacognition. In J. A. Bowden (Ed.), *Student learning: Research into practice—the Marysville symposium.* Parkville, Australia: Centre for the Study of Higher Education, University of Melbourne.

Bloom, B. S., Englehart, M. D., Furst, E. J., Hill, W. H., & Krathwohl, D. R. (1956). *Taxonomy of educational objectives: The classification of goals: Handbook I: Cognitive domain.* New York: David McKay.

Bloom, D., & Sommo, C. (2005, June). *Building learning communities: Early results from the Opening Doors demonstration at Kingsborough Community College.* Retrieved March 13, 2009, from http://www.mdrc.org/publications/410/overview.html

Boice, R. (1996). *First-order principles for college teachers: Ten basic ways to improve the teaching process.* Bolton, MA: Anker.

Bors, D. A., & Stokes, T. L. (1998). Raven's advanced progressive matrices: Norms for first-year university students and the development of a short form. *Educational and Psychological Measurement, 58*(3), 382–398.

Bostrom, M. (2004). *Together for success: Communicating low-wage work as economy, not poverty.* Retrieved April 10, 2009, from http://www.economythatworks.com reports/TogetherforSuccess.pdf

Bourdieu, P. (1984). *Distinction: A social critique of the judgment of taste* (R. Nice, Trans.). Cambridge, MA: Harvard University Press.

Bragg, D. D., Bremer, C. D, Castellano, M., Kirby, C., Mavis, A., Schaad, D., et al. (2007). *A cross-case analysis of career pathway programs that link low-skilled adults to family-sustaining wage careers.* Retrieved April 21, 2009, from http://136.165.122.102/UserFiles/File/pubs/Career_Pathways.pdf

Brock, T., Jenkins, D., Ellwein, T., Miller, J., Gooden, S., Martin, K., et al. (2007, May). *Building a culture of evidence for community college student success: Early progress in the Achieving the Dream Initiative.* Retrieved March 13, 2009, from http://www.mdrc.org/publications/452/overview.html

Brock, T., & Richburg-Hayes, L. (2006, May). *Paying for persistence: Early results of a Louisiana scholarship program for low-income parents attending community college.* Retrieved March 13, 2009, from http://www.mdrc.org/publications/429/overview.html

Brodeur, P. (1985). *Outrageous misconduct: The asbestos industry on trial.* New York: Pantheon Books.

Brookfield, S. D. (1986). *Understanding and facilitating adult learning: A comprehensive analysis of principles and effective practices.* San Francisco: Jossey-Bass.

Brookfield, S. D. (1987). *Developing critical thinkers: Challenging adults to explore alternative ways of thinking and acting.* San Francisco: Jossey-Bass.

Brookfield, S. D. (1990). *The skillful teacher: On technique, trust, and responsiveness in the classroom.* San Francisco: Jossey-Bass.

Brookover, W. B., & Lezotte, L. W. (1979). *Changes in school characteristics coincident with changes in student achievement* (Occasional Paper No. 17). East Lansing, MI: Institute for Research on Teaching, Michigan State University.

Brooks, J. G., & Brooks, M. G. (1993). *In search of understanding: The case for constructivist classrooms.* Alexandria, VA: Association for Supervision and Curriculum Development.

Brophy, J. (1998, May). *Failure syndrome students.* Retrieved March 13, 2009, from http://www.eric.ed.gov/ericdocs/data/ericdocs2sql/content_storage_01/0000019b/80/15/7b/b4.pdf

Brown, J. S., Collins, A., & Duguid, P. (1989). Situated cognition and the culture of learning. *Educational Researcher, 18*(1), 32–42.

Bucks, B. K., Kennickell, A. B., Mach, T. L., & Moore, K. B. (with Fries, G., Grodzicki, D. J., & Windle, R. A.). (2009, February). *Changes in U.S. family finances from 2004 to 2007: Evidence from the Survey of Consumer Finances.* Retrieved April 21, 2009, from http://www.federalreserve.gov/pubs/bulletin/2009/pdf/scf09.pdf

Caine, R. N., & Caine, G. (1991). *Making connections: Teaching and the human brain.* Alexandria, VA: Association for Supervision and Curriculum Development.

Candy, P. C. (1991). *Self-direction for lifelong learning: A comprehensive guide to theory and practice.* San Francisco, CA: Jossey-Bass.

Carey, K. (2008, April). *Graduation rate watch: Making minority student success a priority.* Retrieved April 21, 2009, from http://www.educationsector.org/usr_doc/Graduation_Rate_Watch.pdf

Casazza, M. E., & Silverman, S. L. (1996). *Learning assistance and developmental education: A guide for effective practice.* San Francisco: Jossey-Bass.

Cengage Learning. (n.d.). *Vocabulary development.* Retrieved March 13, 2009, from http://college.hmco.com/instructors/ins_teachtech_foundations_module_vocdev.html

Champy, J. (1995). *Reengineering management: Mandate for new leadership.* New York: HarperCollins.

Choy, S. P. (2000, March). *Low-income students: Who they are and how they pay for their education* (NCES 2000-169). Washington, DC: U.S. Department of Education, National Center for Education Statistics.

Circles campaign. (n.d.). Retrieved March 13, 2009, from http://www.movethemountain.org/circlescampaign.aspx

Circles campaign: Early results and evaluation. (n.d.). (Available from Move the Mountain Leadership Center, 416 Douglas Ave., Ste. 205, Ames, IA 50010)

Coles, W. E. (1988). *The plural I—and after.* Portsmouth, NH: Boynton/Cook.

Coles, W. E. (1992, November). *Keynote address.* Paper presented at Composition Coordinators' Retreat, Kent State University Regional Campus System, Newbury, OH.

College Board. (2007, October 24). *College Board rallies members to help low-income students get college degrees.* Retrieved March 13, 2009, from http://www.collegeboard.com/press/releases/189882.html

Comer, J. (1995). Lecture given at Education Service Center, Region IV, Houston, TX.

Community College Survey of Student Engagement. (2007). *Committing to student engagement: Reflections on CCSSE's first five years: 2007 findings.* Retrieved March 13, 2009, from http://www.ccsse.org/publications/2007NatlRpt-final.pdf

Conley, D. (2008). *College knowledge: What it really takes for students to succeed and what we can do to get them ready.* San Francisco: Jossey-Bass.

Cooper, H. (1984). Models for teacher expectation communication. In J. B. Dusek, V. C. Hall, & W. J. Meyer (Eds.), *Teacher expectancies* (pp. 135–158). Hillsdale, NJ: Erlbaum.

Cotton, K. (1989). *Expectations and student outcomes.* Retrieved March 16, 2009, from http://www.nwrel.org/scpd/sirs/4/cu7.html

Council for Christian Colleges and Universities. (2005, September 2). *Research illuminates students' spiritual search.* Retrieved March 13, 2009, from http://www.cccu.org/news/research_illuminates_students_spiritual_search

Covey, S. R. (1989). *The 7 habits of highly effective people: Powerful lessons in personal change.* New York: Free Press.

Craik, K. J. W. (1943). *The nature of explanation.* Cambridge, UK: Cambridge University Press.

Dean, L. A. (Ed.). (2006). *CAS professional standards for higher education* (6th ed.). Washington, DC: Council for the Advancement of Standards.

DeVol, P. E. (2004). *Getting ahead in a just-gettin'-by world: Building your resources for a better life* (2nd ed.). Highlands, TX: aha! Process.

DeVol, P. E. (2006). *Facilitator notes for getting ahead in a just-gettin'-by world: Building your resources for a better life* (2nd ed.). Highlands, TX: aha! Process.

DeVol, P. E. (2008). *Building bridges communities.* Retrieved March 14, 2009, from http://www.ahaprocess.com/files/BuildingBridgesCommunities_06042008.pdf

DeVol, P. E., & Krodel, K. M. (2010). *Investigations into economic class in America.* Highlands, TX: aha! Process, Inc.

DeVol, P. E., & Krodel, K. M. (2010). *Facilitator notes for investigations into economic class in America.* Highlands, TX: aha! Process, Inc.

DeVol, P. E., Payne, R. K., & Smith, T. D. (2006). *Bridges out of poverty: Strategies for professionals and communities workbook.* Highlands, TX: aha! Process.

DeWitt, T. (Producer). (2007a). *Reading between the lives: Chabot College students talk about reading and more ...* [Motion picture]. (Available from Chabot College, 25555 Hesperian Blvd., Hayward, CA 94545)

DeWitt, T. (Producer). (2007b). *Student responses: English 101A* [Word processor document included with DVD of motion picture *Reading between the lives*]. (Available from Chabot College, 25555 Hesperian Blvd., Hayward, CA 94545)

DeWitt, T. (Producer). (2007c). *Student responses: English 102* [Word processor document included with DVD of motion picture *Reading between the lives*]. (Available from Chabot College, 25555 Hesperian Blvd., Hayward, CA 94545)

Diener, C. I., & Dweck, C. S. (1978). An analysis of learned helplessness: Continuous changes in performance, strategy, and achievement cognitions following failure. *Journal of Personality and Social Psychology, 36,* 451–462.

DiMarco, C. (2000). *Moving through life transitions with power and purpose* (2nd ed.). Upper Saddle River, NJ: Prentice Hall.

Donnelly, J. W., Eburne, N., & Kittleson, M. (2001). *Mental health: Dimensions of self-esteem and emotional well-being.* Boston: Allyn & Bacon.

Douglas, J. W. B. (1964). *The home and the school: A study of ability and attainment in the primary school.* London: MacGibbon & Kee.

Downing, S. (2002, October). *On course workshop II: Innovative strategies for promoting student success across the curriculum.* Paper presented at On Course Workshop, Marriottsville, MD.

Dowst, K. (1980). The epistemic approach: Writing, knowing, and learning. In T. R. Donovan & B. W. McClelland (Eds.), *Eight approaches to teaching composition* (pp. 65–85). Urbana, IL: National Council of Teachers of English.

Drill down. (2009). Retrieved February 17, 2009, from http://www.mindtools.com/pages/article/newTMC_02.htm

Ehrlich, T. (2005, July). *Service learning in undergraduate education: Where is it going?* Retrieved March 14, 2009, from http://www.carnegiefoundation.org/perspectives/sub.asp?key=245&subkey=1251

Engle, J., & Tinto, V. (2008). *Moving beyond access: College success for low-income, first-generation students.* Retrieved March 14, 2009, from http://www.pellinstitute.org/files/COE_MovingBeyondReport_Final.pdf

Evans, G. W. (2004). The environment of childhood poverty. *American Psychologist, 59*(2), 77–92.

Evans, P. (1992). *The verbally abusive relationship: How to recognize it and how to respond.* Avon, MA: Adams Media.

Farrugia, C. (1996). A continuing professional development model for quality assurance in higher education. *Quality Assurance in Higher Education, 4*(2), 28–34.

Feldman, K. A. (1989). The association between student ratings of specific instructional dimensions and student achievement: Refining and extending the synthesis of data from multisection validity studies. *Research in Higher Education, 30,* 583–645.

Feuerstein, R. (1985). Structural cognitive modifiability and Native Americans. In S. Unger (Ed.), *To sing our own songs: Cognition and culture in Indian education* (pp. 21–36). New York: Association on American Indian Affairs.

Fink, L. D. (2003). *Creating significant learning experiences: An integrated approach to designing college courses.* San Francisco: Jossey-Bass.

Flavell, J. H. (1979). Metacognition and cognitive monitoring: A new area of cognitive-developmental inquiry. *American Psychologist, 34*(10), 906–911.

Flowchart: Nomination & confirmation. (2009). Retrieved March 31, 2009, from http://www.smartdraw.com/examples/preview/index.aspx?example=Flowchart_-_Nomination_%26_Confirmation

Frayer, D. A., Fredrick, W. C., & Klausmeier, H. J. (1969). *A schema for testing the level of concept mastery* (Working Paper No. 16). Madison, WI: Wisconsin Research and Development Center for Cognitive Learning.

Freire, P. (1970). *Pedagogy of the oppressed.* New York: Herder and Herder.

Fry, R. (2000). *How to study* (5th ed.). Franklin Lakes, NJ: Career Press.

Gee, J. P. (1987). What is literacy? *Teaching and Learning: The Journal of Natural Inquiry, 2*(1), 3–11.

Gillespie, R. J., & Nyholm, R. S. (1957). Inorganic stereochemistry. *Quart. Rev. Chem. Soc., 11,* 339–380.

Gilliland, H. (1995). *Teaching the Native American* (3rd ed.). Dubuque, IA: Kendall/Hunt.

Glaser, R., Lesgold, A., & Lajoie, S. (1987). Toward a cognitive theory for the measurement of achievement. In R. Ronning, J. Glover, J. Conoley, & J. Witt (Eds.), *The influence of cognitive psychology on testing* (pp. 45–85). Hillsdale, NJ: Erlbaum.

Glasser, W. (1998). *Choice theory: A new psychology of personal freedom.* New York: HarperCollins.

Glennerster, H. (2002). United States poverty studies and poverty measurement: The past twenty-five years. *Social Service Review, 76,* 83–107.

Goleman, D. (1995). *Emotional intelligence: Why it can matter more than IQ.* New York: Bantam Books.

Good, T. L. (1987). Two decades of research on teacher expectations: Findings and future directions. *Journal of Teacher Education, 38*(4), 32–47.

Gorski, P. (2005). *Savage unrealities: Uncovering classism in Ruby Payne's framework* [Abridged version]. Retrieved March 14, 2009, from http://www.edchange.org/publications/Savage_Unrealities_abridged.pdf

Graves, M. F., & Watts-Taffe, S. M. (2002). The place of word-consciousness in a research-based vocabulary program. In A. E. Farstrup & S. J. Samuels (Eds.), *What research has To say about reading instruction* (3rd ed., pp. 140–165). Newark, DE: International Reading Association.

Greenspan, S. I., & Benderly, B. L. (1997). *The growth of the mind and the endangered origins of intelligence.* Reading, MA: Addison-Wesley.

Habermas, J. (1971). *Knowledge and human interest* (J. J. Shapiro, Trans.). Boston: Beacon Press.

Harris, J. R. (1998). *The nurture assumption: Why children turn out the way they do.* New York: Free Press.

Hart, B., & Risley, T. R. (1995). *Meaningful differences in the everyday experience of young American children.* Baltimore: P. H. Brookes.

Higher Education Research Institute. (2005). *The spiritual life of college students: A national study of college students' search for meaning and purpose.* Retrieved March 30, 2009, from http://spirituality.ucla.edu/spirituality/reports/FINAL_REPORT.pdf

Hirumi, A., & Bowers, D. R. (1991). Enhancing motivation and acquisition of coordinate concepts by using concept trees. *Journal of Educational Research, 84*(5), 273–279.

Hoover, E. (2004, July 23). *For American Indians, the keys to college: A summer workshop helps unlock the admissions process.* Retrieved March 30, 2009, from http://collegehorizons.org/index.php?page=press-chrons-of-higher-edu

Horn, L., Peter, K., & Rooney, K. (2002, July). *Profile of undergraduates in U.S. postsecondary institutions: 1999–2000* (NCES 2002-168). Washington, DC: U.S. Department of Education, National Center for Education Statistics.

Hutchings, P. (Ed.). (2000). *Opening lines: Approaches to the scholarship of teaching and learning.* Menlo Park, CA: Carnegie Foundation for the Advancement of the Scholarship of Teaching.

Hyerle, D. (1996). *Visual tools for transforming information into knowledge.* Alexandria, VA: Association for Supervision and Curriculum Development.

Jacobs, D. C. (2008, October 24). *Learning as a community endeavor.* Plenary speech at The Professional Organization and Development Network and The National Council for Staff, Program, and Organizational Development Conference, Reno, NV.

Jacobs, J. (2007). Income equity and workforce development: Balancing the earnings scale. *Community College Journal, 77,* 22–24.

Jaschik, S. (2007, March 22). *Community colleges and graduation rates.* Retrieved March 16, 2009, from http://www.insidehighereducation.com/news/2007/03/22/ccdata

Jaschik, S. (2008, June 2). *Many adults left behind.* Retrieved March 16, 2009, from http://www.insidehighered.com/news/2008/06/02/adults

Jenkins, D., & Spence, C. (2006). *The career pathways how-to guide.* Retrieved March 16, 2009, from http://www.workforcestrategy.org/publications/WSC_howto_10.16.06.pdf

Joos, M. (1967). The styles of the five clocks. In R. D. Abraham & R. C. Troike (Eds.), *Language and cultural diversity in American education* (pp. 145–149). Englewood Cliffs, NJ: Prentice Hall.

Keller, J. M. (1979). Motivation and instructional design: A theoretical perspective. *Journal of Instructional Development, 2*(4), 26–34.

Keller, J. M. (1983). Motivational design of instruction. In C. M. Reigeluth (Ed.), *Instructional design theories and models: An overview of their current status* (pp. 383–434). Hillsdale, NJ: Erlbaum.

Kirsch, I., Braun, H., Yamamoto, K., & Sum, K. (2007). *America's perfect storm: Three forces changing our nation's future.* Princeton, NJ: Educational Testing Service, Policy Information Center.

Knowles, M. S. (1990). *The adult learner: A neglected species* (4th ed.). Houston, TX: Gulf.

Krodel, K. (2008). *Career pathways final report.* Unpublished document, Youngstown State University, OH.

Krodel, K., Becker, K., Ingle, H., & Jakes, S. (2008). *Helping under-resourced learners succeed at the college and university level: What works, what doesn't, and why.* Retrieved March 16, 2009, from http://www.ahaprocess.com/files/ HelpingUnderResourcedLearnersSucceed_whitepaper02042009.pdf

Land, R., Meyer, J., & Smith, J. (2008). *Threshold concepts within the disciplines.* Rotterdam, the Netherlands: Sense.

Lave, J., & Wenger, E. (1991). *Situated learning: Legitimate peripheral participation.* New York: Cambridge University Press.

Learning strategies database. (n.d.). Retrieved April 3, 2009, from http://www. muskingum.edu/~cal/database/general/organization.html#Strategies

Leathwood, C. (2006). Gender, equity and the discourse of the independent learner in higher education. *Higher Education, 52*(4), 611–633.

Lederman, D. (2008, June 16). *Double whammy of disadvantage.* Retrieved March 16, 2009, from http://www.insidehighered.com/news/2008/06/16/first

Lederman, D., & Heggen, J. (2008, May 27). *As institutional researchers meet, studies galore.* Retrieved March 16, 2009, from http://www.insidehighered.com/ news/2008/05/27/air

Liebowitz, M., & Taylor, J. C. (2004, November). *Breaking through: Helping low-skilled adults enter and succeed in college and careers.* Retrieved March 16, 2009, from http://eric.ed.gov/ERICDocs/data/ericdocs2sql/content_storage_01/0000019b/80/1b/b0/0d.pdf

Lindeman, E. C. (1961). *The meaning of adult education.* Norman, OK: Oklahoma Research Center for Continuing Professional and Higher Education.

Lui, M., Robles, B., Leondar-Wright, B., Brewer, R., & Adamson, R. (2006). *The color of wealth: The story behind the U.S. racial wealth divide.* New York: New Press.

MacEachren, A. M. (1995). *How maps work: Representation, visualization and design.* New York: Guilford Press.

Mackler, B. (1969). Grouping in the ghetto. *Education and Urban Society, 2*(1), 80–96.

Marzano, R. J. (1992). Toward a theory-based review of research in vocabulary. In C. Gordon, G. Labercane, and W. R. McEachern (Eds.), *Elementary reading: Process and practice* (pp. 29–45). New York: Ginn.

Marzano, R. J. (2007). *The art and science of teaching: A comprehensive framework for effective instruction.* Alexandria, VA: Association for Supervision and Curriculum Development.

Maslow, A. H. (1970). *Motivation and personality* (2nd ed.). New York: Harper & Row.

Matte, N. L., & Henderson, S. H. G. (1995). *Success, your style! Right- and left-brain techniques for learning.* Belmont, CA: Wadsworth.

Mattessich, P., & Monsey, B. R. (1992). *Collaboration: What makes it work.* St. Paul, MN: Amherst H. Wilder Foundation.

Mattessich, P., Murray-Close, M., Monsey, B. R., & Wilder Research Center. (2004). *Collaboration: What makes it work* (2nd ed.). St. Paul, MN: Fieldstone Alliance.

McKeachie, W. J. (2002). *McKeachie's teaching tips: Strategies, research, and theory for college and university teachers* (11th ed.). Boston: Houghton Mifflin.

McSwain, C., & Davis, R. (2007, July). *College access for the working poor: Overcoming burdens to succeed in higher education.* Retrieved March 16, 2009, from http://www.cpec.ca.gov/CompleteReports/ExternalDocuments/College_Access_for_the_Working_Poor_2007_Report.pdf

Menec, V. H., & Perry, R. P. (1995). Disciplinary differences in perceptions of success: Modifying misperceptions with attributional retraining. In M. D. Svinicki (Series Ed.) & N. Hativa & M. Marincovich (Vol. Eds.), *New directions for teaching and learning #64* (pp. 105–112). San Francisco: Jossey-Bass.

Menec, V. H., Perry, R. P., Struthers, C. W., Schonwetter, D. J, Hechter, F. J., & Eichholz, B. L. (1994). Assisting at-risk college students with attributional retraining and effective teaching. *Journal of Applied Social Psychology, 24,* 675–701.

Mental models for English/language arts: Grades 6–12. (2007). Highlands, TX: aha! Process.

Mental models for social studies/history: Grades 6–12. (2008). Highlands, TX: aha! Process.

Merchant, D. A. (1986). *Community college faculty and student perceptions of Feuerstein's cognitive deficiencies.* Unpublished doctoral dissertation, Kent State University, OH.

Mezirow, J. (1981). A critical theory of adult learning and education. *Adult Education, 32*(1), 3–24.

Mezirow, J., & Associates (Eds.). (1990). *Fostering critical reflection in adulthood: A guide to transformative and emancipatory learning.* San Francisco: Jossey-Bass.

Miller, W. R., & Rollnick, S. (2002). *Motivational interviewing: Preparing people for change* (2nd ed.). New York: Guilford Press.

Miringoff, M., & Miringoff, M.-L. (1999). *The social health of the nation: How America is really doing.* New York: Oxford University Press.

Montano-Harmon, M. R. (1991). Discourse features of written Mexican Spanish: Current research in contrastive rhetoric and its implications. *Hispania, 74*(2), 417–425.

Morrison, E. (2006). *New models of economic development: White paper version 0.5.* Retrieved March 16, 2009, from http://www.i-open.org/_Media/I-Open_White_Paper_2.pdf

Mosse, D. (2005). Power relations and poverty reduction. In R. Alsop (Ed.), *Power, rights, and poverty: Concepts and connections* (pp. 51–67). Washington, DC: The International Bank for Reconstruction and Development/The World Bank.

Moustakas, C. E. (1966). *The authentic teacher: Sensitivity and awareness in the classroom.* Cambridge, MA: Howard A. Doyle.

Nagy, W. E., & Scott, J. A. (2000). Vocabulary processes. In M. L. Kamil, P. B. Mosenthal, P. D. Pearson, & R. Barr (Eds.), *Handbook of reading research: Vol. III* (pp. 269–284). Mahwah, NJ: Erlbaum.

Nilson, L. B. (2003). *Teaching at its best: A research-based resource for college instructors* (2nd ed.). Bolton, MA: Anker.

Nuhfer, E. (1993). Bottom-line disclosure and assessment. *Teaching Professor, 7*(7), 8.

Nuhfer, E., & Knipp, D. (2003). *The knowledge survey: A tool for all reasons.* Retrieved April 27, 2009, from http://www.isu.edu/ctl/facultydev/KnowS_files/KnowS.htm

O'Connor, A. (2001). *Poverty knowledge: Social science, social policy, and the poor in twentieth century U.S. history.* Princeton, NJ: Princeton University Press.

Palmer, P. J. (1998). *The courage to teach: Exploring the inner landscape of a teacher's life.* San Francisco: Jossey-Bass.

Parnell, D. P. (1995). *Why do I have to learn this? Teaching the way people learn best.* Waco, TX: Cord Communications.

Parsad, B., & Lewis, L. (2003). *Remedial education at degree-granting postsecondary institutions in fall 2000.* Retrieved March 16, 2009, from http://nces.ed.gov/pubs2004/2004010.pdf

Patterson, F., & Longsworth, C. R. (1966). *The making of a college: Plans for a new departure in higher education.* Cambridge, MA: MIT Press.

Pauk, W. (1974). *How to study in college* (2nd ed.). Boston: Houghton Mifflin.

Payne, R. K. (1996). *A framework for understanding poverty.* Baytown, TX: RFT.

Payne, R. K. (2001). *Trainer certification manual: A framework for understanding poverty.* Highlands, TX: aha! Process.

Payne, R. K. (2002). *Understanding learning: The how, the why, the what.* Highlands, TX: aha! Process.

Payne, R. K. (2005a). *Crossing the tracks for love: What to do when you and your partner grew up in different worlds.* Highlands, TX: aha! Process.

Payne, R. K. (2005b). *A framework for understanding poverty* (4th rev. ed.). Highlands, TX: aha! Process.

Payne, R. K. (2005c). *Learning structures* (3rd rev. ed.). Highlands, TX: aha! Process.

Payne, R. K. (2008a). *PowerPoint presentation on preventing dropouts.* Highlands, TX: aha! Process.

Payne, R. K. (2008b). *Under-resourced learners: 8 strategies to boost student achievement.* Highlands, TX: aha! Process.

Payne, R. K., & DeVol, P. E. (2005). *Toward a deeper understanding of issues surrounding poverty: A response to critiques of A Framework for Understanding Poverty.* Retrieved March 16, 2009, from http://www.ahaprocess.com/files/Deeper_Understanding_of_Framework_2005.pdf

Payne, R. K., DeVol, P. E., & Smith, T. D. (2001). *Bridges out of poverty: Trainer certification manual.* Highlands, TX: aha! Process.

Payne, R. K., DeVol, P. E., & Smith, T. D. (2006). *Bridges out of poverty: Strategies for professionals and communities* (3rd rev. ed.). Highlands, TX: aha! Process.

Pellino, K. M. (2007). *The effects of poverty on teaching and learning.* Retrieved March 16, 2009, from http://www.teach-nology.com/tutorials/teaching/poverty/print.htm

Perry, R. P. (1999). Teaching for success: Assisting helpless students in their academic development. *Education Canada, 39,* 16–19.

Perry, R. P., Hechter, F. J., Menec, V. H., & Weinberg, L. (1993). Enhancing achievement motivation and performance in college students: An attributional retraining perspective. *Research in Higher Education, 34,* 687–723.

Perry, W. G. (1970). *Forms of intellectual and ethical development in the college years: A scheme.* New York: Holt, Rinehart, & Winston.

Perry, W. G. (1981). Cognitive and ethical growth: The making of meaning. In A. W. Chickering (Ed.), *The modern American college: Responding to the new realities of diverse students and a changing society* (pp. 76–116). San Francisco: Jossey-Bass.

Pfarr, J. R. (2009). *Tactical communication: Law enforcement tools for successful encounters with people from poverty, middle class, and wealth.* Highlands, TX: aha! Process.

Pikulski, J. J., & Templeton, S. (2004). *Teaching and developing vocabulary: Key to long-term reading success.* Retrieved March 16, 2009, from www.eduplace.com/state/author/pik_temp.pdf

Pingree, A. (2009, Winter). Teaching, learning, and spirituality in the college classroom. *POD Network News,* 8–11.

Pintrich, P. R. (1995). Understanding self-regulated learning. In M. D. Svinicki (Series Ed.) & P. R. Pintrich (Vol. Ed.), *New directions for teaching and learning #63* (pp. 3–12). San Francisco: Jossey-Bass.

Pintrich, P. R., Walters, C., & Baxter, G. P. (2000). Assessing metacognition and self-regulated learning. In G. Schraw & J. C. Impara (Eds.), *Issues in the measurement of metacognition* (pp. 43–97). Lincoln, NE: Buros Institute of Mental Measurements.

Putnam, R. D. (2000). *Bowling alone: The collapse and revival of American community.* New York: Simon & Schuster.

Rank, M. R. (2005). *One nation, underprivileged: Why American poverty affects us all.* New York: Oxford University Press.

Robinson, G. (2001). *Community colleges broadening horizons through service learning, 2000–2003.* Retrieved March 16, 2009, from http://webadmin.aacc.nche.edu/Publications/Briefs/Documents/05012001broadening horizons.pdf

Roderick, M., Nagaoka, J., Coca, V., & Moeller, E. (2008, March). *From high school to the future: Potholes on the road to college.* Retrieved March 16, 2009, from: http://ccsr.uchicago.edu/publications/CCSR_Potholes_Report.pdf

Rodriguez, R. (2005). The achievement of desire. In D. Bartholomae & A. Petrosky (Eds.), *Ways of reading: An anthology for writers* (pp. 561–581). Boston/New York: Bedford/St. Martins.

Rose, M. (1989). *Lives on the boundary: The struggles and achievements of America's underprepared.* New York: Free Press.

Rosenthal, R., & Jacobson, L. (1968). *Pygmalion in the classroom: Teacher expectations and pupils' intellectual development.* New York: Holt, Rinehart, & Winston.

Rowe, M. B. (1969). Science, silence, and sanctions. *Science and Children, 6*(6), 11–13.

Roy, J. (2005, October 12). *Low income hinders college attendance for even the highest achieving students.* Retrieved March 16, 2009, from http://www.epi.org/economic_snapshots/entry/webfeatures_snapshots_20051012/

Saroyan, A. (2000). The lecturer: Working with large groups. In J. L. Bess (Ed.), *Teaching alone, teaching together: Transforming the structure of teams for teaching* (pp. 87–107). San Francisco: Jossey-Bass.

Shankman, M. L., & Allen, S. J. (2008). *Group savvy: Interpreting the situation and/or networks of an organization* [Tomorrow's professor message #902]. Retrieved March 27, 2009, from http://cgi.stanford.edu/~dept-ctl/cgi-bin/tomprof/postings.php

Sharron, H., & Coulter, M. (2004). *Changing children's minds: Feuerstein's revolution in the teaching of intelligence.* Highlands, TX: aha! Process.

Shaughnessy, M. P. (1977). *Errors and expectations: A guide for the teacher of basic writing.* New York: Oxford University Press.

Shipler, D. K. (2004). *The working poor: Invisible in America.* New York: Alfred A. Knopf.

Shulman, L. S. (1986). Those who understand: Knowledge growth in teaching. *Educational Researcher, 15*(2), 4–14.

Singham, M. (2005). *The achievement gap in U.S. education: Canaries in the mine.* Lanham, MD: Rowan & Littlefield Education.

Singham, M. (2007). Death to the syllabus! *Liberal Education, 93*(4), 52–56.

Slocumb, P. D., & Payne, R. K. (2000). *Removing the mask: Giftedness in poverty.* Highlands, TX: aha! Process.

Smart, J. C., & Feldman, K. A. (1998). 'Accentuation effects' of dissimilar academic departments: An application and exploration of Holland's theory. *Research in Higher Education, 39*(4), 385–418.

Smart, J. C., Feldman, K. A., & Ethington, C. A. (2000). *Academic disciplines: Holland's theory and the study of college students and faculty.* Nashville, TN: Vanderbilt University Press.

Smith, F. (1985). *Reading without nonsense* (2nd ed.). New York: Teachers College Press.

Smith, F. (1986). *Insult to intelligence: The bureaucratic invasion of our classrooms.* Portsmouth, NH: Heinemann.

Sternberg, R. J. (1989). *The triarchic mind: A new theory of human intelligence.* New York: Penguin.

Sturrock, C. (2008, March 31). Low-income students feel left out at Stanford. *San Francisco Chronicle,* p. B1.

Surowiecki, J. (2005). *The wisdom of crowds.* New York: Anchor.

Swanborn, M. S. L., & de Glopper, K. (1999). Incidental word learning while reading: A meta-analysis. *Review of Educational Research, 69*(3), 261–285.

Tarule, J. M. (1988). Voices of returning women: Ways of knowing. *New Directions for Adult and Continuing Education, 39,* 19–33.

Tinto, V. (2004, April 20). *Access without support is not opportunity: Rethinking the first year of college for low-income students.* Retrieved March 16, 2009, from http://pathways.syr.edu/documents/2004AACRAOSpeech.pdf

UNICEF. (2007). *Child poverty in perspective: An overview of child well-being in rich countries.* Retrieved March 16, 2009, from http://www.unicef-irc.org/publications/pdf/rc7_eng.pdf

Valenzuela, C., & Addington, J. (2006a). *Four features of racism.* (Available from Minnesota Collaborative Anti-Racism Initiative, 1671 Summit Ave., St. Paul, MN 55105)

Valenzuela, C., & Addington, J. (2006b). *Systemic racism: Daily strategies for survival and beyond.* (Available from Minnesota Collaborative Anti-Racism Initiative, 1671 Summit Ave., St. Paul, MN 55105)

Vella, J. (2002). *Learning to listen, learning to teach: The power of dialogue in educating adults* (Rev. ed.). San Francisco: Jossey-Bass.

Walker, J. (1989). Getting them unstuck: Some strategies for the teaching of reading in science. *School Science and Mathematics, 80*(2), 130–135.

Walter, T. L., Siebert, A., & Smith, L. N. (2000). *Student success: How to succeed in college and still have time for your friends* (8th ed.). Fort Worth, TX: Harcourt Brace.

Weiner, B. (1986). *An attributional theory of motivation and emotion.* New York: Springer.

Wenger, E. (1998). *Communities of practice: Learning, meaning, and identity.* New York: Cambridge University Press.

Wiggins, G., & McTighe, J. (2005). *Understanding by design* (2nd expanded ed.). Alexandria, VA: Association for Supervision and Curriculum Development.

Williams, T. R., & Butterfield, E. C. (1992). Advance organizers: A review of the research—part I. *Journal of Technical Writing and Communication, 22*(3), 259–272.

Wingspread declaration on school connections. (2004). *The Journal of School Health, 74,* 233–234.

Wirth, K. R., & Perkins, D. (n.d.). *Knowledge surveys: An indispensable course design and assessment tool.* Retrieved March 16, 2009, from www.macalester.edu/geology/wirth/WirthPerkinsKS.pdf

Word atlas: Mapping your way to SAT success. (1981). (Available from Townsend Learning Center, 1667 E. 40th St., Ste. 1B, Cleveland, OH 44103)

Zimmerman, B. J., & Paulsen, A. S. (1995). Self-monitoring during collegiate studying: An invaluable tool for academic self-regulation. In M. D. Svinicki (Series Ed.) & P. R. Pintrich (Vol. Ed.), *New directions for teaching and learning #63* (pp. 13–27). San Francisco: Jossey-Bass.

Zull, J. (2002). *The art of changing the brain: Enriching the practice of teaching by exploring the biology of learning.* Sterling, VA: Stylus.

INDEX

NOTE: Page numbers in *italics* refer to figures or tables not otherwise referenced in the text.

About the Authors

Karen A. Becker, Ph.D., has taught developmental courses for more than 20 years and presently serves as coordinator of the Reading and Study Skills Center at Youngstown State University. She taught developmental reading and writing courses, as well as education courses, at a number of Ohio two- and four-year colleges and universities. As a program director and curriculum designer for the Business and Industry Division at Columbus State Community College, she helped start a summer college for elementary and middle school students. Dr. Becker has continued to create similar programs serving under-resourced college students from Ohio and New Mexico, in addition to early college high school students using *Getting Ahead.* Her research interests include the use of reading and writing as vehicles for learning, which she has been sharing with college faculty and staff through professional development. A certified trainer in *A Framework for Understanding Poverty* and *Bridges Out of Poverty,* Dr. Becker is uniquely familiar with the challenges facing under-resourced postsecondary students.

Karla M. Krodel, M.B.A., holds an undergraduate nursing degree from the University of Pittsburgh, as well as a master's degree from Kent State University. In her current position as director of the Youngstown State University Metro Credit Education Outreach, she helps create partnerships that bring college programs to under-served populations. YSU Metro Credit was an early adopter of *Getting Ahead* for college students and has already trained 300 college and trade school students in the *Getting Ahead* concepts. Previously Ms. Krodel was a charge nurse on inpatient psychiatric units, a program coordinator in county health department clinics, and director of a regional lead poison program. More recently she joined the YSU staff as a grant writer, workforce development program director, and research associate in the Urban Studies Department. Ms. Krodel is also a certified trainer in the *Bridges Out of Poverty* program, a key resource in the creation of this book.

Bethanie H. Tucker, Ed.D., is a trainer and consultant with a diverse career in education spanning nearly four decades, including teaching positions in elementary classrooms, Title I reading, gifted education, and adjunct faculty at the University of Virginia. Since 1990 she has been a professor of education at Averett University. Author of several books, she is the creator of *Tucker Signing Strategies,* an approach to teaching letter-sound recognition to struggling readers. This technique has been introduced to teachers in most U.S. states, as well as Australia and China. Dr. Tucker's training and consulting expertise includes reading-related presentations, *A Framework for Understanding Poverty, Learning Structures,* and *Under-Resourced Learners.* Formerly a full-need scholarship college student herself, she "made it through" thanks to caring professors who provided the resources she needed to succeed. Dr. Tucker's experiences, along with the research of Dr. Ruby Payne and other scholars worldwide, constitute the foundation for her contributions to this book.